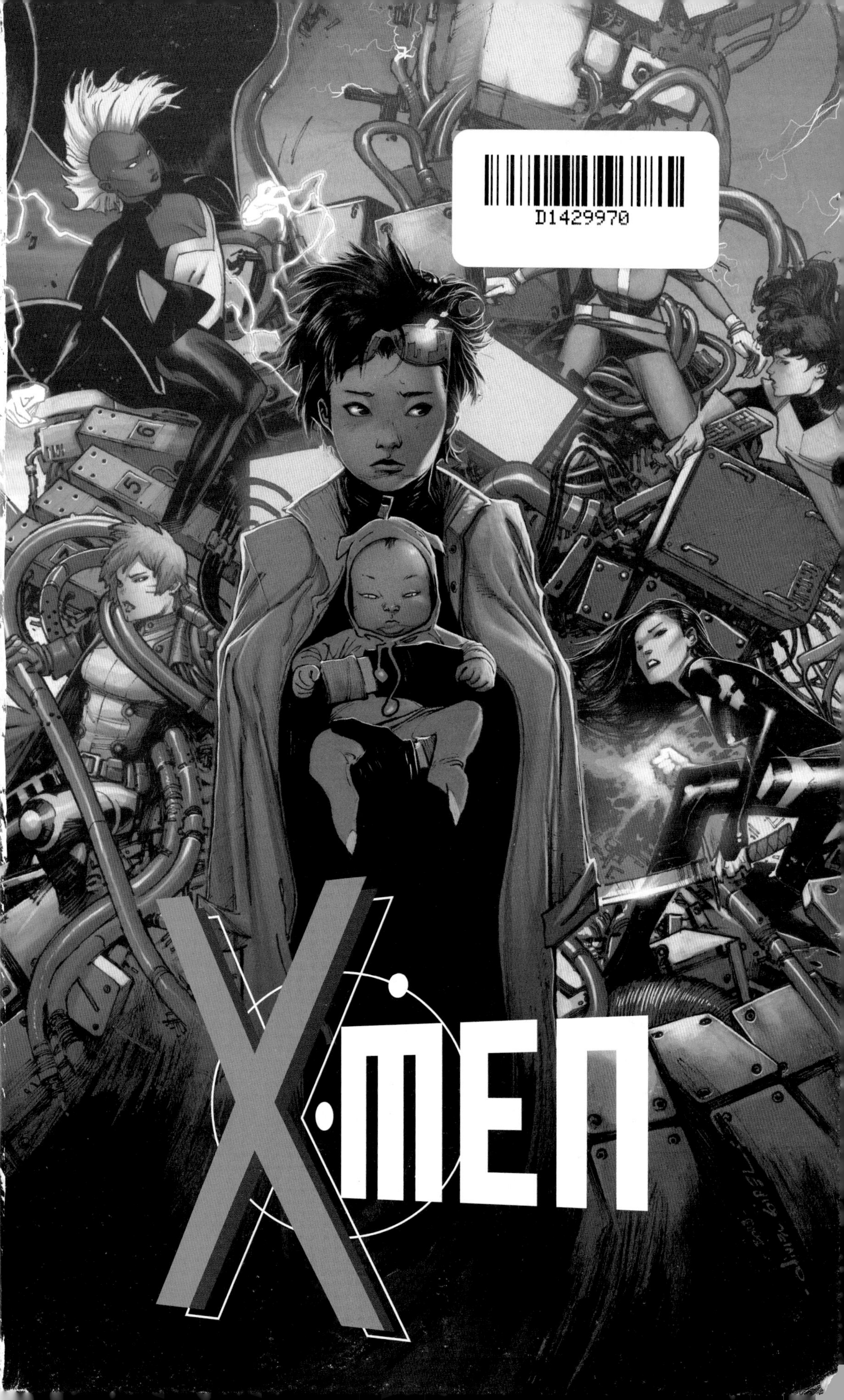
X-MEN

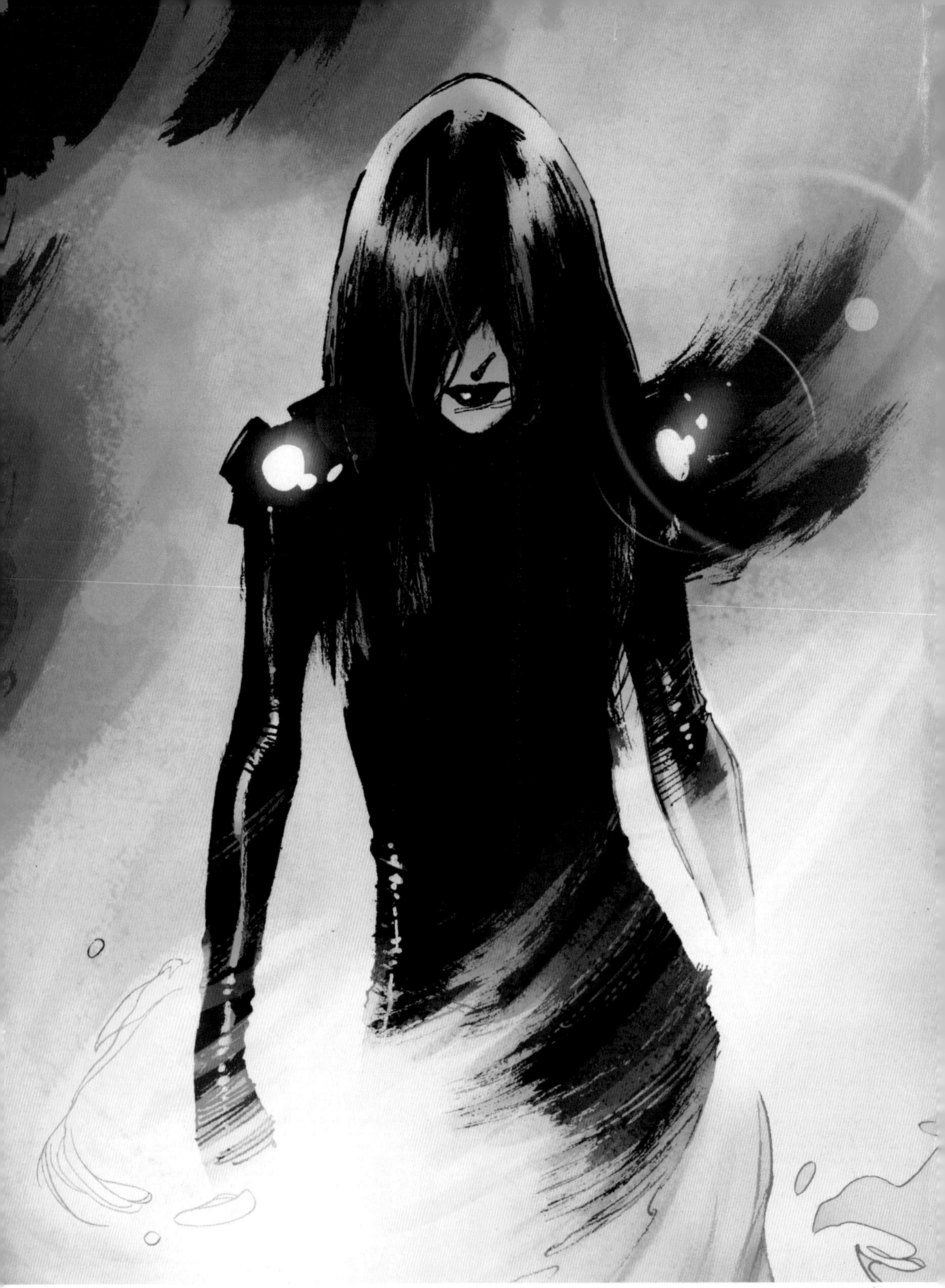

PRIMER

STORM **ROGUE** **PSYLOCKE** **KITTY PRYDE** **RACHEL GREY** **JUBILEE**

BRIAN WOOD
WRITER

X-MEN #1-3

OLIVIER
COIPEL
PENCILER

MARK
MORALES,
OLIVIER COIPEL &
SCOTT HANNA
INKERS

LAURA
MARTIN,
MATT MILLA &
CHRISTINA STRAIN
COLORISTS

COVER ART: OLIVIER COIPEL WITH LAURA MARTIN (#1 & #3) & FRANK MARTIN (#2)

X-MEN #4

DAVID
LOPEZ
PENCILER

CAM
SMITH
WITH NORMAN LEE
INKERS

CRIS
PETER,
MATT MILLA &
CHRISTINA STRAIN
COLORISTS

COVER ART: TERRY DODSON & RACHEL DODSON

UNCANNY X-MEN #244

CHRIS
CLAREMONT
WRITER

MARC
SILVESTRI
PENCILER

DAN
GREEN
INKER

GLYNIS
OLIVER
COLORIST

TOM
ORZECHOWSKI
LETTERER

BOB
HARRAS
EDITOR

COVER ART: MARC SILVESTRI & DAN GREEN

COLLECTION EDITOR: **JENNIFER GRÜNWALD** ASSISTANT EDITORS: **ALEX STARBUCK** & **NELSON RIBEIRO**
EDITOR, SPECIAL PROJECTS: **MARK D. BEAZLEY** SENIOR EDITOR, SPECIAL PROJECTS: **JEFF YOUNGQUIST**
SVP OF PRINT & DIGITAL PUBLISHING SALES: **DAVID GABRIEL** BOOK DESIGN: **JEFF POWELL**

EDITOR IN CHIEF: **AXEL ALONSO** CHIEF CREATIVE OFFICER: **JOE QUESADA**
PUBLISHER: **DAN BUCKLEY** EXECUTIVE PRODUCER: **ALAN FINE**

X-MEN VOL. 1: PRIMER. Contains material originally published in magazine form as X-MEN 1-4 and UNCANNY X-MEN #244. First printing 2013. ISBN# 978-0-7851-6800-3. Published by MARVEL WORLDWIDE, INC., a subsidiary of MARVEL ENTERTAINMENT, LLC. OFFICE OF PUBLICATION: 135 West 50th Street, New York, NY 10020. Copyright © 1989 and 2013 Marvel Characters, Inc. All rights reserved. All characters featured in this issue and the distinctive names and likenesses thereof, and all related indicia are trademarks of Marvel Characters, Inc. No similarity between any of the names, characters, persons, and/or institutions in this magazine with those of any living or dead person or institution is intended, and any such similarity which may exist is purely coincidental. **Printed in the U.S.A.** ALAN FINE, EVP - Office of the President, Marvel Worldwide, Inc. and EVP & CMO Marvel Characters B.V.; DAN BUCKLEY, Publisher & President - Print, Animation & Digital Divisions; JOE QUESADA, Chief Creative Officer; TOM BREVOORT, SVP of Publishing; DAVID BOGART, SVP of Operations & Procurement, Publishing; C.B. CEBULSKI, SVP of Creator & Content Development; DAVID GABRIEL, SVP of Print & Digital Publishing Sales; JIM O'KEEFE, VP of Operations & Logistics; DAN CARR, Executive Director of Publishing Technology; SUSAN CRESPI, Editorial Operations Manager; ALEX MORALES, Publishing Operations Manager; STAN LEE, Chairman Emeritus. For information regarding advertising in Marvel Comics or on Marvel.com, please contact Niza Disla, Director of Marvel Partnerships, at ndisla@marvel.com. For Marvel subscription inquiries, please call 800-217-9158. Manufactured between 9/27/2013 and 11/4/2013 by QUAD/GRAPHICS, VERSAILLES, KY, USA.

10 9 8 7 6 5 4 3 2 1

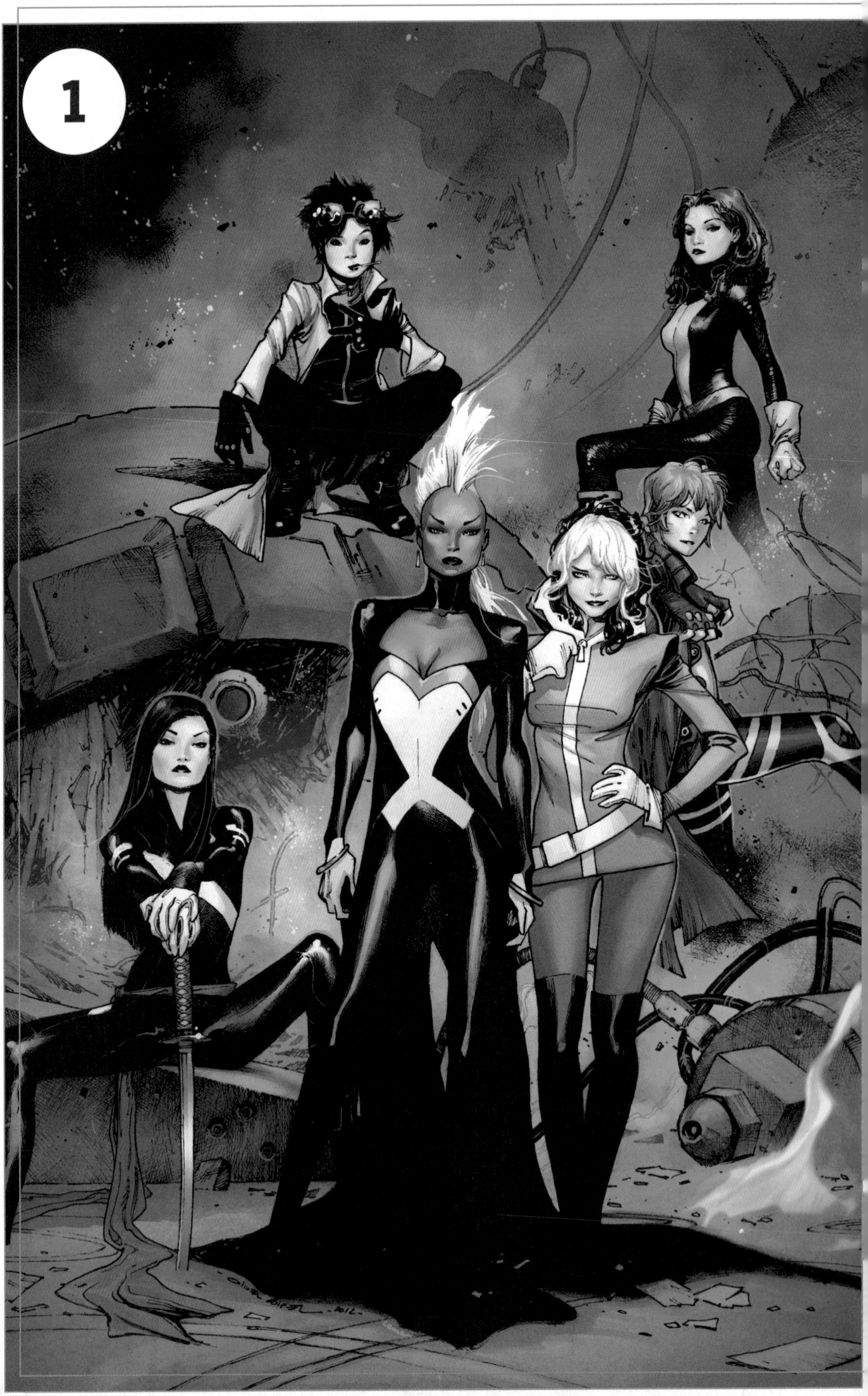
1

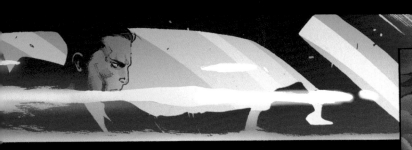

BEFORE THERE WAS
ANYTHING ELSE, THERE
WERE TWO SIBLINGS.

PERFECT TWINS,
IN THRALL TO
THEIR BIOLOGICAL
IMPERATIVES.

DOMINANCE.

REPLICATION.

SURVIVAL.

ONE WAS FORCED OUT, TO
EVOLVE ON HER OWN, TO FIND
HER OWN PLACE IN THE INFANT
COSMOS. THE OTHER, THE
VICTOR, WOULD COME TO
INHERIT PRIMORIDAL EARTH.

PLUNK

EVEN TO THE MOST ANCIENT
OF LIFEFORMS, A BILLION
YEARS IS NOT INSIGNIFICANT.
BUT AGAINST NEARLY
IMPOSSIBLE ODDS, BOTH
SIBLINGS THRIVED.

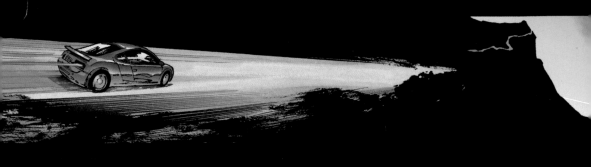

THE FEMALE, AND
THE MALE, THE
ONE WHO CAST
HER OUT.

SHE NEVER FORGOT.
CODED INTO HER DNA
WAS A FOURTH
IMPERATIVE.

REVENGE.

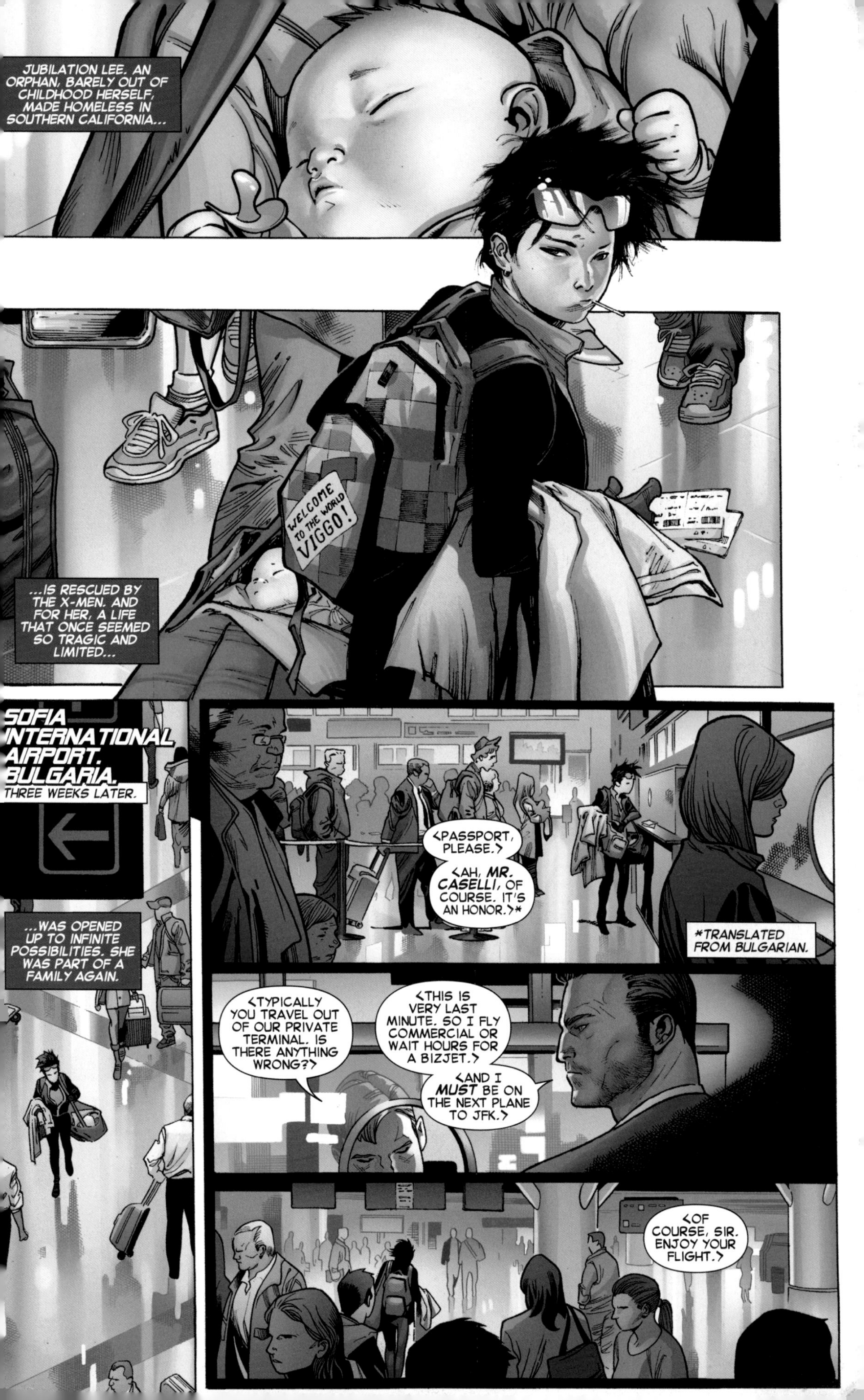
JUBILATION LEE. AN ORPHAN, BARELY OUT OF CHILDHOOD HERSELF, MADE HOMELESS IN SOUTHERN CALIFORNIA...
WELCOME TO THE WORLD VIGGO!
...IS RESCUED BY THE X-MEN. AND FOR HER, A LIFE THAT ONCE SEEMED SO TRAGIC AND LIMITED...
SOFIA INTERNATIONAL AIRPORT. BULGARIA.
THREE WEEKS LATER.
...WAS OPENED UP TO INFINITE POSSIBILITIES. SHE WAS PART OF A FAMILY AGAIN.
<PASSPORT, PLEASE.>
<AH, MR. CASELLI, OF COURSE. IT'S AN HONOR.>*
*TRANSLATED FROM BULGARIAN.
<TYPICALLY YOU TRAVEL OUT OF OUR PRIVATE TERMINAL. IS THERE ANYTHING WRONG?>
<THIS IS VERY LAST MINUTE. SO I FLY COMMERCIAL OR WAIT HOURS FOR A BIZJET.>
<AND I MUST BE ON THE NEXT PLANE TO JFK.>
<OF COURSE, SIR. ENJOY YOUR FLIGHT.>

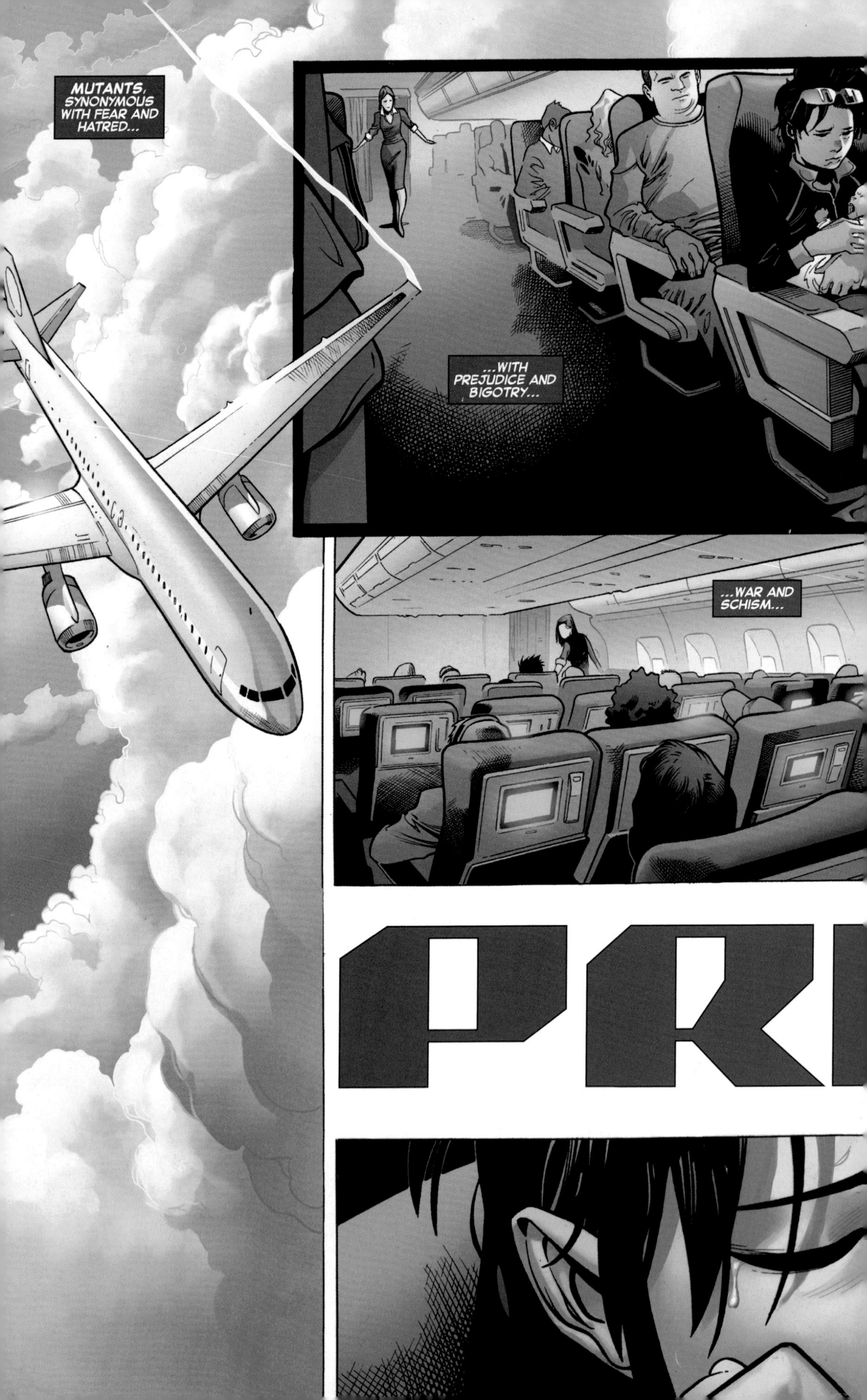
MUTANTS, SYNONYMOUS WITH FEAR AND HATRED...
...WITH PREJUDICE AND BIGOTRY...
...WAR AND SCHISM...
PR

...VIOLENCE AND DECIMATION...

...ALIENATION, SHAME, AND SECLUSION.

BUT JUBILEE HAS JUST ONE WORD TO DESCRIBE THE X-MEN:

MER

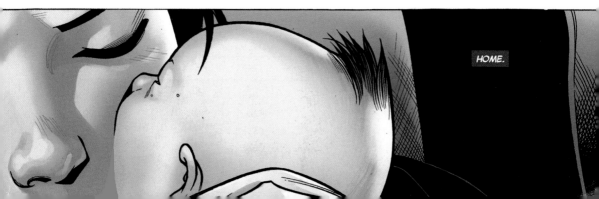

HOME.

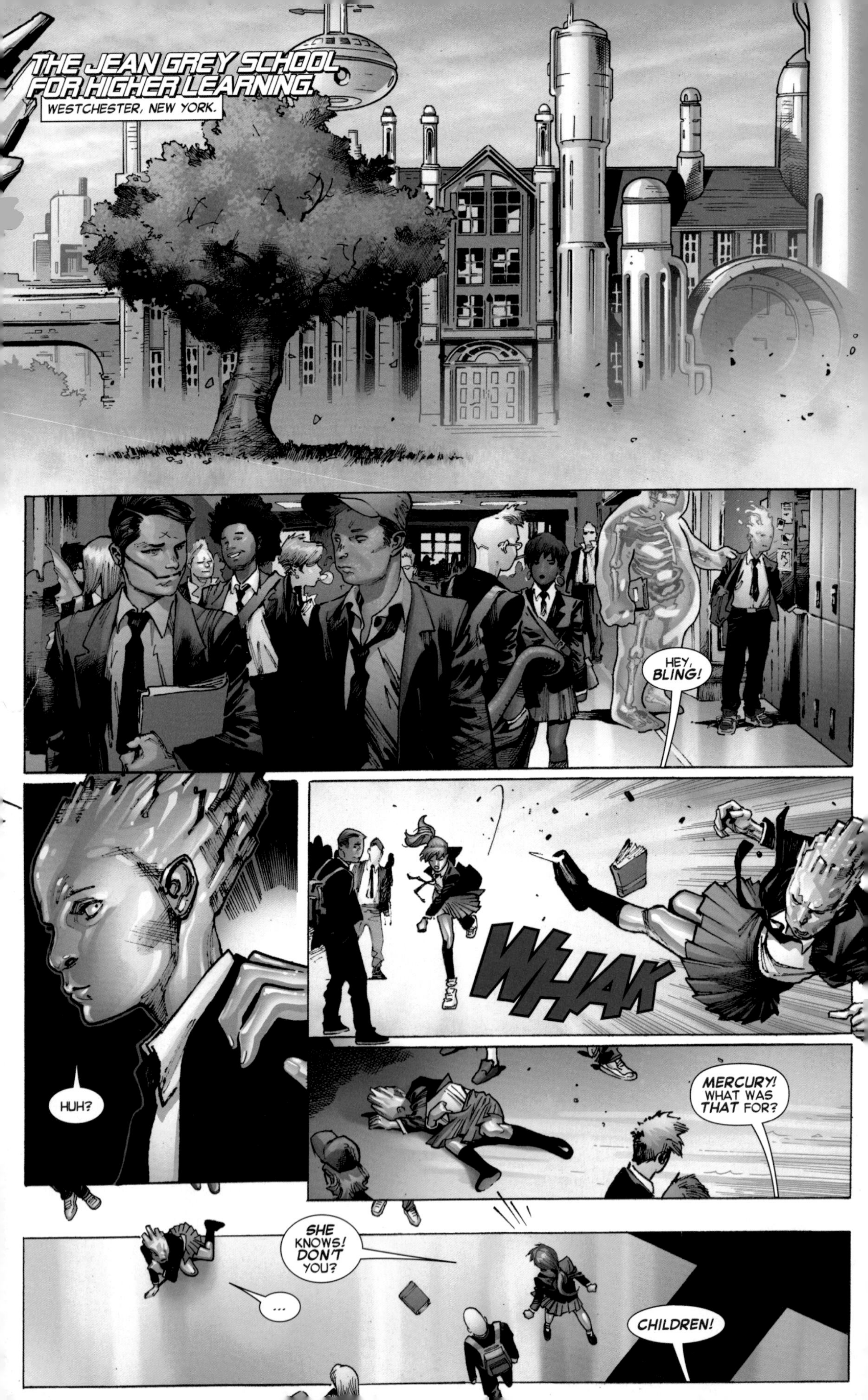
THE JEAN GREY SCHOOL FOR HIGHER LEARNING.
WESTCHESTER, NEW YORK.
HEY, BLING!
HUH?
WHAK
MERCURY! WHAT WAS THAT FOR?
SHE KNOWS! DON'T YOU?
...
CHILDREN!

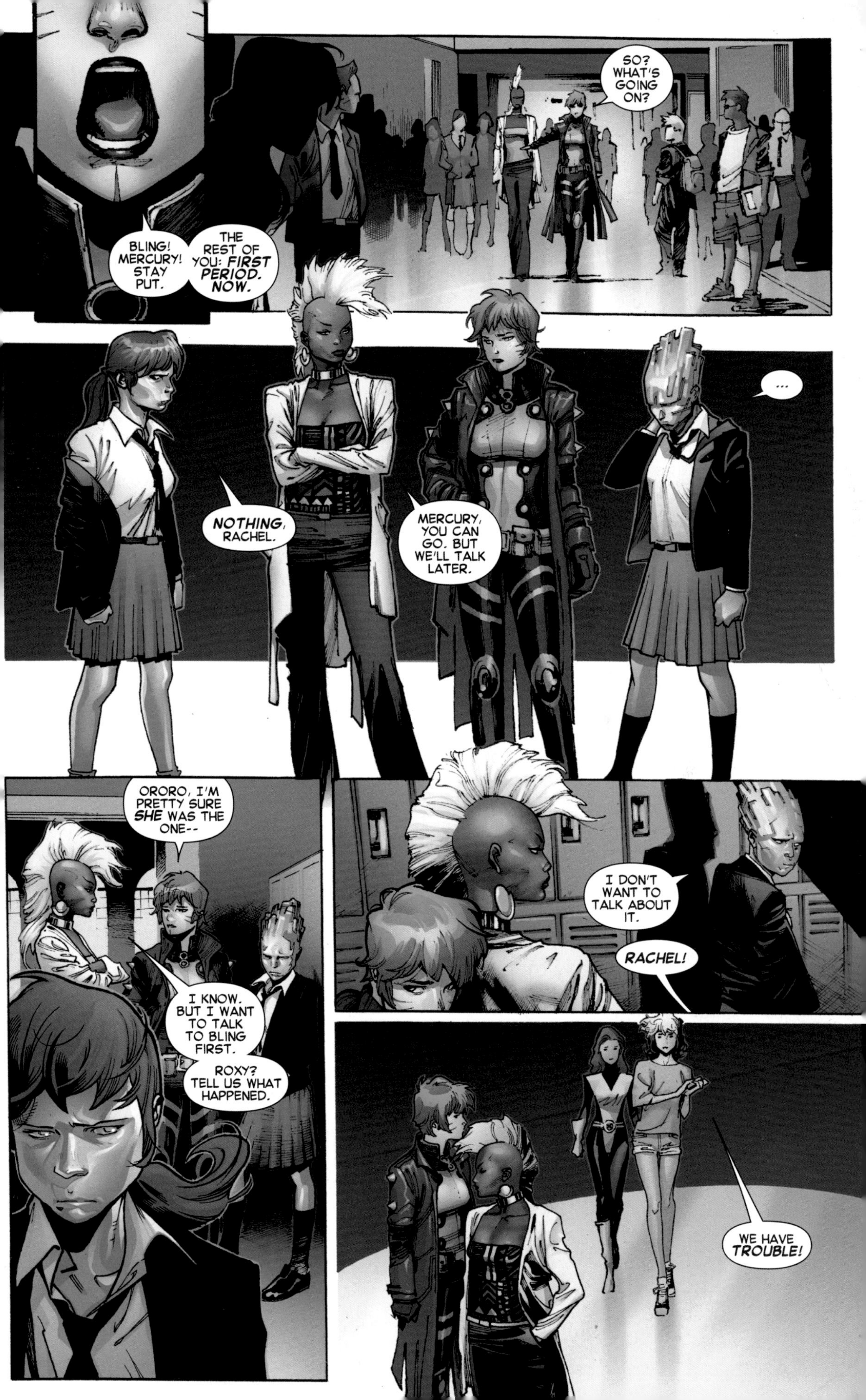
SO? WHAT'S GOING ON?
BLING! MERCURY! STAY PUT.
THE REST OF YOU: FIRST PERIOD. NOW.
...
NOTHING, RACHEL.
MERCURY, YOU CAN GO. BUT WE'LL TALK LATER.
ORORO, I'M PRETTY SURE SHE WAS THE ONE--
I KNOW. BUT I WANT TO TALK TO BLING FIRST.
ROXY? TELL US WHAT HAPPENED.
I DON'T WANT TO TALK ABOUT IT.
RACHEL!
WE HAVE TROUBLE!

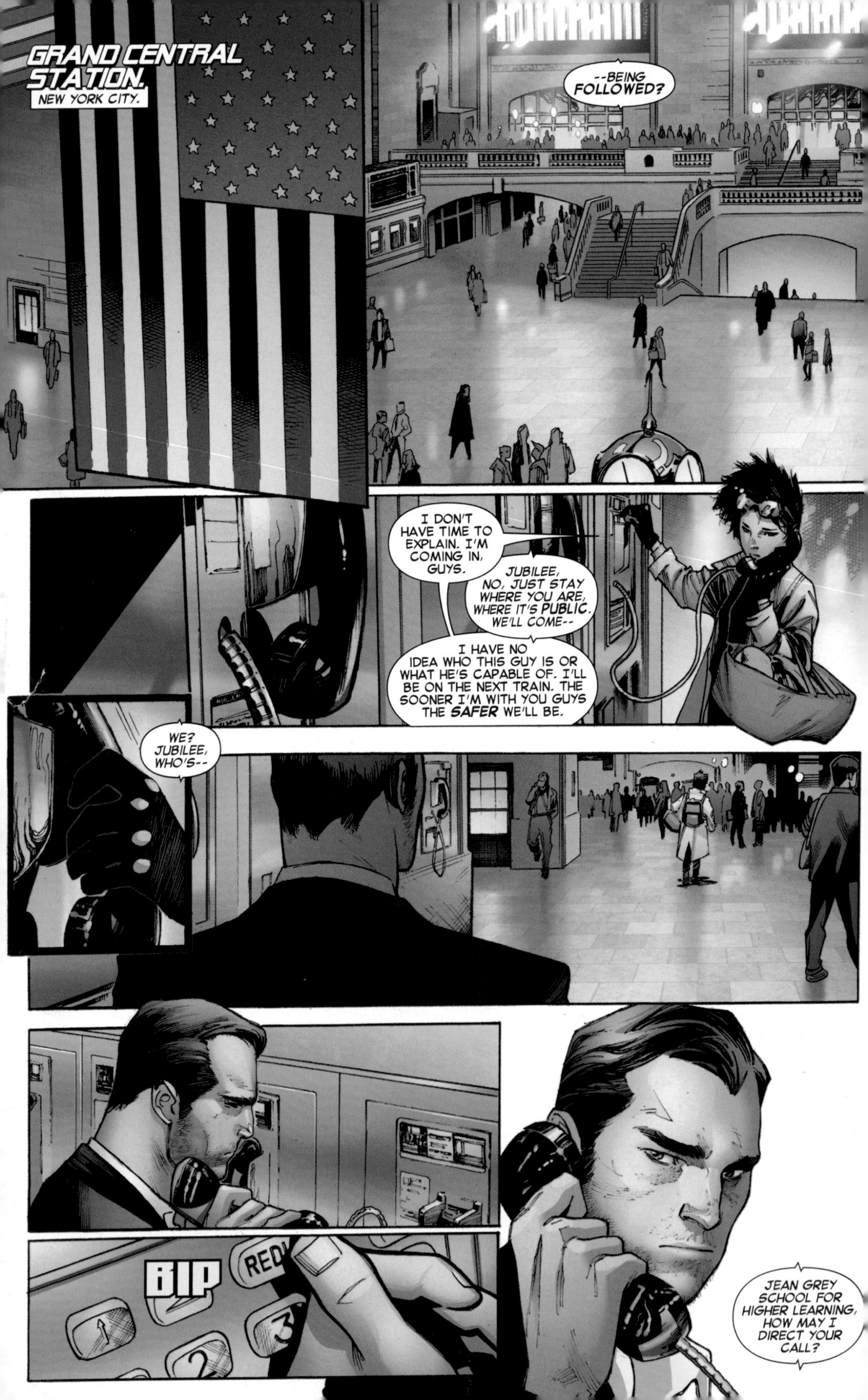
GRAND CENTRAL STATION.
NEW YORK CITY.
--BEING FOLLOWED?
I DON'T HAVE TIME TO EXPLAIN. I'M COMING IN, GUYS.
JUBILEE, NO, JUST STAY WHERE YOU ARE, WHERE IT'S PUBLIC. WE'LL COME--
I HAVE NO IDEA WHO THIS GUY IS OR WHAT HE'S CAPABLE OF. I'LL BE ON THE NEXT TRAIN. THE SOONER I'M WITH YOU GUYS THE SAFER WE'LL BE.
WE? JUBILEE, WHO'S--
BIP
JEAN GREY SCHOOL FOR HIGHER LEARNING, HOW MAY I DIRECT YOUR CALL?

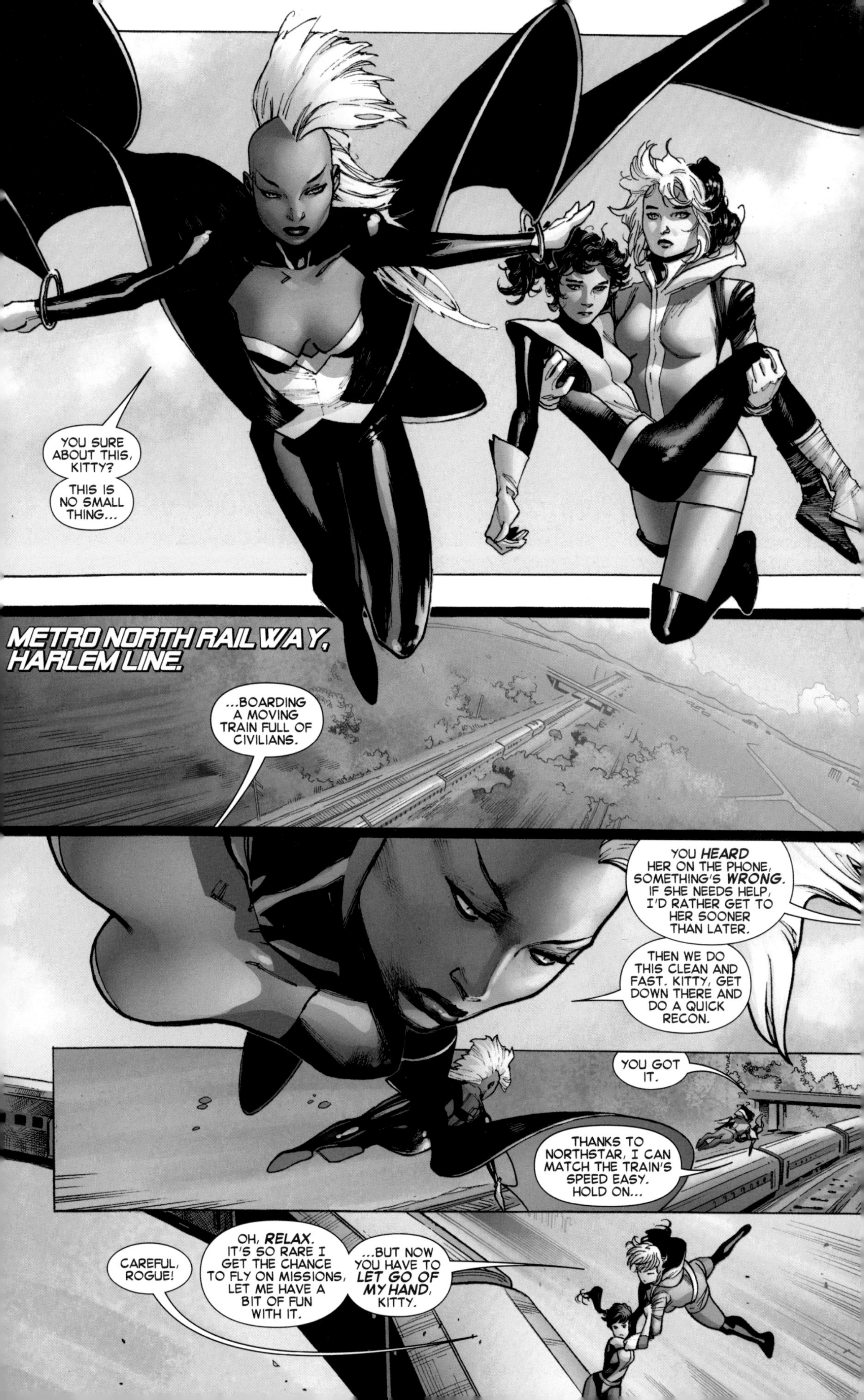
YOU SURE ABOUT THIS, KITTY?
THIS IS NO SMALL THING...
METRO NORTH RAILWAY, HARLEM LINE.
...BOARDING A MOVING TRAIN FULL OF CIVILIANS.
YOU HEARD HER ON THE PHONE, SOMETHING'S WRONG. IF SHE NEEDS HELP, I'D RATHER GET TO HER SOONER THAN LATER.
THEN WE DO THIS CLEAN AND FAST. KITTY, GET DOWN THERE AND DO A QUICK RECON.
YOU GOT IT.
THANKS TO NORTHSTAR, I CAN MATCH THE TRAIN'S SPEED EASY. HOLD ON...
CAREFUL, ROGUE!
OH, RELAX. IT'S SO RARE I GET THE CHANCE TO FLY ON MISSIONS, LET ME HAVE A BIT OF FUN WITH IT.
...BUT NOW YOU HAVE TO LET GO OF MY HAND, KITTY.

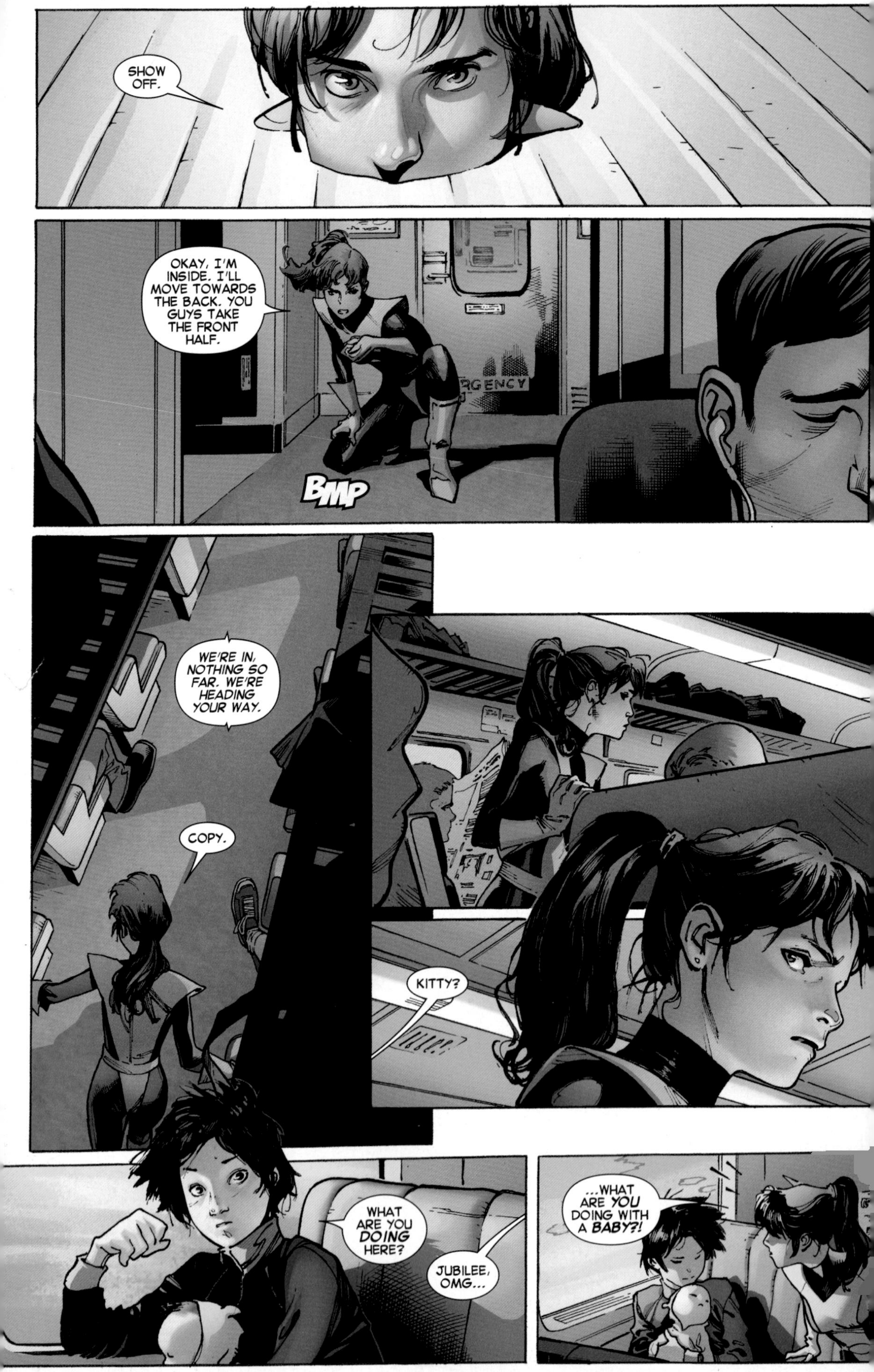
SHOW OFF.
OKAY, I'M INSIDE. I'LL MOVE TOWARDS THE BACK. YOU GUYS TAKE THE FRONT HALF.
ERGENCY
BMP
WE'RE IN, NOTHING SO FAR. WE'RE HEADING YOUR WAY.
COPY.
KITTY?
WHAT ARE YOU DOING HERE?
JUBILEE, OMG...
...WHAT ARE YOU DOING WITH A BABY?!

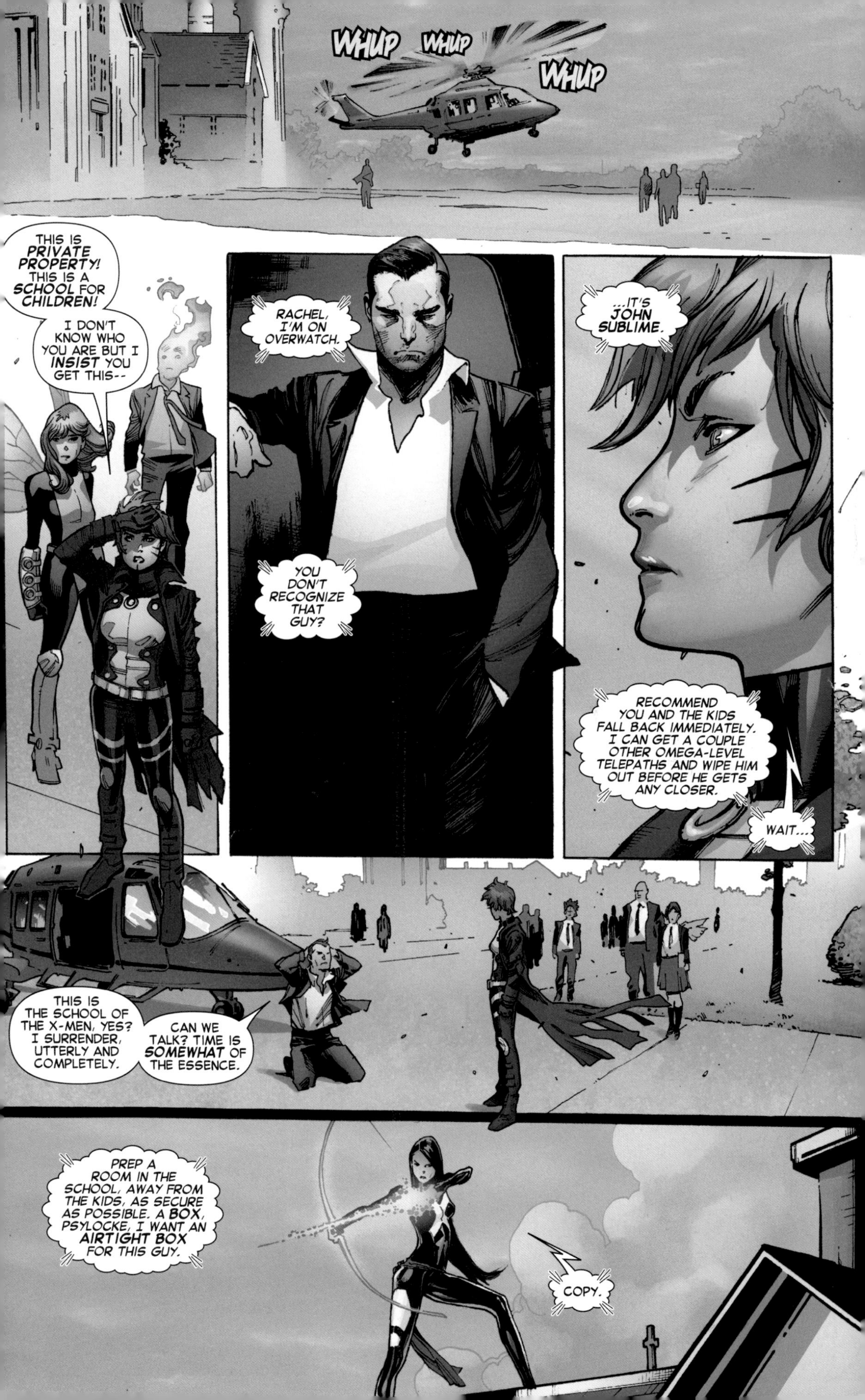
WHUP WHUP WHUP
THIS IS PRIVATE PROPERTY! THIS IS A SCHOOL FOR CHILDREN!
I DON'T KNOW WHO YOU ARE BUT I INSIST YOU GET THIS--
RACHEL, I'M ON OVERWATCH.
YOU DON'T RECOGNIZE THAT GUY?
...IT'S JOHN SUBLIME.
RECOMMEND YOU AND THE KIDS FALL BACK IMMEDIATELY. I CAN GET A COUPLE OTHER OMEGA-LEVEL TELEPATHS AND WIPE HIM OUT BEFORE HE GETS ANY CLOSER.
WAIT...
THIS IS THE SCHOOL OF THE X-MEN, YES? I SURRENDER, UTTERLY AND COMPLETELY.
CAN WE TALK? TIME IS SOMEWHAT OF THE ESSENCE.
PREP A ROOM IN THE SCHOOL, AWAY FROM THE KIDS, AS SECURE AS POSSIBLE. A BOX, PSYLOCKE, I WANT AN AIRTIGHT BOX FOR THIS GUY.
COPY.

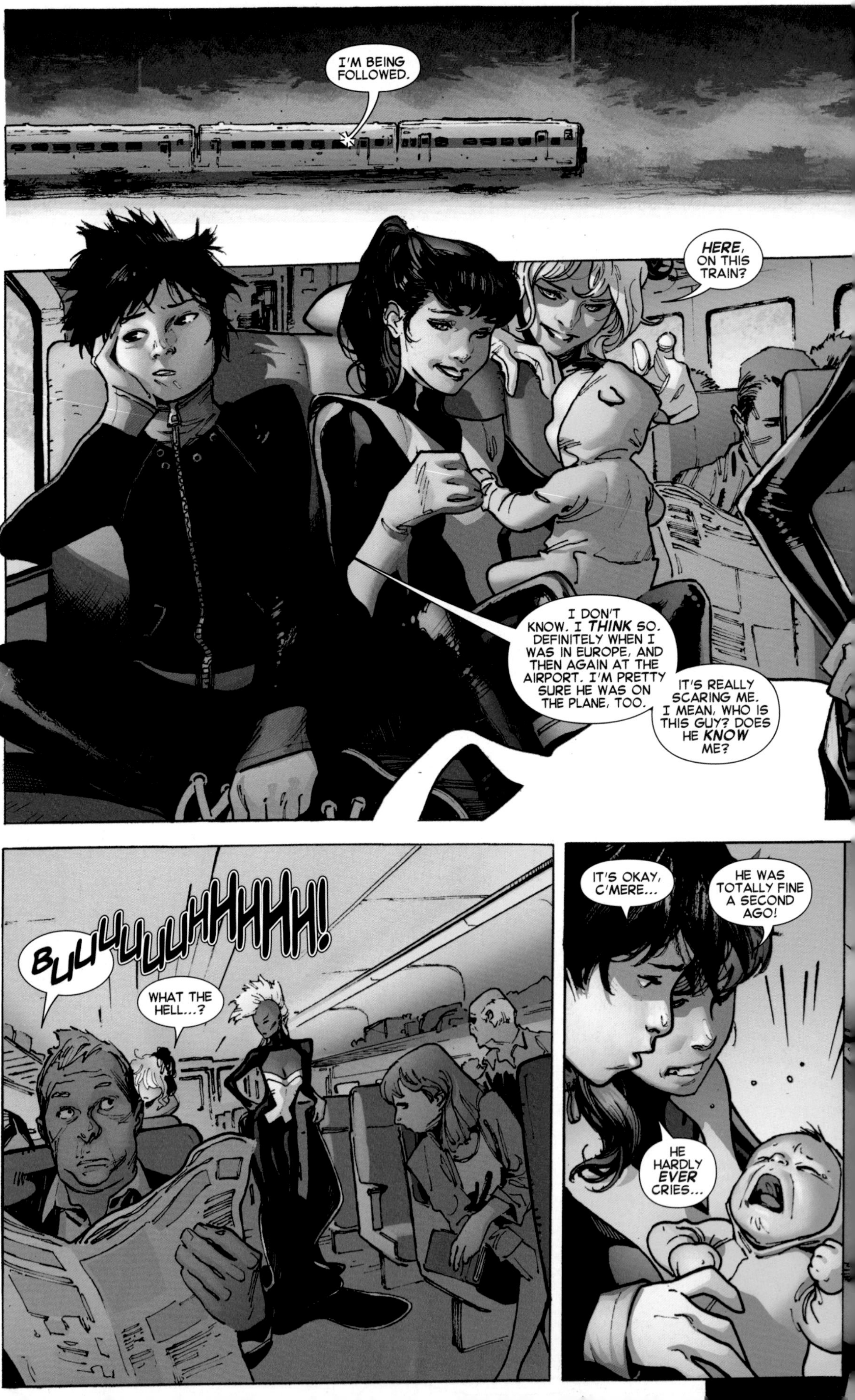
I'M BEING FOLLOWED.
HERE, ON THIS TRAIN?
I DON'T KNOW. I THINK SO. DEFINITELY WHEN I WAS IN EUROPE, AND THEN AGAIN AT THE AIRPORT. I'M PRETTY SURE HE WAS ON THE PLANE, TOO.
IT'S REALLY SCARING ME. I MEAN, WHO IS THIS GUY? DOES HE KNOW ME?
BLUUUUUUHHHHHH!
WHAT THE HELL...?
IT'S OKAY, C'MERE...
HE WAS TOTALLY FINE A SECOND AGO!
HE HARDLY EVER CRIES...

IS THIS CONNECTED TO THE INFANT? DOES THE BABY *BELONG* TO *SOMEONE*, JUBILEE?

HE'S MINE. SORTA.

BUT I DIDN'T *KIDNAP* HIM, STORM. HE'S AN ORPHAN, I *RESCUED* HIM. THERE WAS THIS TERRORIST BOMBING, BUT SOME PEOPLE SAID THEY SAW A METEORITE... I DUNNO, IT'S A LONG STORY.

I WANTED TO BRING HIM TO THE X-MEN. LIKE YOU ALL DID FOR ME.

I JUST WANT TO BE HOME. I WANT HIM TO HAVE A HOT MEAL AND A REAL BED TO SLEEP IN. HE WAS LIVING IN SOME ORPHANAGE, I THINK?

I WANT DR. REYES TO CHECK HIM OUT, MAKE SURE HE'S OKAY.

BUH

BABIES HATE ME!

HE JUST WANTS HIS MOMMY.

OR TO TOUCH THAT SPEAKER. HEY, DON'T TOUCH, THAT'S DIRTY.

BUH!

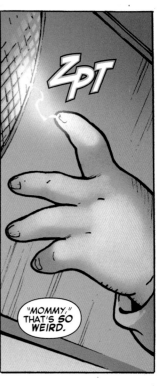

ZPT

"MOMMY," THAT'S SO WEIRD.

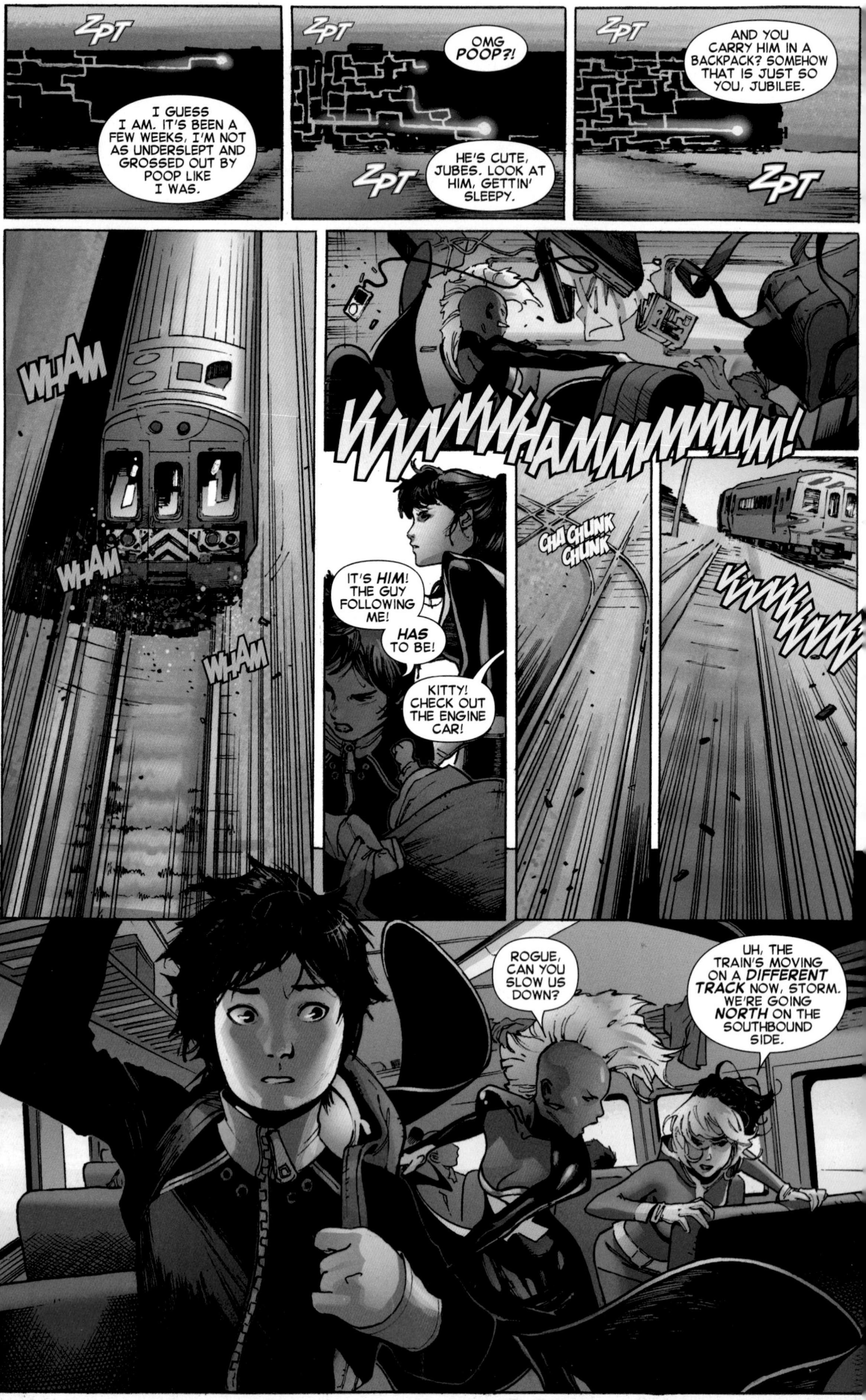
ZPT
I GUESS I AM. IT'S BEEN A FEW WEEKS, I'M NOT AS UNDERSLEPT AND GROSSED OUT BY POOP LIKE I WAS.
ZPT
OMG POOP?!
HE'S CUTE, JUBES. LOOK AT HIM, GETTIN' SLEEPY.
ZPT
ZPT
AND YOU CARRY HIM IN A BACKPACK? SOMEHOW THAT IS JUST SO YOU, JUBILEE.
ZPT
WHAM
WHAM
WHAM
VVVVWHAMMMMMM!
IT'S HIM! THE GUY FOLLOWING ME!
HAS TO BE!
KITTY! CHECK OUT THE ENGINE CAR!
CHA CHUNK CHUNK
VVVVVVVV
ROGUE, CAN YOU SLOW US DOWN?
UH, THE TRAIN'S MOVING ON A DIFFERENT TRACK NOW, STORM. WE'RE GOING NORTH ON THE SOUTHBOUND SIDE.

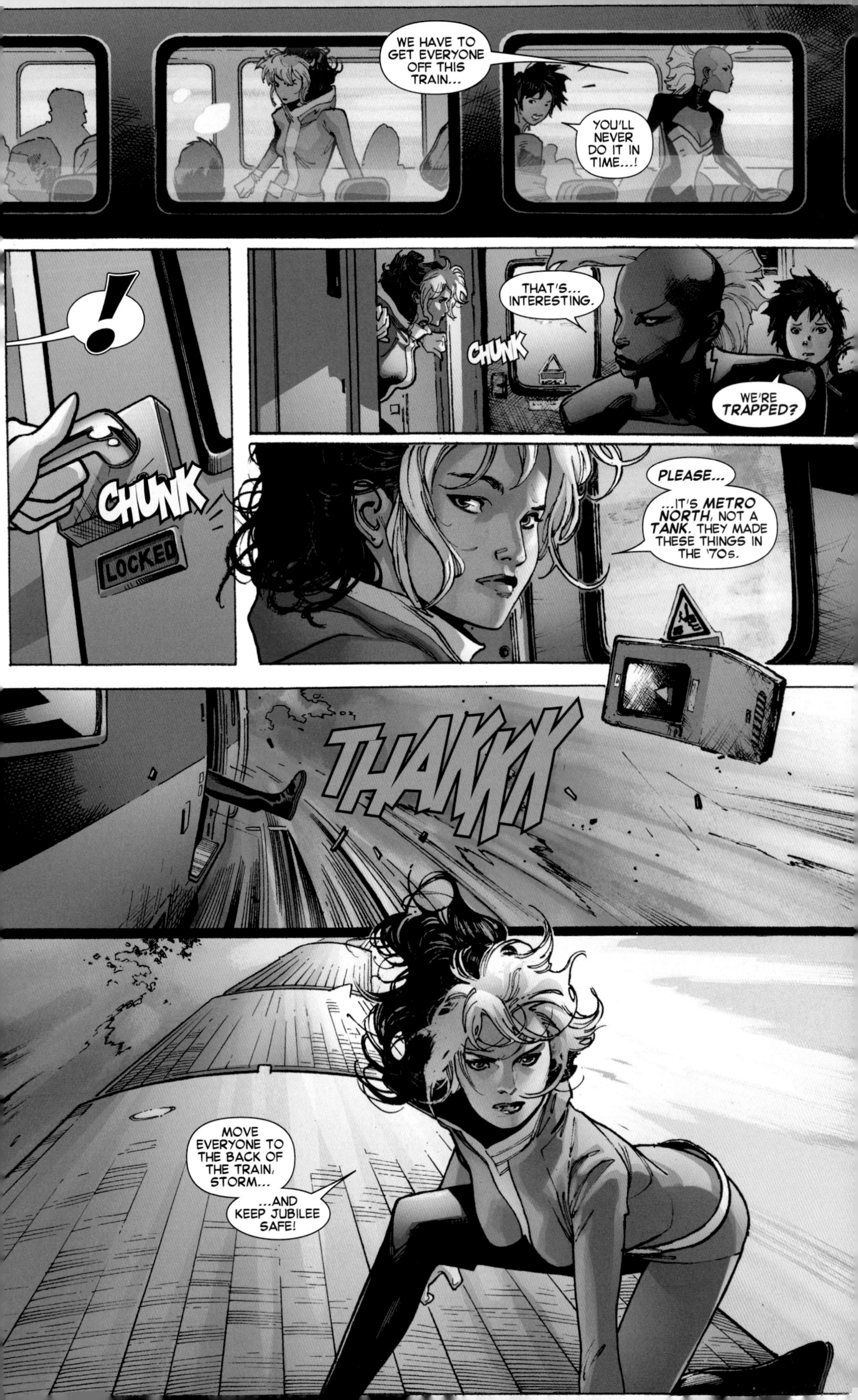
WE HAVE TO GET EVERYONE OFF THIS TRAIN...
YOU'LL NEVER DO IT IN TIME...!
!
CHUNK
LOCKED
THAT'S... INTERESTING.
CHUNK
WE'RE TRAPPED?
PLEASE...
...IT'S METRO NORTH, NOT A TANK. THEY MADE THESE THINGS IN THE '70s.
THAKKK
MOVE EVERYONE TO THE BACK OF THE TRAIN, STORM...
...AND KEEP JUBILEE SAFE!

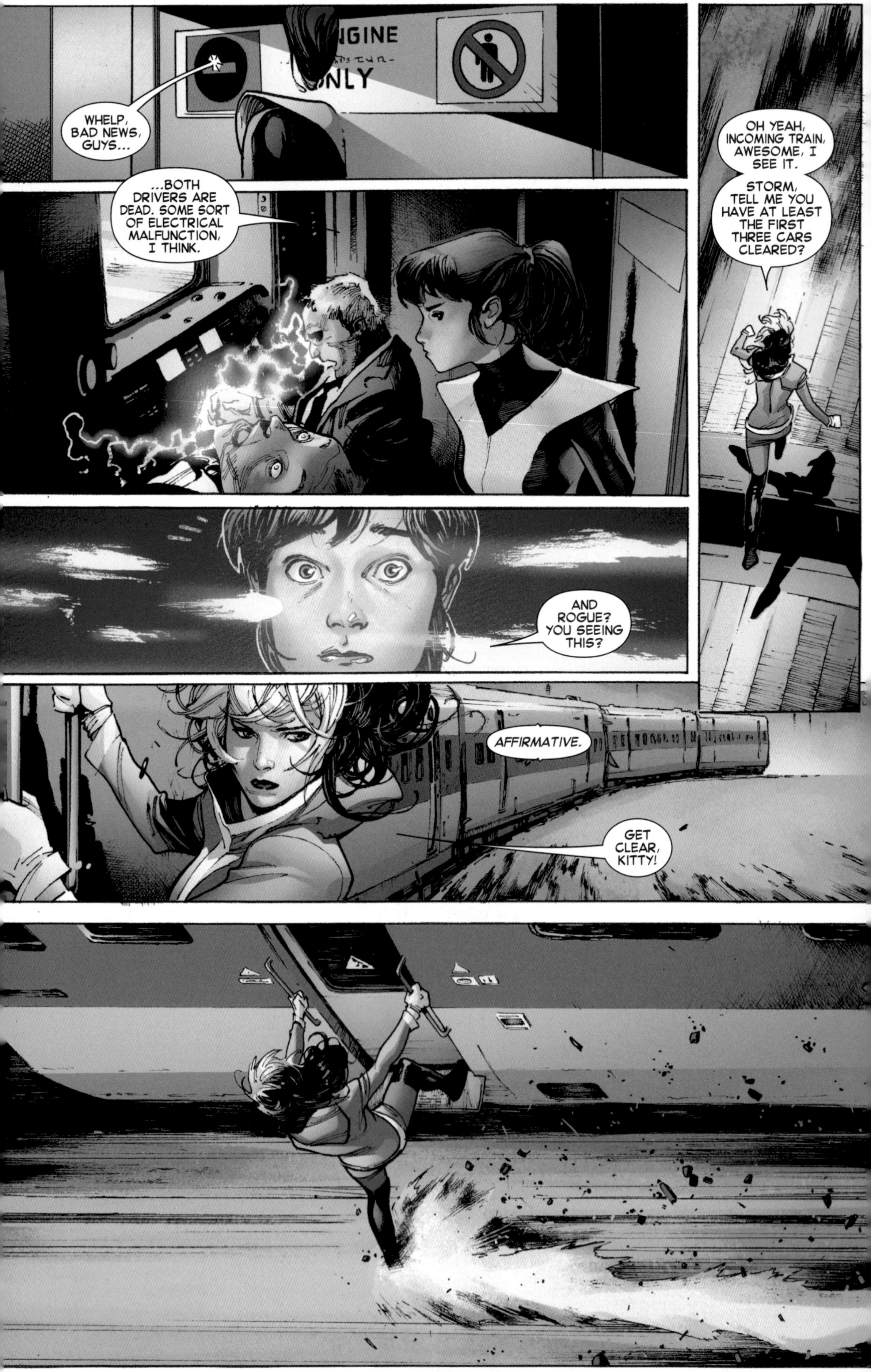
WHELP, BAD NEWS, GUYS...
...BOTH DRIVERS ARE DEAD. SOME SORT OF ELECTRICAL MALFUNCTION, I THINK.
OH YEAH, INCOMING TRAIN, AWESOME, I SEE IT.
STORM, TELL ME YOU HAVE AT LEAST THE FIRST THREE CARS CLEARED?
AND ROGUE? YOU SEEING THIS?
AFFIRMATIVE.
GET CLEAR, KITTY!

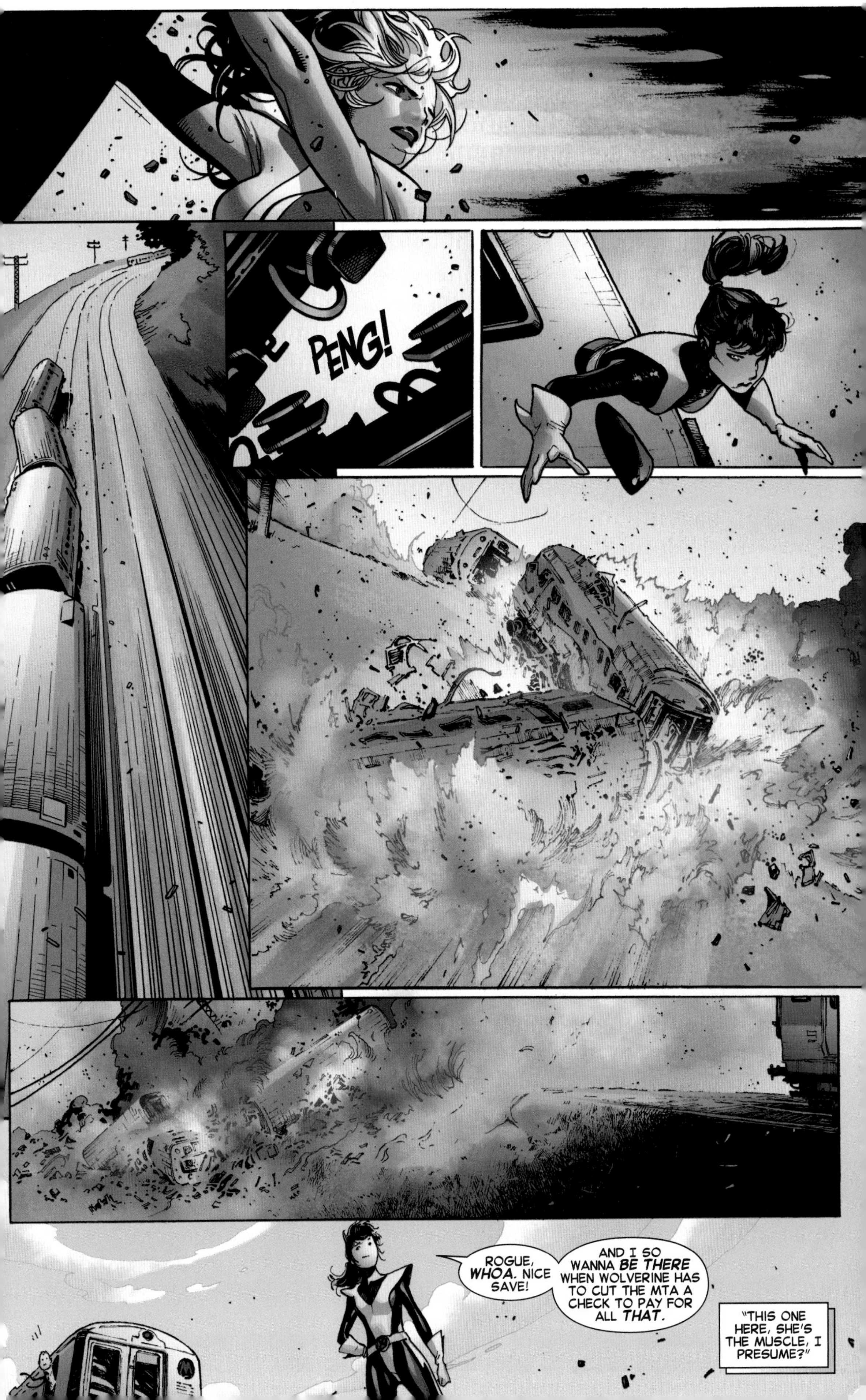
PENG!
ROGUE, WHOA. NICE SAVE!
AND I SO WANNA BE THERE WHEN WOLVERINE HAS TO CUT THE MTA A CHECK TO PAY FOR ALL THAT.
"THIS ONE HERE, SHE'S THE MUSCLE, I PRESUME?"

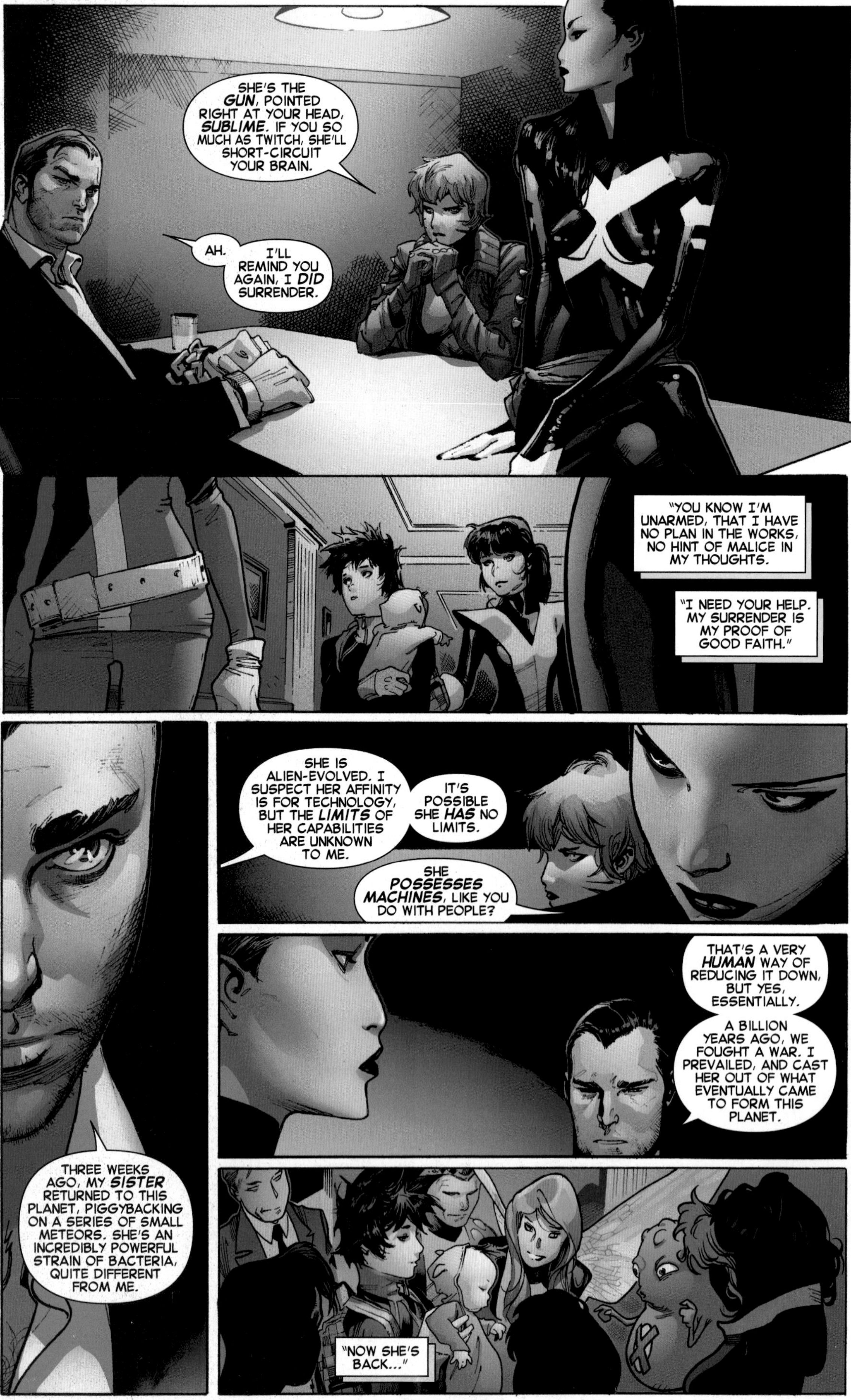

SHE'S THE GUN, POINTED RIGHT AT YOUR HEAD, SUBLIME. IF YOU SO MUCH AS TWITCH, SHE'LL SHORT-CIRCUIT YOUR BRAIN.
AH.
I'LL REMIND YOU AGAIN, I DID SURRENDER.
"YOU KNOW I'M UNARMED, THAT I HAVE NO PLAN IN THE WORKS, NO HINT OF MALICE IN MY THOUGHTS.
"I NEED YOUR HELP. MY SURRENDER IS MY PROOF OF GOOD FAITH."
SHE IS ALIEN-EVOLVED. I SUSPECT HER AFFINITY IS FOR TECHNOLOGY, BUT THE LIMITS OF HER CAPABILITIES ARE UNKNOWN TO ME.
IT'S POSSIBLE SHE HAS NO LIMITS.
SHE POSSESSES MACHINES, LIKE YOU DO WITH PEOPLE?
THAT'S A VERY HUMAN WAY OF REDUCING IT DOWN, BUT YES, ESSENTIALLY.
A BILLION YEARS AGO, WE FOUGHT A WAR. I PREVAILED, AND CAST HER OUT OF WHAT EVENTUALLY CAME TO FORM THIS PLANET.
THREE WEEKS AGO, MY SISTER RETURNED TO THIS PLANET, PIGGYBACKING ON A SERIES OF SMALL METEORS. SHE'S AN INCREDIBLY POWERFUL STRAIN OF BACTERIA, QUITE DIFFERENT FROM ME.
"NOW SHE'S BACK..."

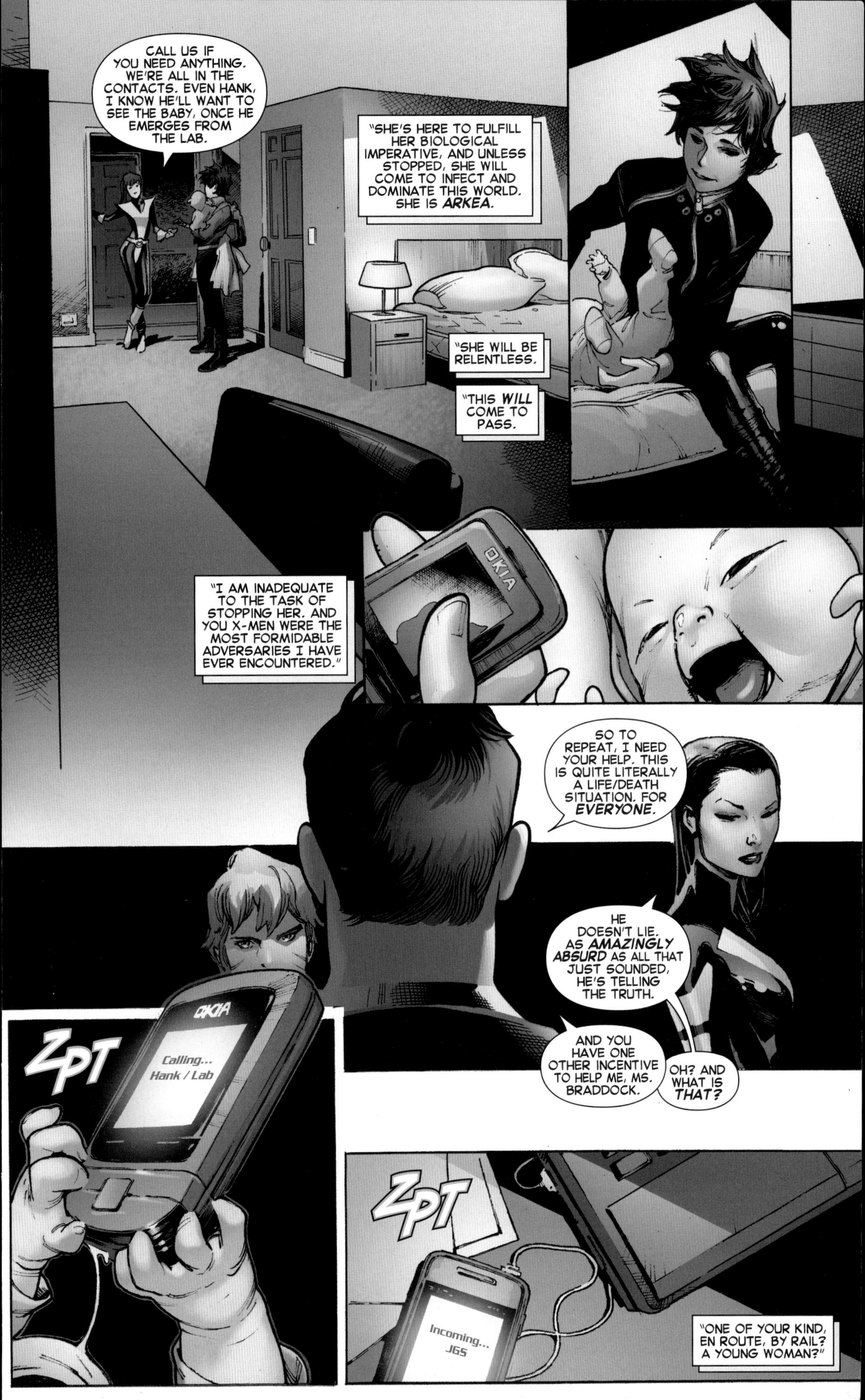
CALL US IF YOU NEED ANYTHING. WE'RE ALL IN THE CONTACTS. EVEN HANK, I KNOW HE'LL WANT TO SEE THE BABY, ONCE HE EMERGES FROM THE LAB.
"SHE'S HERE TO FULFILL HER BIOLOGICAL IMPERATIVE, AND UNLESS STOPPED, SHE WILL COME TO INFECT AND DOMINATE THIS WORLD. SHE IS ARKEA.
"SHE WILL BE RELENTLESS.
"THIS WILL COME TO PASS.
"I AM INADEQUATE TO THE TASK OF STOPPING HER. AND YOU X-MEN WERE THE MOST FORMIDABLE ADVERSARIES I HAVE EVER ENCOUNTERED."
OKIA
SO TO REPEAT, I NEED YOUR HELP. THIS IS QUITE LITERALLY A LIFE/DEATH SITUATION. FOR EVERYONE.
HE DOESN'T LIE. AS AMAZINGLY ABSURD AS ALL THAT JUST SOUNDED, HE'S TELLING THE TRUTH.
AND YOU HAVE ONE OTHER INCENTIVE TO HELP ME, MS. BRADDOCK.
OH? AND WHAT IS THAT?
ZPT
OKIA
Calling...
Hank / Lab
ZPT
Incoming...
JGS
"ONE OF YOUR KIND, EN ROUTE, BY RAIL? A YOUNG WOMAN?"

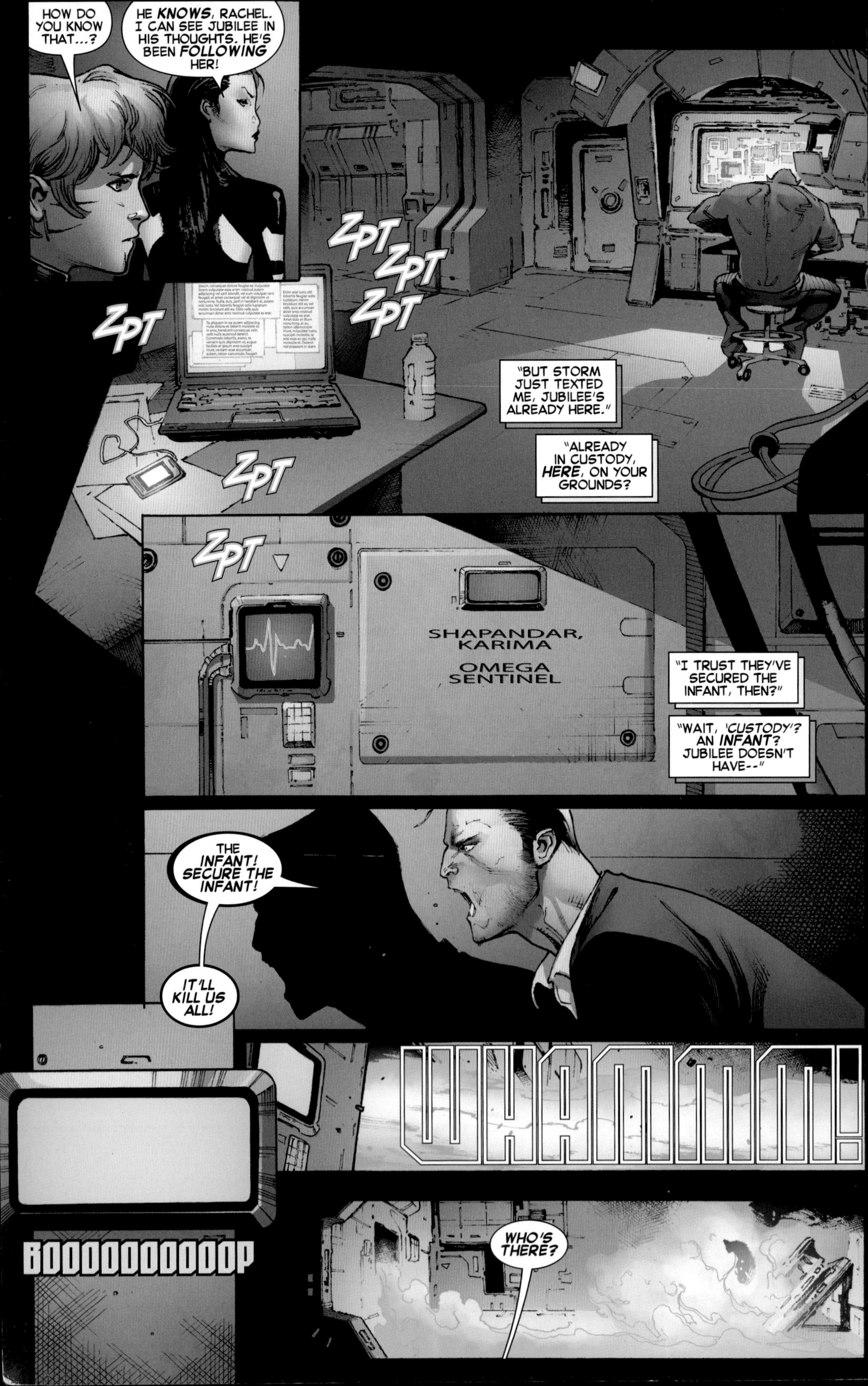
HOW DO YOU KNOW THAT...?
HE KNOWS, RACHEL. I CAN SEE JUBILEE IN HIS THOUGHTS. HE'S BEEN FOLLOWING HER!
ZPT
ZPT
ZPT
ZPT
"BUT STORM JUST TEXTED ME, JUBILEE'S ALREADY HERE."
"ALREADY IN CUSTODY, HERE, ON YOUR GROUNDS?
ZPT
ZPT
SHAPANDAR, KARIMA
OMEGA SENTINEL
"I TRUST THEY'VE SECURED THE INFANT, THEN?"
"WAIT, 'CUSTODY'? AN INFANT? JUBILEE DOESN'T HAVE--"
THE INFANT! SECURE THE INFANT!
IT'LL KILL US ALL!
WHAMMM!
BOOOOOOOOOOP
WHO'S THERE?

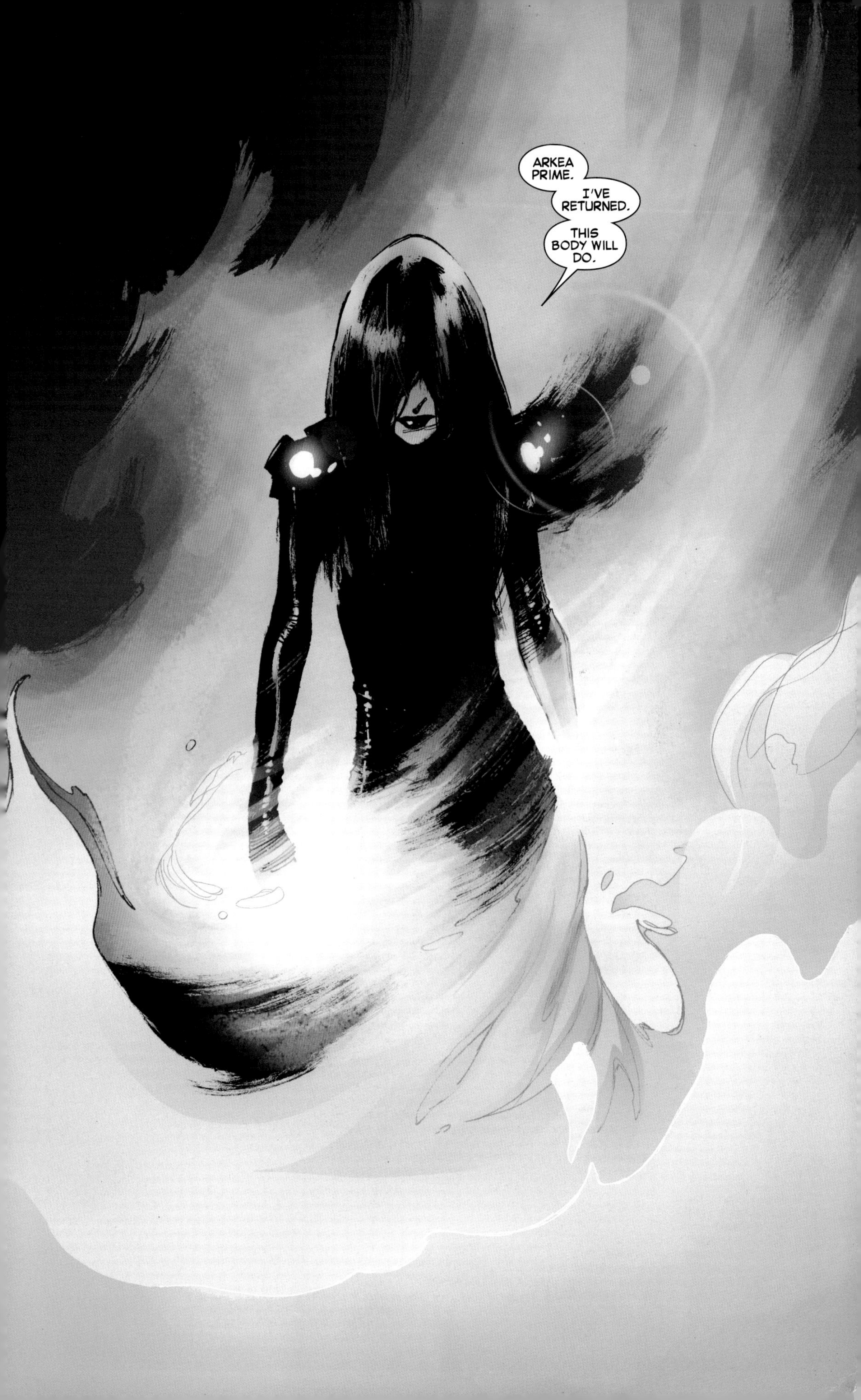
ARKEA PRIME.
I'VE RETURNED.
THIS BODY WILL DO.

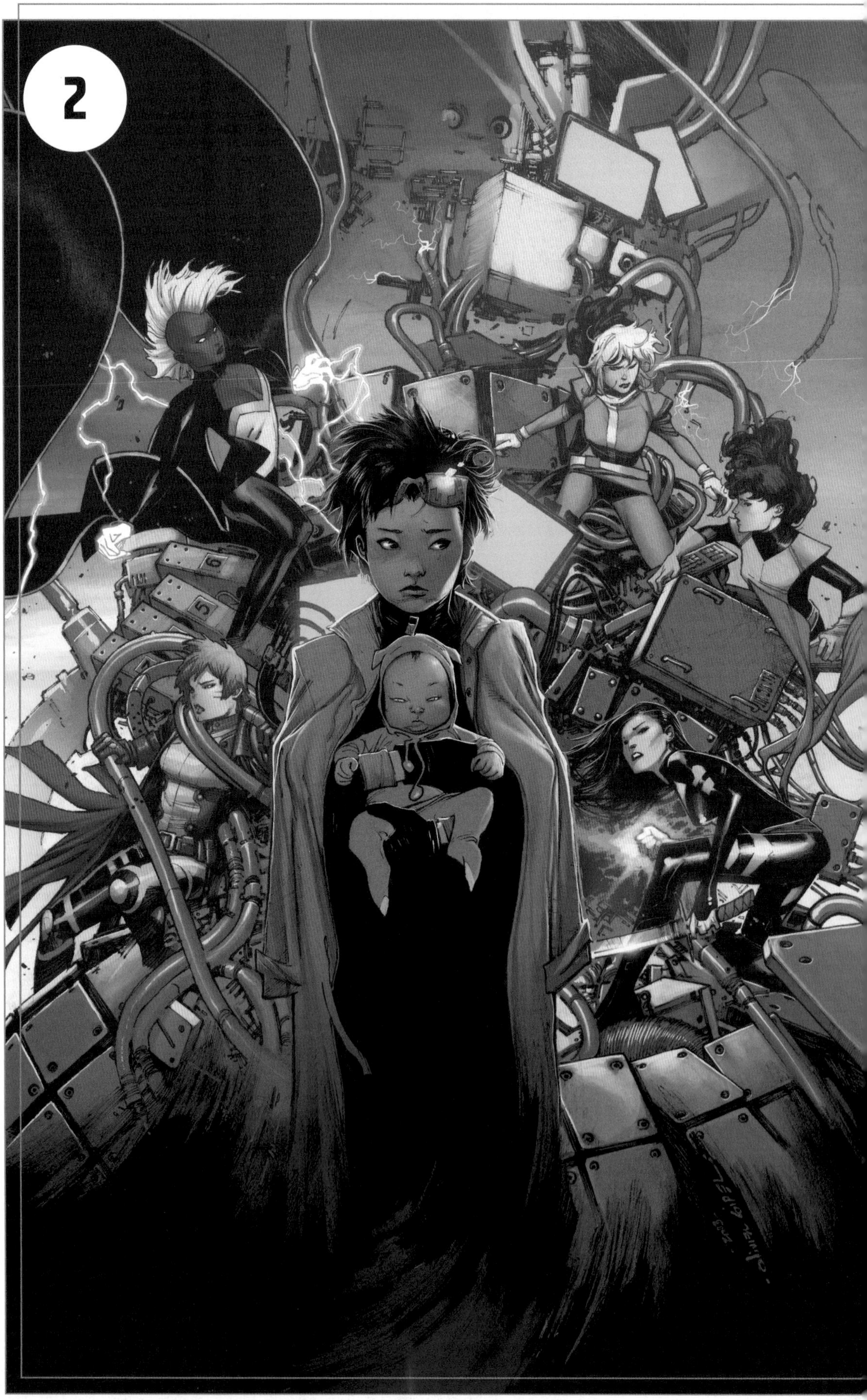
2

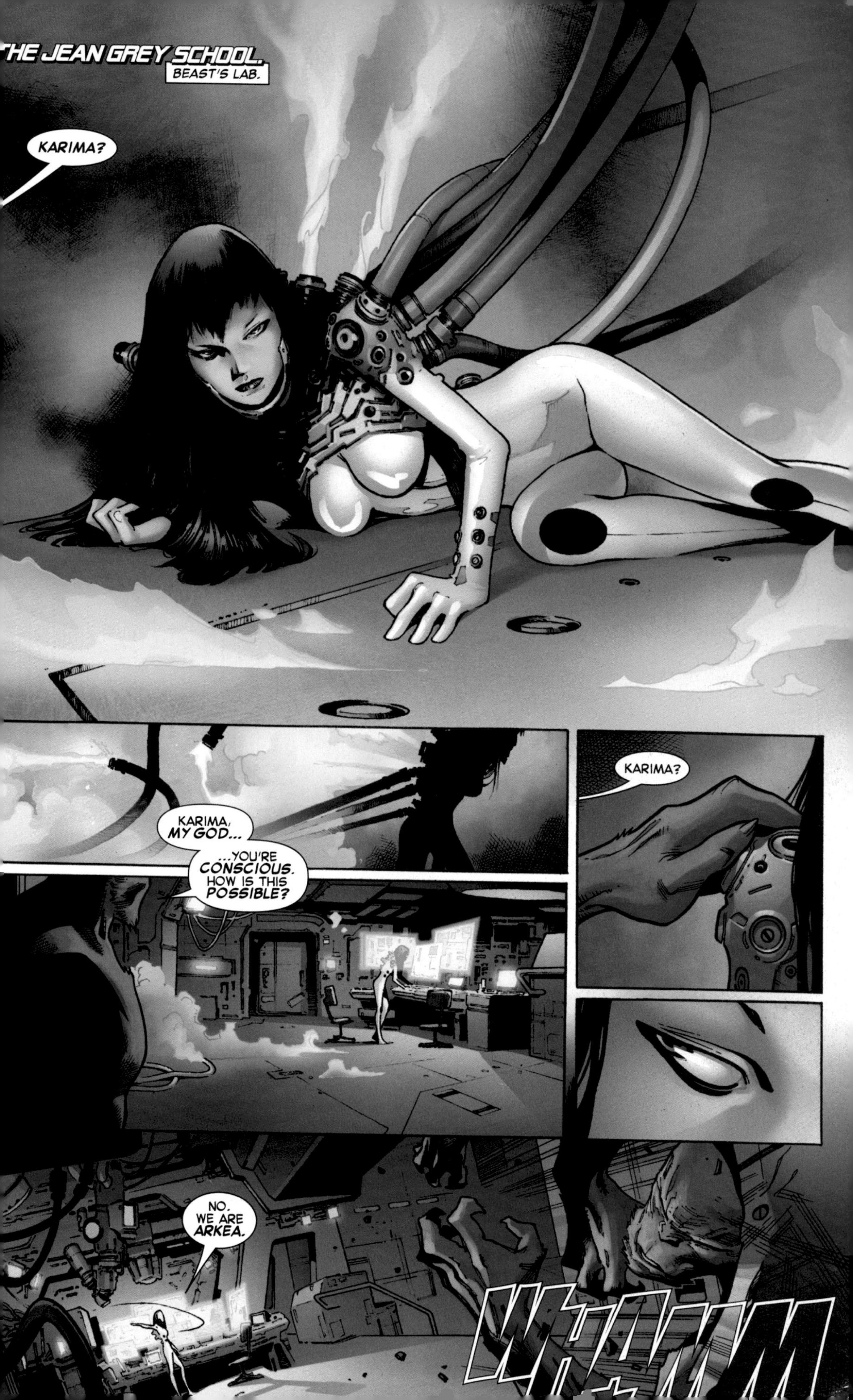
THE JEAN GREY SCHOOL.
BEAST'S LAB.
KARIMA?
KARIMA, MY GOD...
...YOU'RE CONSCIOUS. HOW IS THIS POSSIBLE?
KARIMA?
NO. WE ARE ARKEA.
WHAMM

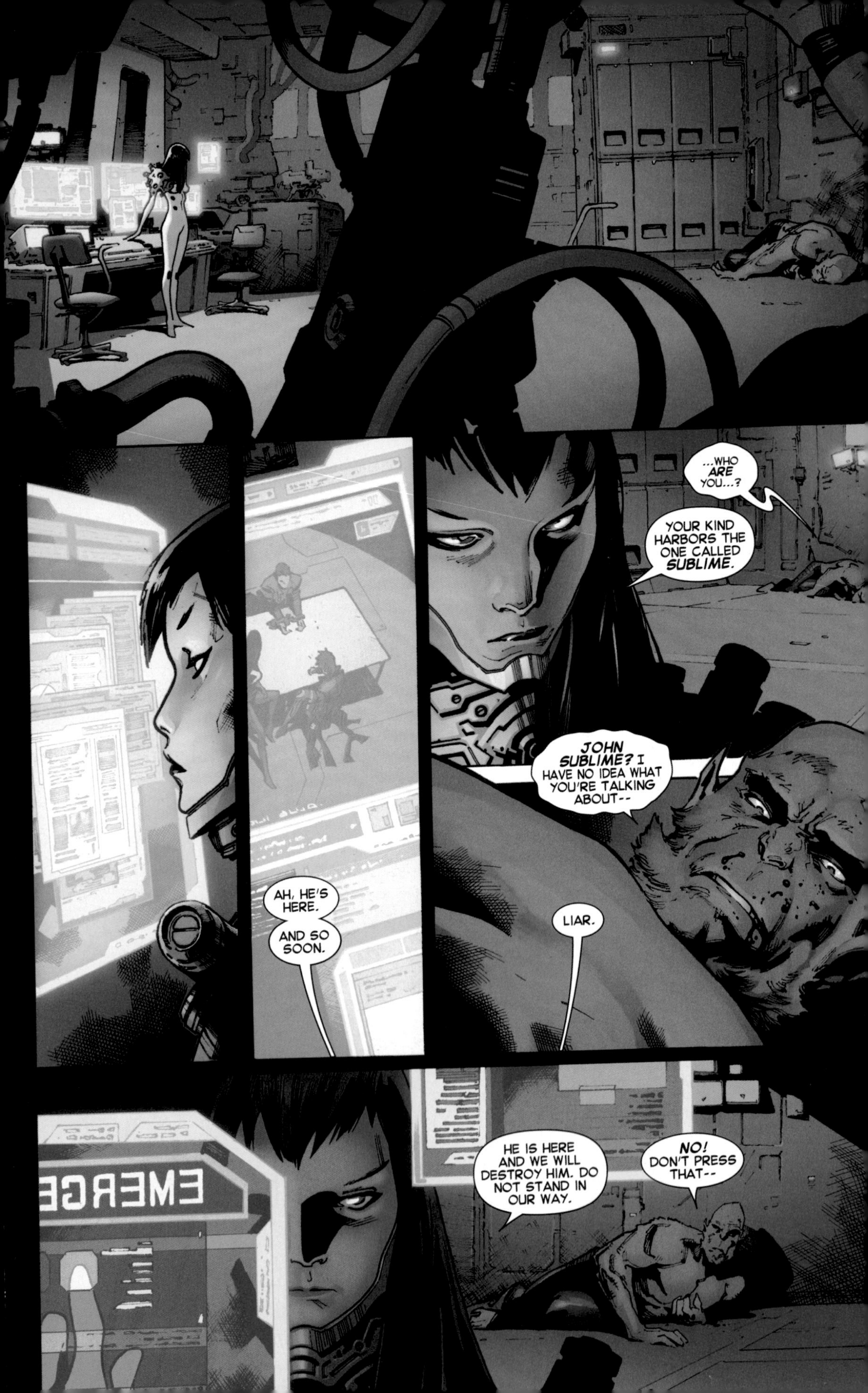
...WHO ARE YOU...?
YOUR KIND HARBORS THE ONE CALLED SUBLIME.
JOHN SUBLIME? I HAVE NO IDEA WHAT YOU'RE TALKING ABOUT--
LIAR.
AH, HE'S HERE.
AND SO SOON.
EMERGE
HE IS HERE AND WE WILL DESTROY HIM. DO NOT STAND IN OUR WAY.
NO! DON'T PRESS THAT--

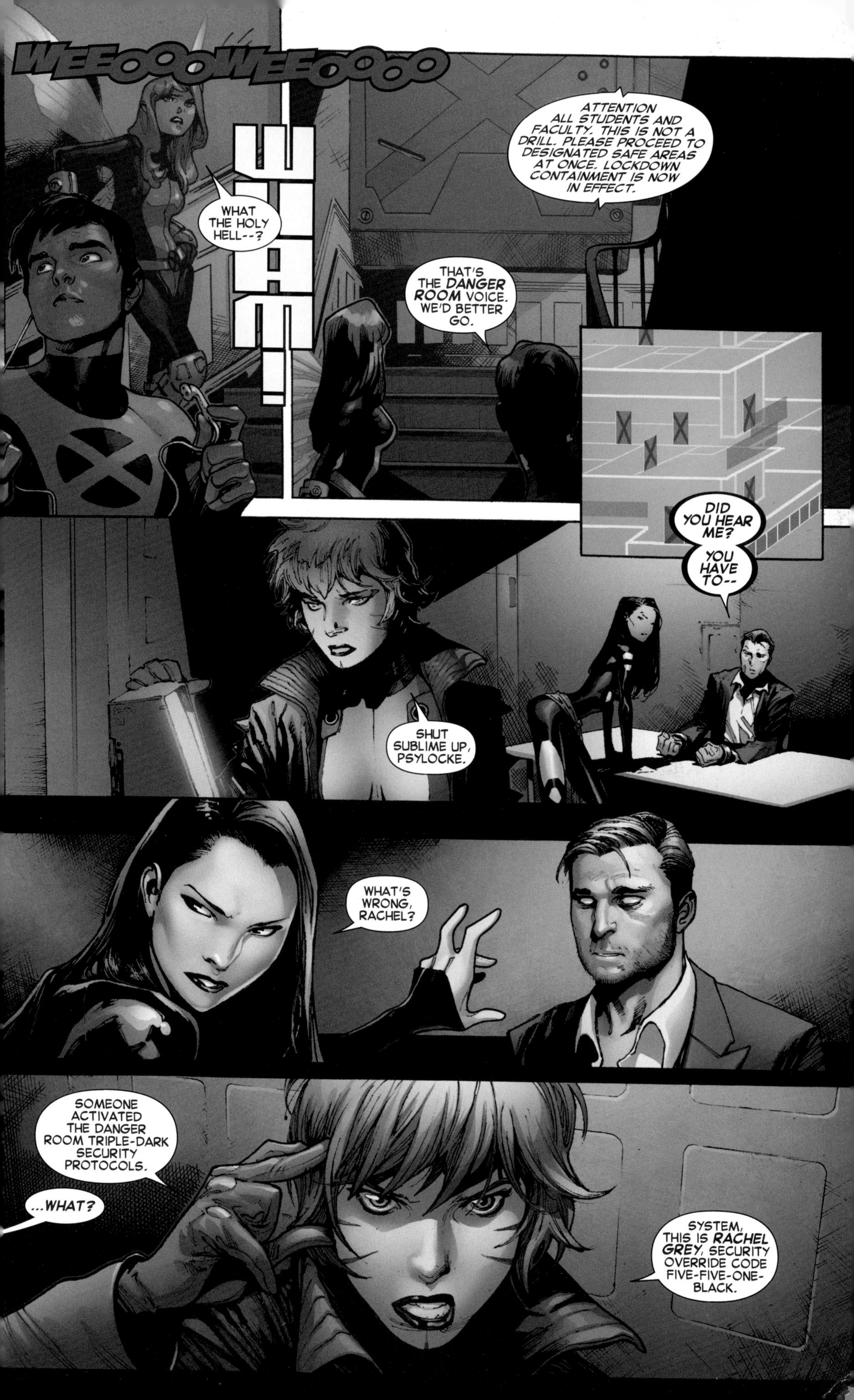
WEEOOOOWEEOOOOO
WHAT THE HOLY HELL--?
WHAM!
ATTENTION ALL STUDENTS AND FACULTY. THIS IS NOT A DRILL. PLEASE PROCEED TO DESIGNATED SAFE AREAS AT ONCE. LOCKDOWN CONTAINMENT IS NOW IN EFFECT.
THAT'S THE DANGER ROOM VOICE. WE'D BETTER GO.
DID YOU HEAR ME?
YOU HAVE TO--
SHUT SUBLIME UP, PSYLOCKE.
WHAT'S WRONG, RACHEL?
SOMEONE ACTIVATED THE DANGER ROOM TRIPLE-DARK SECURITY PROTOCOLS.
...WHAT?
SYSTEM, THIS IS RACHEL GREY, SECURITY OVERRIDE CODE FIVE-FIVE-ONE-BLACK.

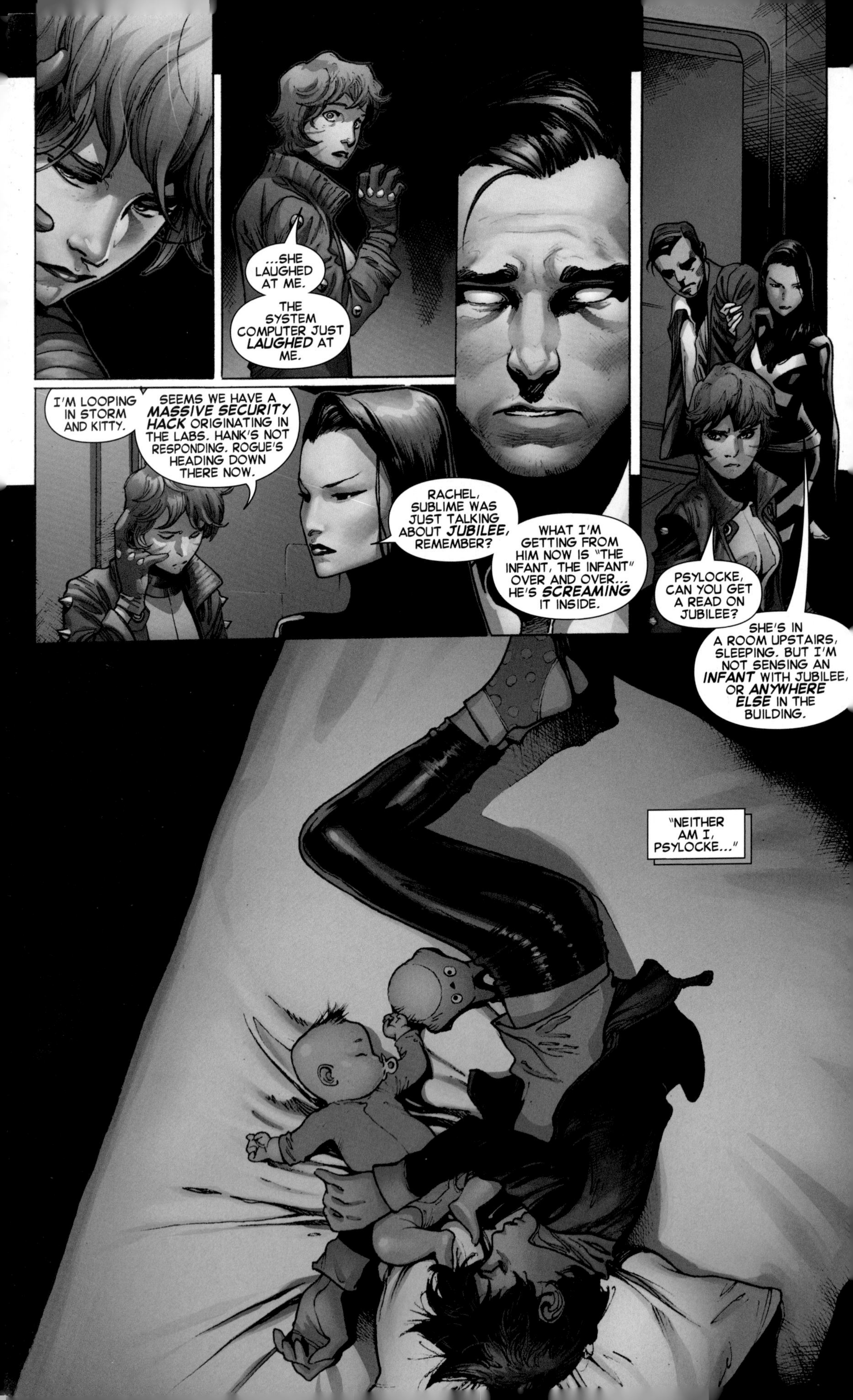
...SHE LAUGHED AT ME.
THE SYSTEM COMPUTER JUST LAUGHED AT ME.
I'M LOOPING IN STORM AND KITTY.
SEEMS WE HAVE A MASSIVE SECURITY HACK ORIGINATING IN THE LABS. HANK'S NOT RESPONDING. ROGUE'S HEADING DOWN THERE NOW.
RACHEL, SUBLIME WAS JUST TALKING ABOUT JUBILEE, REMEMBER?
WHAT I'M GETTING FROM HIM NOW IS "THE INFANT, THE INFANT" OVER AND OVER... HE'S SCREAMING IT INSIDE.
PSYLOCKE, CAN YOU GET A READ ON JUBILEE?
SHE'S IN A ROOM UPSTAIRS, SLEEPING. BUT I'M NOT SENSING AN INFANT WITH JUBILEE, OR ANYWHERE ELSE IN THE BUILDING.
"NEITHER AM I, PSYLOCKE..."

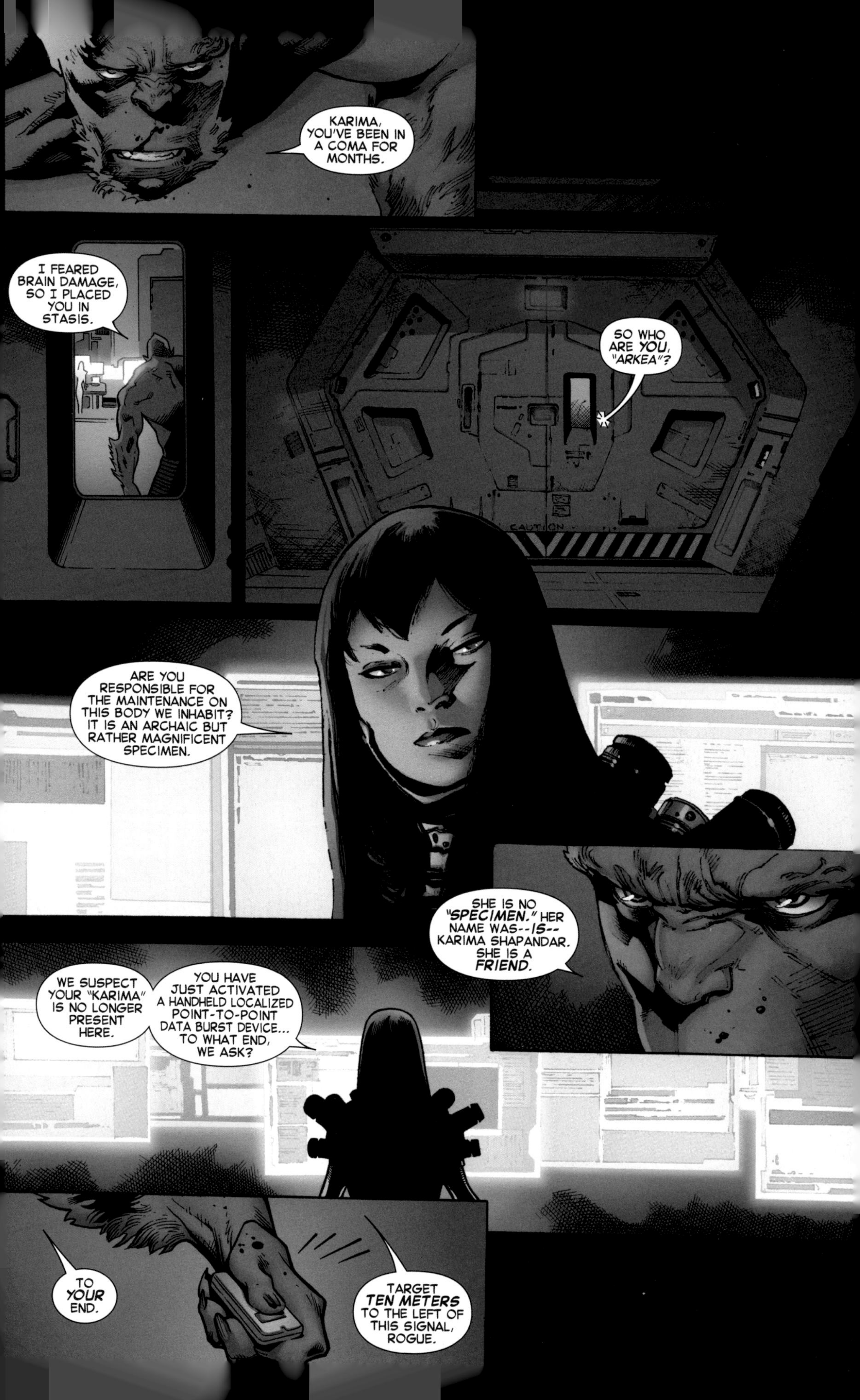
KARIMA, YOU'VE BEEN IN A COMA FOR MONTHS.
I FEARED BRAIN DAMAGE, SO I PLACED YOU IN STASIS.
SO WHO ARE YOU, "ARKEA"?
CAUTION
ARE YOU RESPONSIBLE FOR THE MAINTENANCE ON THIS BODY WE INHABIT? IT IS AN ARCHAIC BUT RATHER MAGNIFICENT SPECIMEN.
SHE IS NO "SPECIMEN." HER NAME WAS--IS--KARIMA SHAPANDAR. SHE IS A FRIEND.
WE SUSPECT YOUR "KARIMA" IS NO LONGER PRESENT HERE.
YOU HAVE JUST ACTIVATED A HANDHELD LOCALIZED POINT-TO-POINT DATA BURST DEVICE... TO WHAT END, WE ASK?
TO YOUR END.
TARGET TEN METERS TO THE LEFT OF THIS SIGNAL, ROGUE.

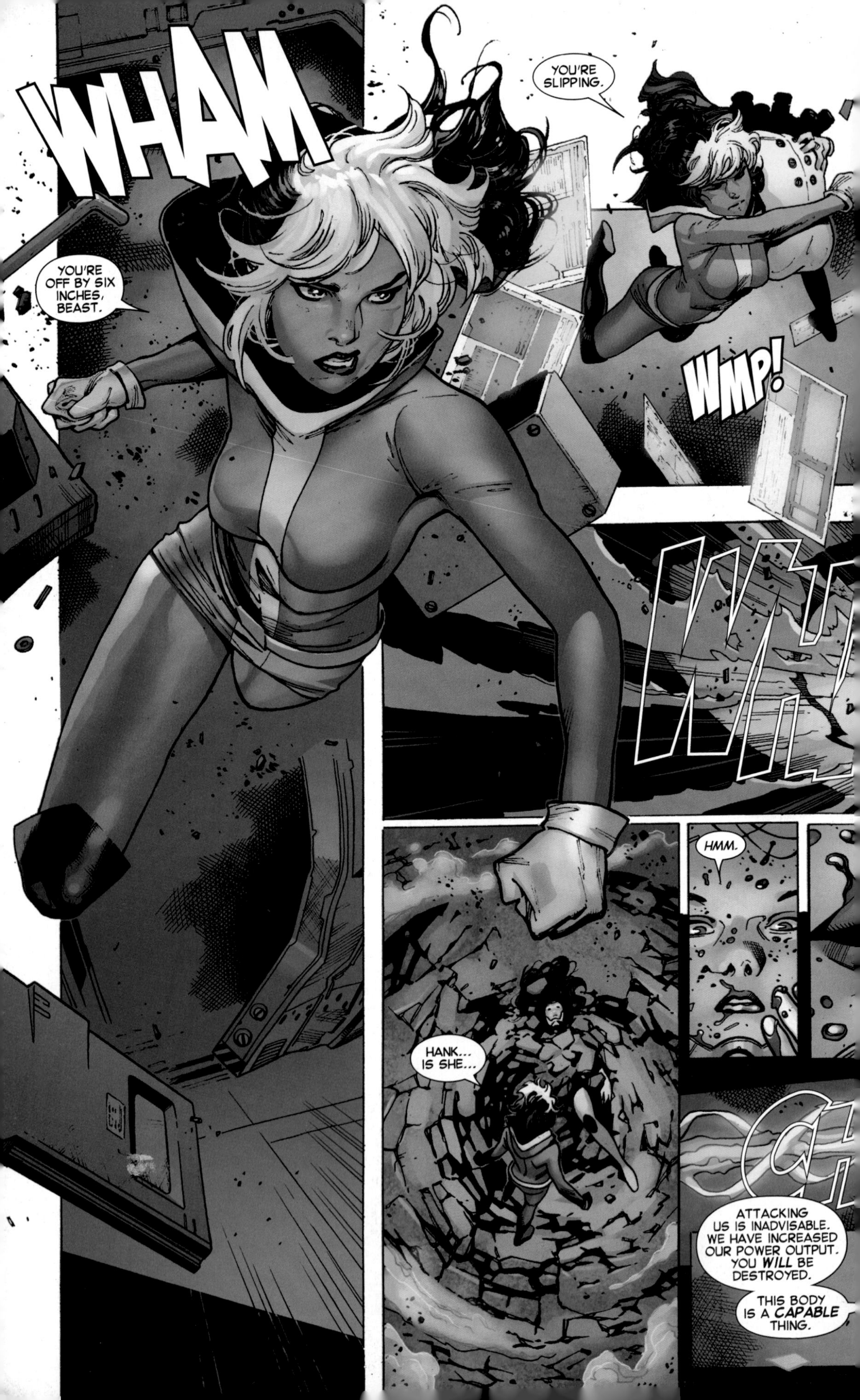
WHAM
YOU'RE OFF BY SIX INCHES, BEAST.
YOU'RE SLIPPING.
WMP!
HANK... IS SHE...
HMM.
ATTACKING US IS INADVISABLE. WE HAVE INCREASED OUR POWER OUTPUT. YOU *WILL* BE DESTROYED.
THIS BODY IS A *CAPABLE* THING.

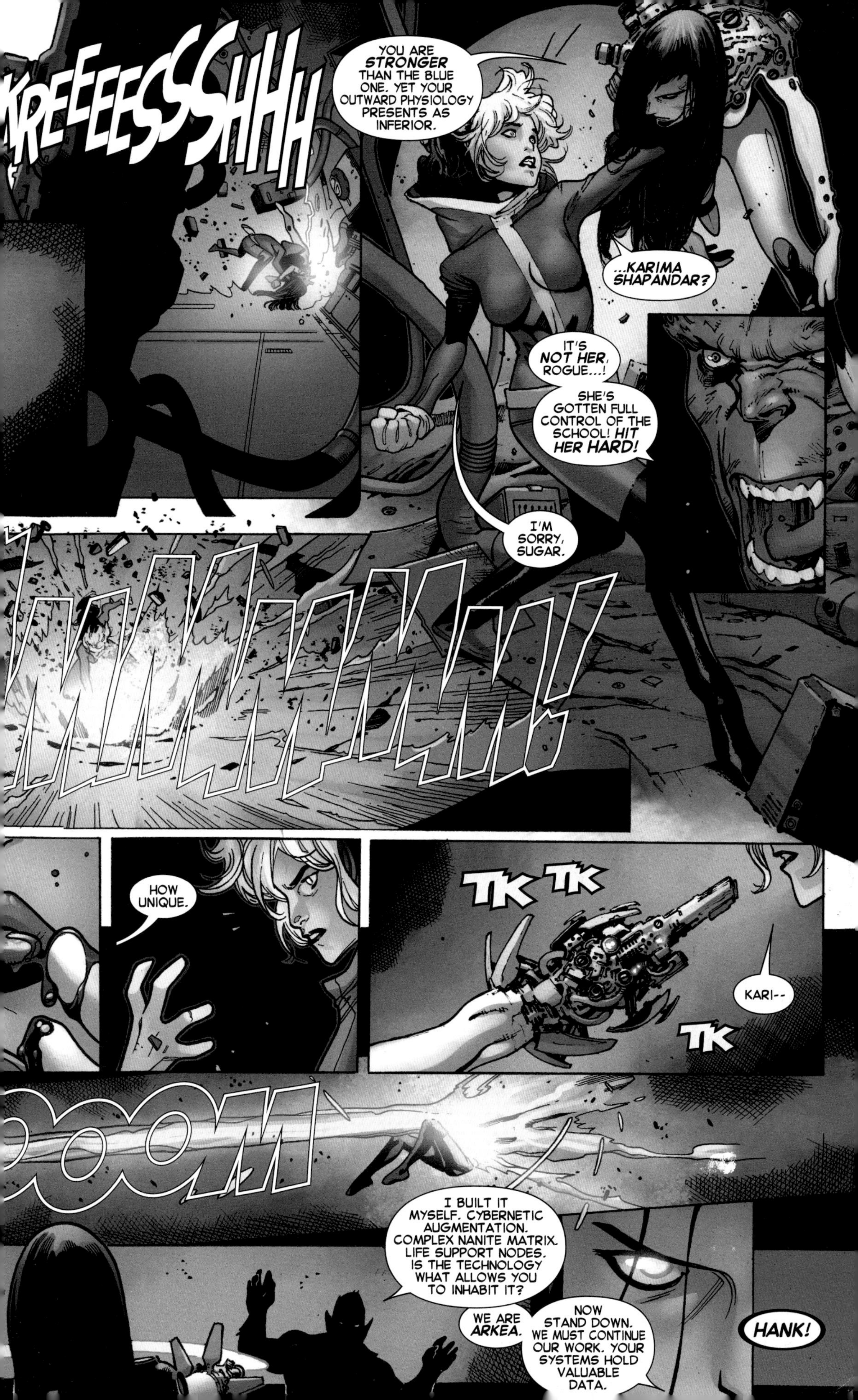
KREEEESSSHHH
YOU ARE STRONGER THAN THE BLUE ONE. YET YOUR OUTWARD PHYSIOLOGY PRESENTS AS INFERIOR.
...KARIMA SHAPANDAR?
IT'S NOT HER, ROGUE...!
SHE'S GOTTEN FULL CONTROL OF THE SCHOOL! HIT HER HARD!
I'M SORRY, SUGAR.
HOW UNIQUE.
TK TK
KARI--
TK
I BUILT IT MYSELF. CYBERNETIC AUGMENTATION. COMPLEX NANITE MATRIX. LIFE SUPPORT NODES. IS THE TECHNOLOGY WHAT ALLOWS YOU TO INHABIT IT?
WE ARE ARKEA.
NOW STAND DOWN. WE MUST CONTINUE OUR WORK. YOUR SYSTEMS HOLD VALUABLE DATA.
HANK!

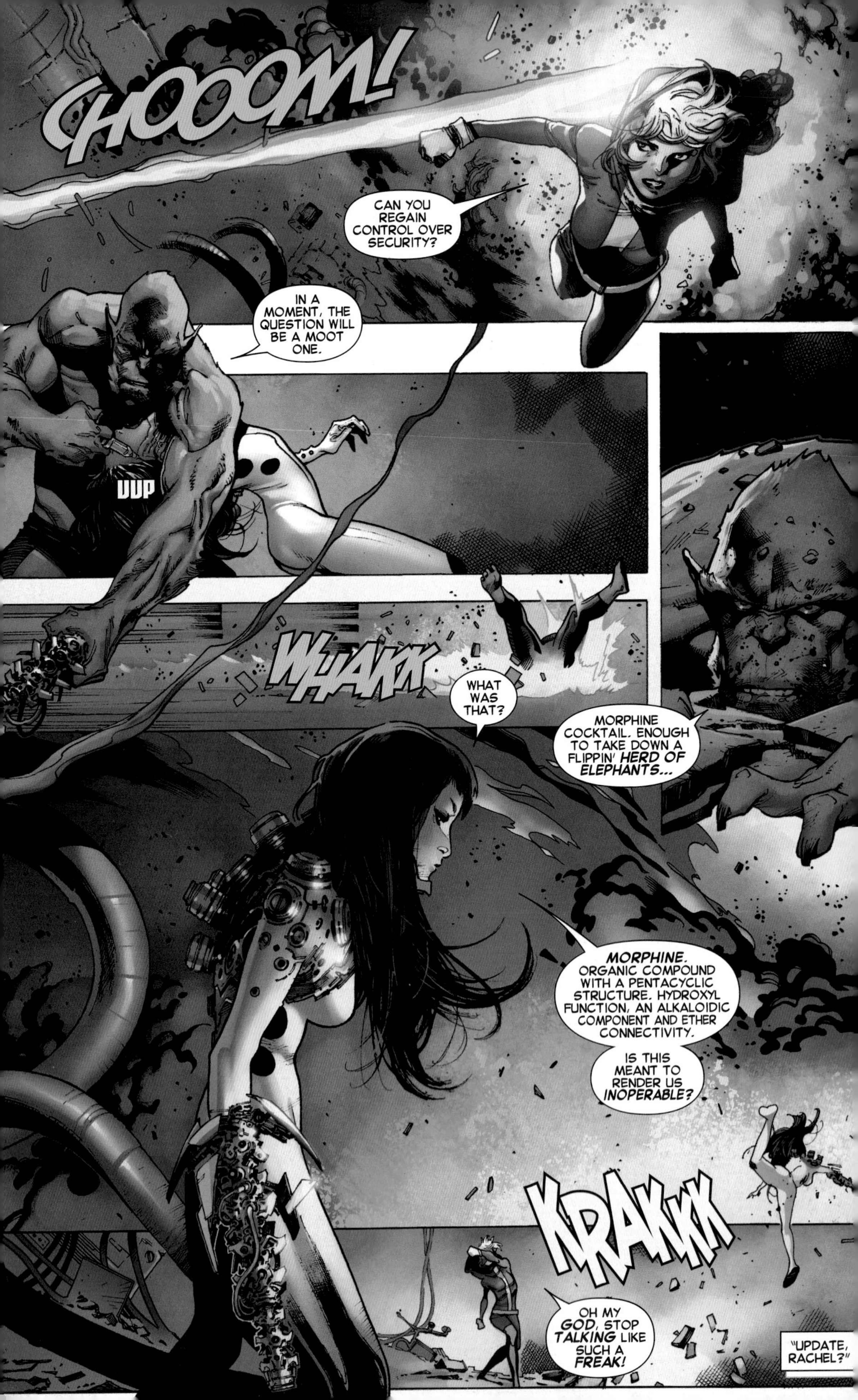
CHOOOM!
CAN YOU REGAIN CONTROL OVER SECURITY?
IN A MOMENT, THE QUESTION WILL BE A MOOT ONE.
VVP
WHAKK
WHAT WAS THAT?
MORPHINE COCKTAIL. ENOUGH TO TAKE DOWN A FLIPPIN' HERD OF ELEPHANTS...
MORPHINE. ORGANIC COMPOUND WITH A PENTACYCLIC STRUCTURE. HYDROXYL FUNCTION, AN ALKALOIDIC COMPONENT AND ETHER CONNECTIVITY.
IS THIS MEANT TO RENDER US INOPERABLE?
KRAKKK
OH MY GOD, STOP TALKING LIKE SUCH A FREAK!
"UPDATE, RACHEL?"

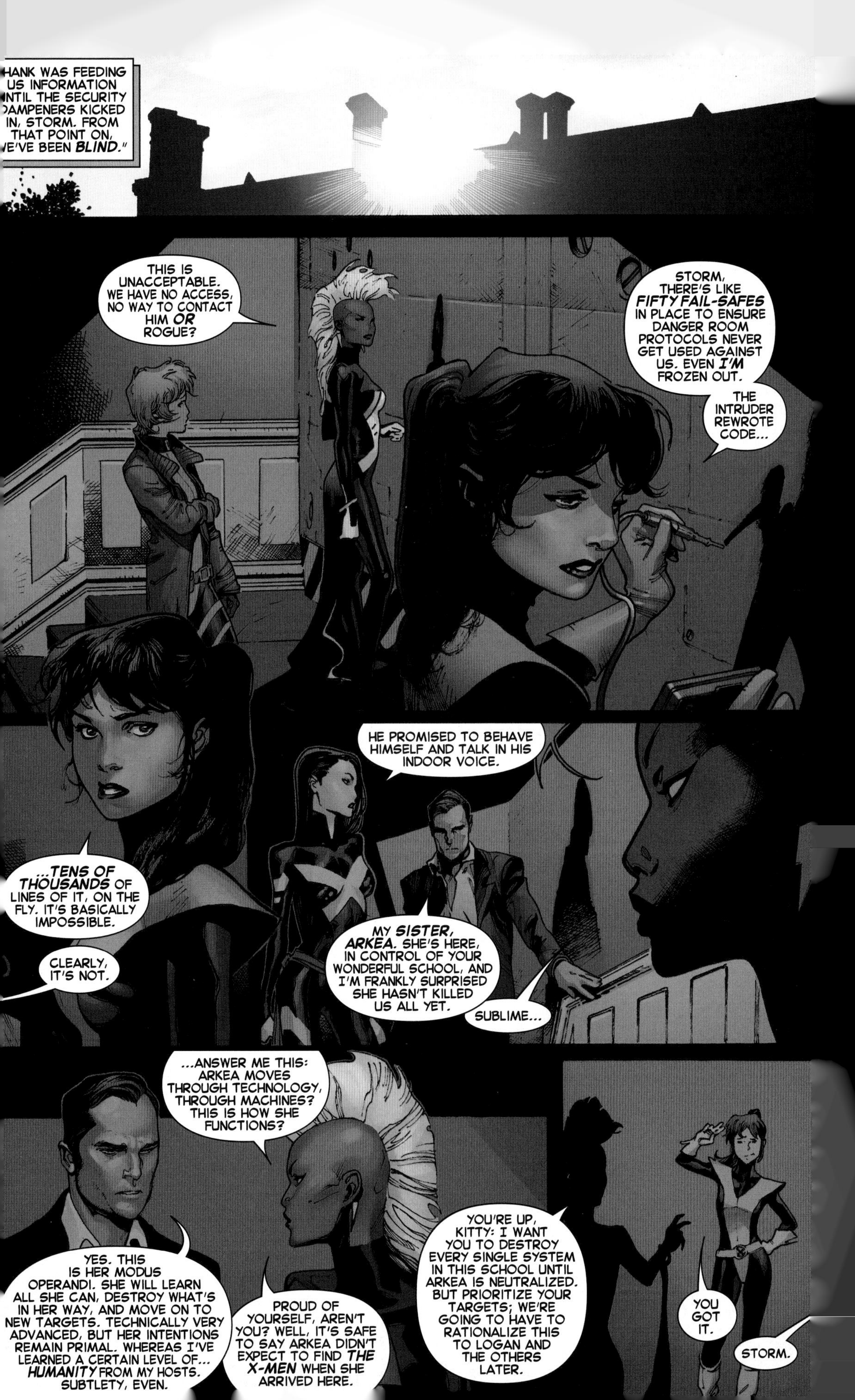
HANK WAS FEEDING US INFORMATION UNTIL THE SECURITY DAMPENERS KICKED IN, STORM. FROM THAT POINT ON, WE'VE BEEN BLIND."
THIS IS UNACCEPTABLE. WE HAVE NO ACCESS, NO WAY TO CONTACT HIM OR ROGUE?
STORM, THERE'S LIKE FIFTY FAIL-SAFES IN PLACE TO ENSURE DANGER ROOM PROTOCOLS NEVER GET USED AGAINST US. EVEN I'M FROZEN OUT.
THE INTRUDER REWROTE CODE...
...TENS OF THOUSANDS OF LINES OF IT, ON THE FLY. IT'S BASICALLY IMPOSSIBLE.
CLEARLY, IT'S NOT.
HE PROMISED TO BEHAVE HIMSELF AND TALK IN HIS INDOOR VOICE.
MY SISTER, ARKEA. SHE'S HERE, IN CONTROL OF YOUR WONDERFUL SCHOOL, AND I'M FRANKLY SURPRISED SHE HASN'T KILLED US ALL YET.
SUBLIME...
...ANSWER ME THIS: ARKEA MOVES THROUGH TECHNOLOGY, THROUGH MACHINES? THIS IS HOW SHE FUNCTIONS?
YES. THIS IS HER MODUS OPERANDI. SHE WILL LEARN ALL SHE CAN, DESTROY WHAT'S IN HER WAY, AND MOVE ON TO NEW TARGETS. TECHNICALLY VERY ADVANCED, BUT HER INTENTIONS REMAIN PRIMAL. WHEREAS I'VE LEARNED A CERTAIN LEVEL OF... HUMANITY FROM MY HOSTS. SUBTLETY, EVEN.
PROUD OF YOURSELF, AREN'T YOU? WELL, IT'S SAFE TO SAY ARKEA DIDN'T EXPECT TO FIND THE X-MEN WHEN SHE ARRIVED HERE.
YOU'RE UP, KITTY: I WANT YOU TO DESTROY EVERY SINGLE SYSTEM IN THIS SCHOOL UNTIL ARKEA IS NEUTRALIZED. BUT PRIORITIZE YOUR TARGETS; WE'RE GOING TO HAVE TO RATIONALIZE THIS TO LOGAN AND THE OTHERS LATER.
YOU GOT IT.
STORM.

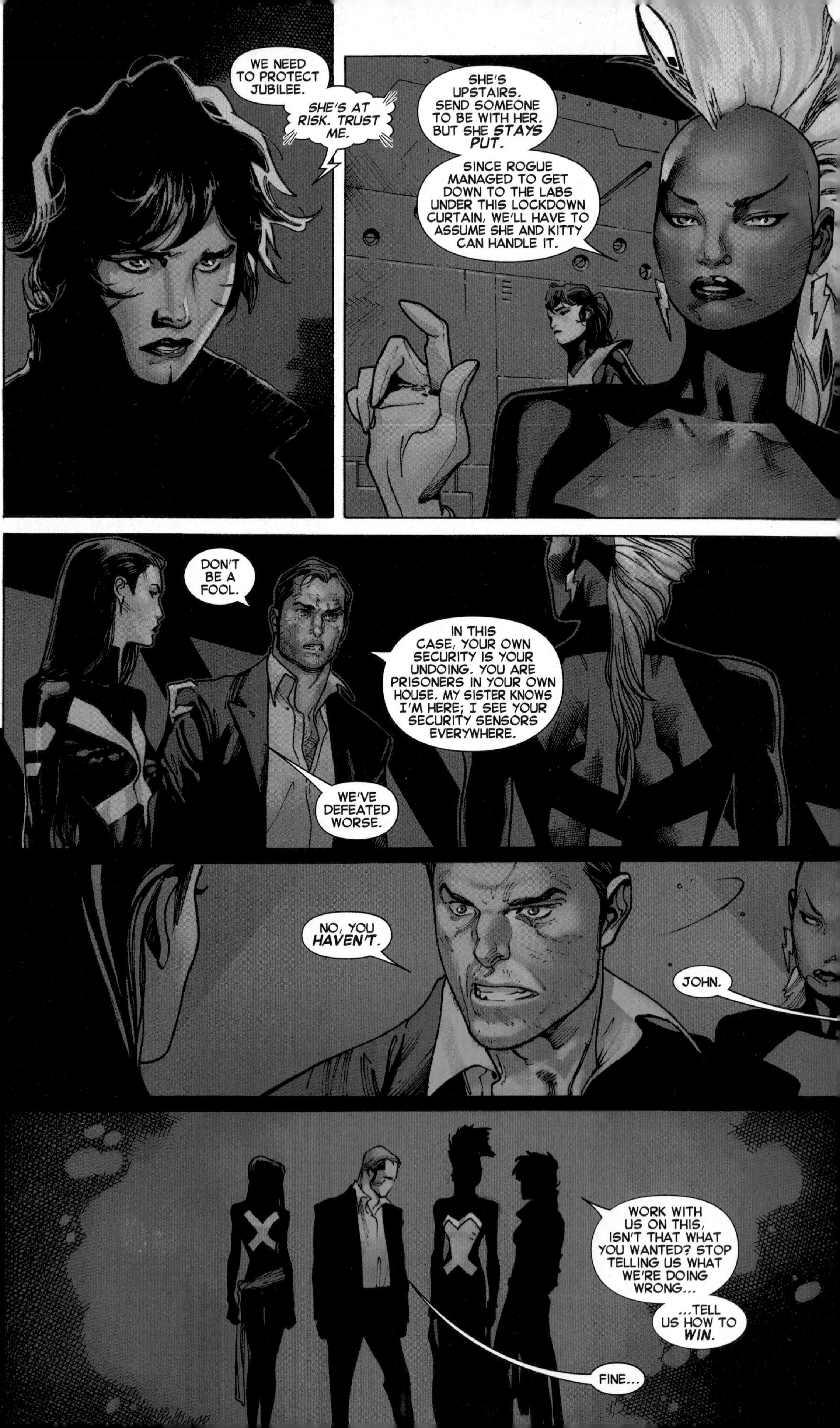

WE NEED TO PROTECT JUBILEE.
SHE'S AT RISK. TRUST ME.
SHE'S UPSTAIRS. SEND SOMEONE TO BE WITH HER. BUT SHE STAYS PUT.
SINCE ROGUE MANAGED TO GET DOWN TO THE LABS UNDER THIS LOCKDOWN CURTAIN, WE'LL HAVE TO ASSUME SHE AND KITTY CAN HANDLE IT.
DON'T BE A FOOL.
IN THIS CASE, YOUR OWN SECURITY IS YOUR UNDOING. YOU ARE PRISONERS IN YOUR OWN HOUSE. MY SISTER KNOWS I'M HERE; I SEE YOUR SECURITY SENSORS EVERYWHERE.
WE'VE DEFEATED WORSE.
NO, YOU HAVEN'T.
JOHN.
WORK WITH US ON THIS, ISN'T THAT WHAT YOU WANTED? STOP TELLING US WHAT WE'RE DOING WRONG...
...TELL US HOW TO WIN.
FINE...

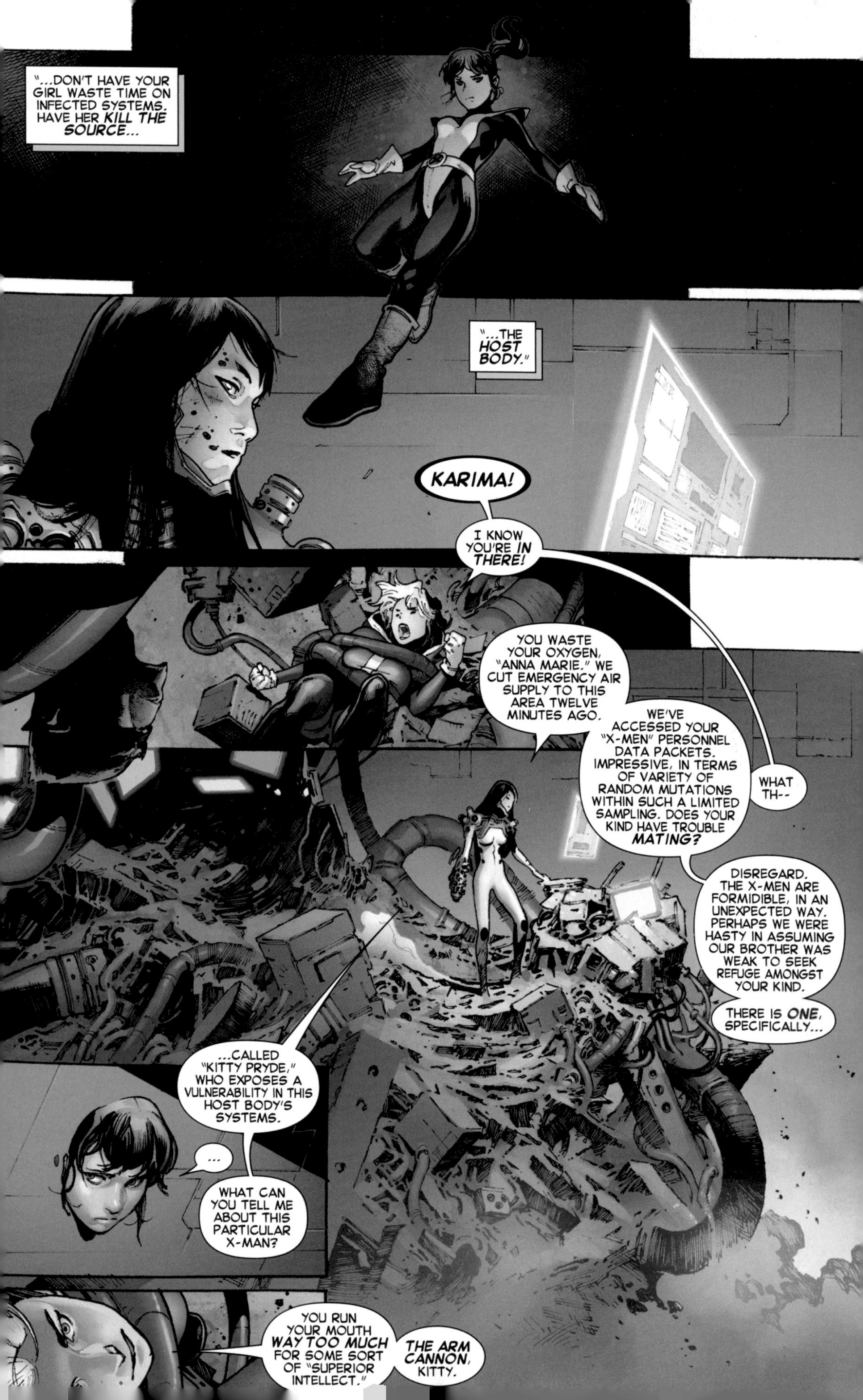
"...DON'T HAVE YOUR GIRL WASTE TIME ON INFECTED SYSTEMS. HAVE HER KILL THE SOURCE...
"...THE HOST BODY."
KARIMA!
I KNOW YOU'RE IN THERE!
YOU WASTE YOUR OXYGEN, "ANNA MARIE." WE CUT EMERGENCY AIR SUPPLY TO THIS AREA TWELVE MINUTES AGO.
WE'VE ACCESSED YOUR "X-MEN" PERSONNEL DATA PACKETS. IMPRESSIVE, IN TERMS OF VARIETY OF RANDOM MUTATIONS WITHIN SUCH A LIMITED SAMPLING. DOES YOUR KIND HAVE TROUBLE MATING?
WHAT TH--
DISREGARD. THE X-MEN ARE FORMIDIBLE, IN AN UNEXPECTED WAY. PERHAPS WE WERE HASTY IN ASSUMING OUR BROTHER WAS WEAK TO SEEK REFUGE AMONGST YOUR KIND.
THERE IS ONE, SPECIFICALLY...
...CALLED "KITTY PRYDE," WHO EXPOSES A VULNERABILITY IN THIS HOST BODY'S SYSTEMS.
...
WHAT CAN YOU TELL ME ABOUT THIS PARTICULAR X-MAN?
YOU RUN YOUR MOUTH WAY TOO MUCH FOR SOME SORT OF "SUPERIOR INTELLECT."
THE ARM CANNON, KITTY.

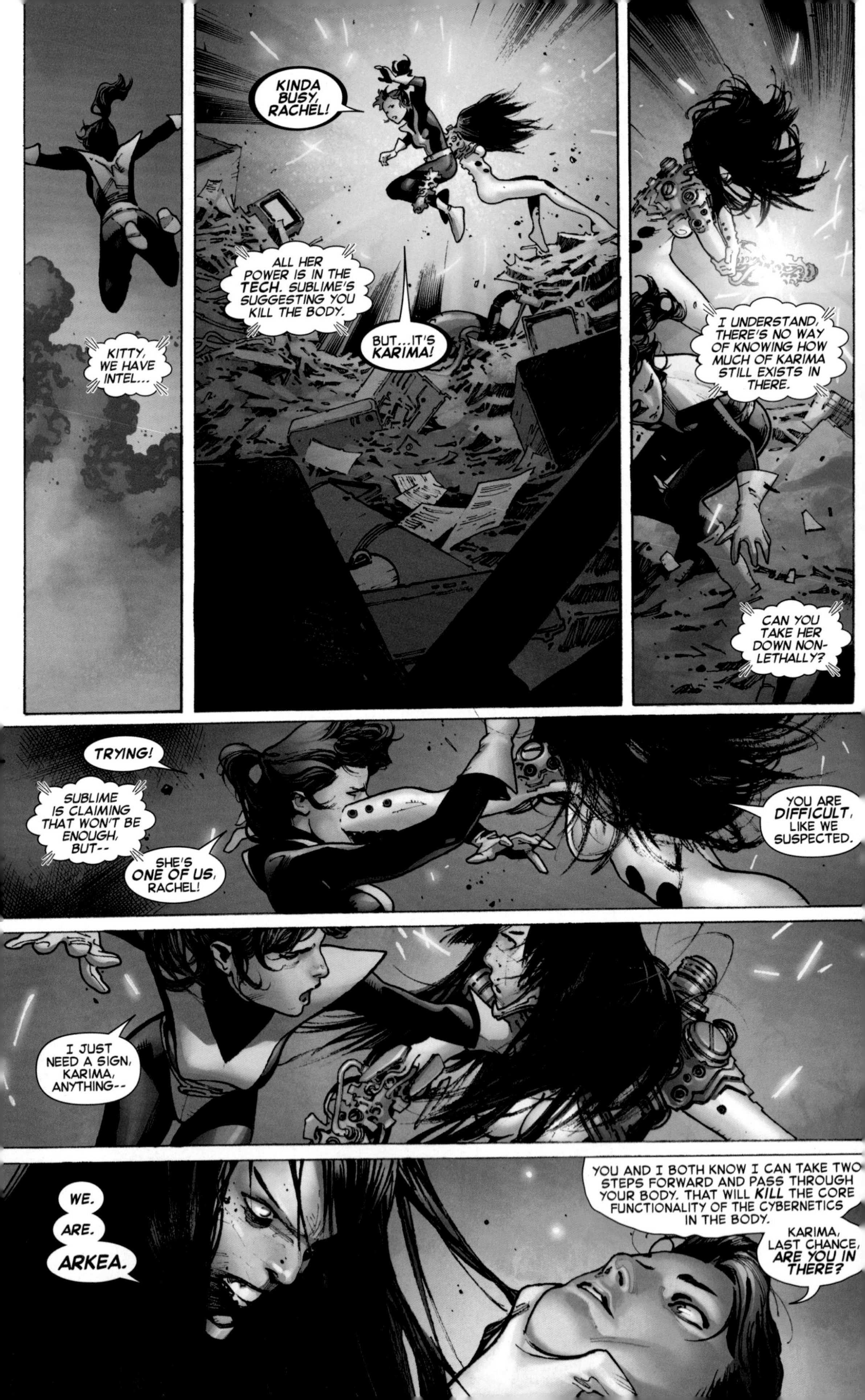
KINDA BUSY, RACHEL!
ALL HER POWER IS IN THE TECH. SUBLIME'S SUGGESTING YOU KILL THE BODY.
KITTY, WE HAVE INTEL...
BUT...IT'S KARIMA!
I UNDERSTAND, THERE'S NO WAY OF KNOWING HOW MUCH OF KARIMA STILL EXISTS IN THERE.
CAN YOU TAKE HER DOWN NON-LETHALLY?
TRYING!
SUBLIME IS CLAIMING THAT WON'T BE ENOUGH, BUT--
SHE'S ONE OF US, RACHEL!
YOU ARE DIFFICULT, LIKE WE SUSPECTED.
I JUST NEED A SIGN, KARIMA, ANYTHING--
WE.
ARE.
ARKEA.
YOU AND I BOTH KNOW I CAN TAKE TWO STEPS FORWARD AND PASS THROUGH YOUR BODY. THAT WILL KILL THE CORE FUNCTIONALITY OF THE CYBERNETICS IN THE BODY.
KARIMA, LAST CHANCE, ARE YOU IN THERE?

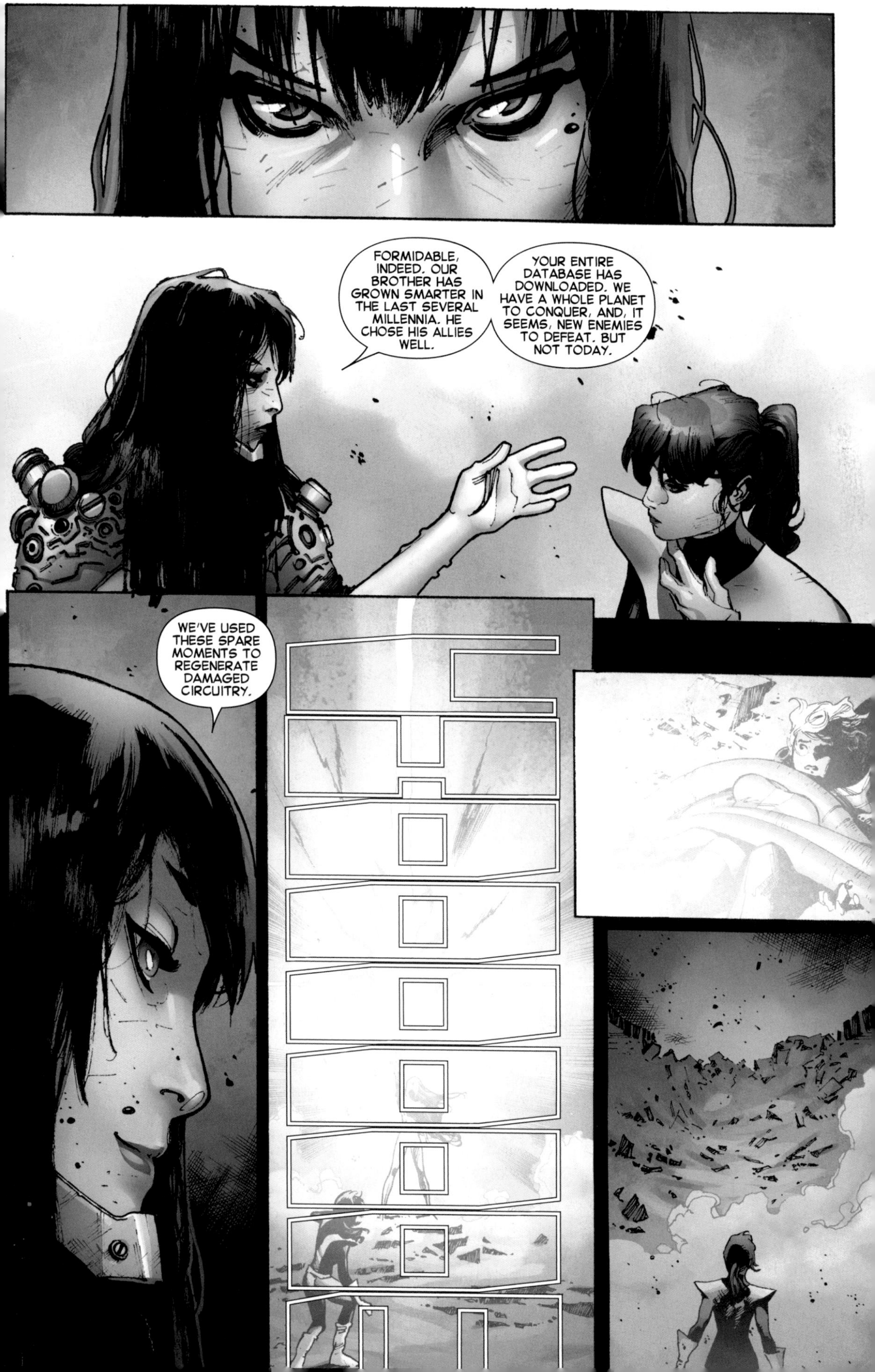
FORMIDABLE, INDEED. OUR BROTHER HAS GROWN SMARTER IN THE LAST SEVERAL MILLENNIA. HE CHOSE HIS ALLIES WELL.
YOUR ENTIRE DATABASE HAS DOWNLOADED. WE HAVE A WHOLE PLANET TO CONQUER, AND, IT SEEMS, NEW ENEMIES TO DEFEAT. BUT NOT TODAY.
WE'VE USED THESE SPARE MOMENTS TO REGENERATE DAMAGED CIRCUITRY.

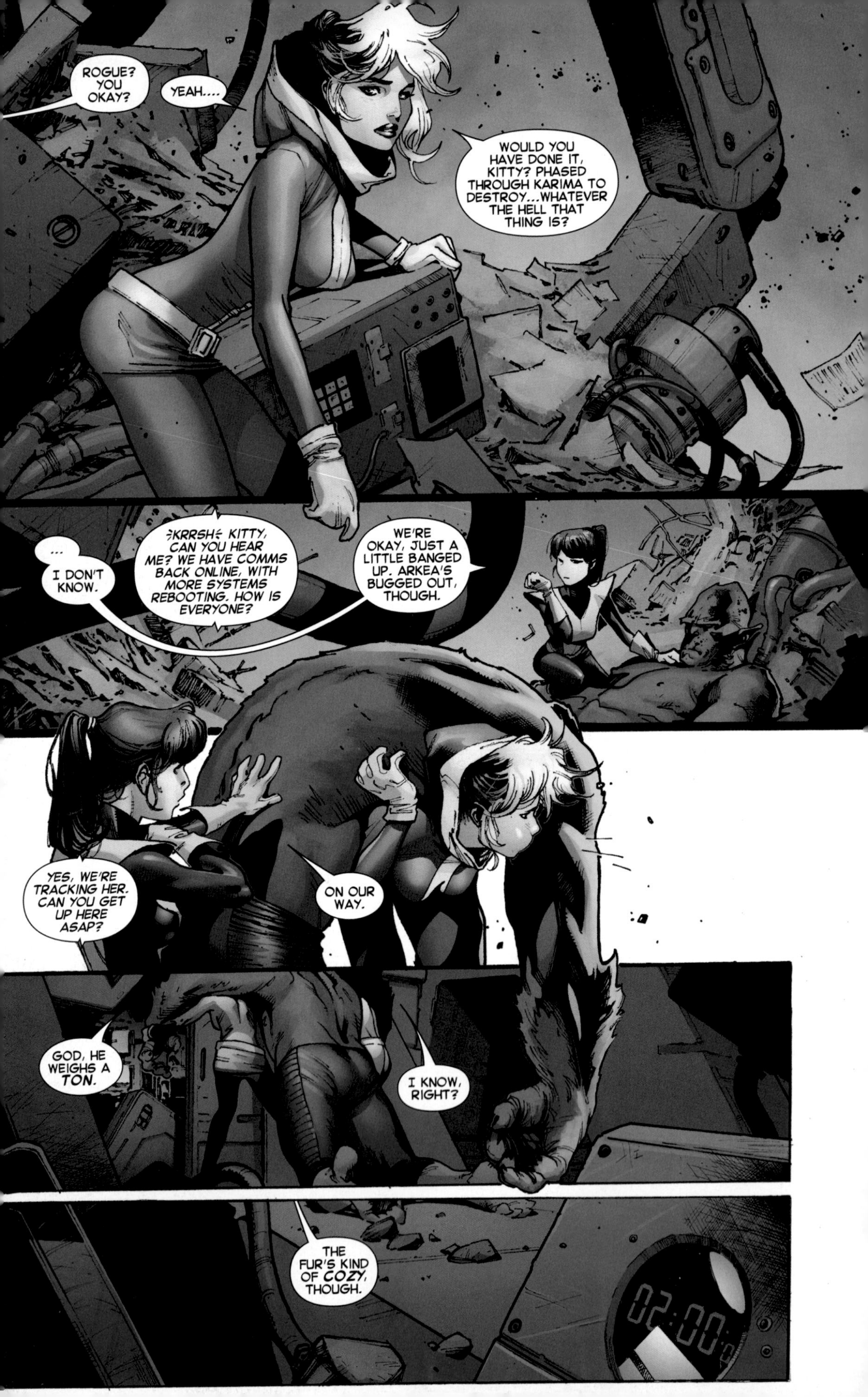
ROGUE? YOU OKAY?
YEAH....
WOULD YOU HAVE DONE IT, KITTY? PHASED THROUGH KARIMA TO DESTROY...WHATEVER THE HELL THAT THING IS?
... I DON'T KNOW.
KRRSH KITTY, CAN YOU HEAR ME? WE HAVE COMMS BACK ONLINE, WITH MORE SYSTEMS REBOOTING. HOW IS EVERYONE?
WE'RE OKAY, JUST A LITTLE BANGED UP. ARKEA'S BUGGED OUT, THOUGH.
YES, WE'RE TRACKING HER. CAN YOU GET UP HERE ASAP?
ON OUR WAY.
GOD, HE WEIGHS A *TON*.
I KNOW, RIGHT?
THE FUR'S KIND OF *COZY*, THOUGH.
02:00

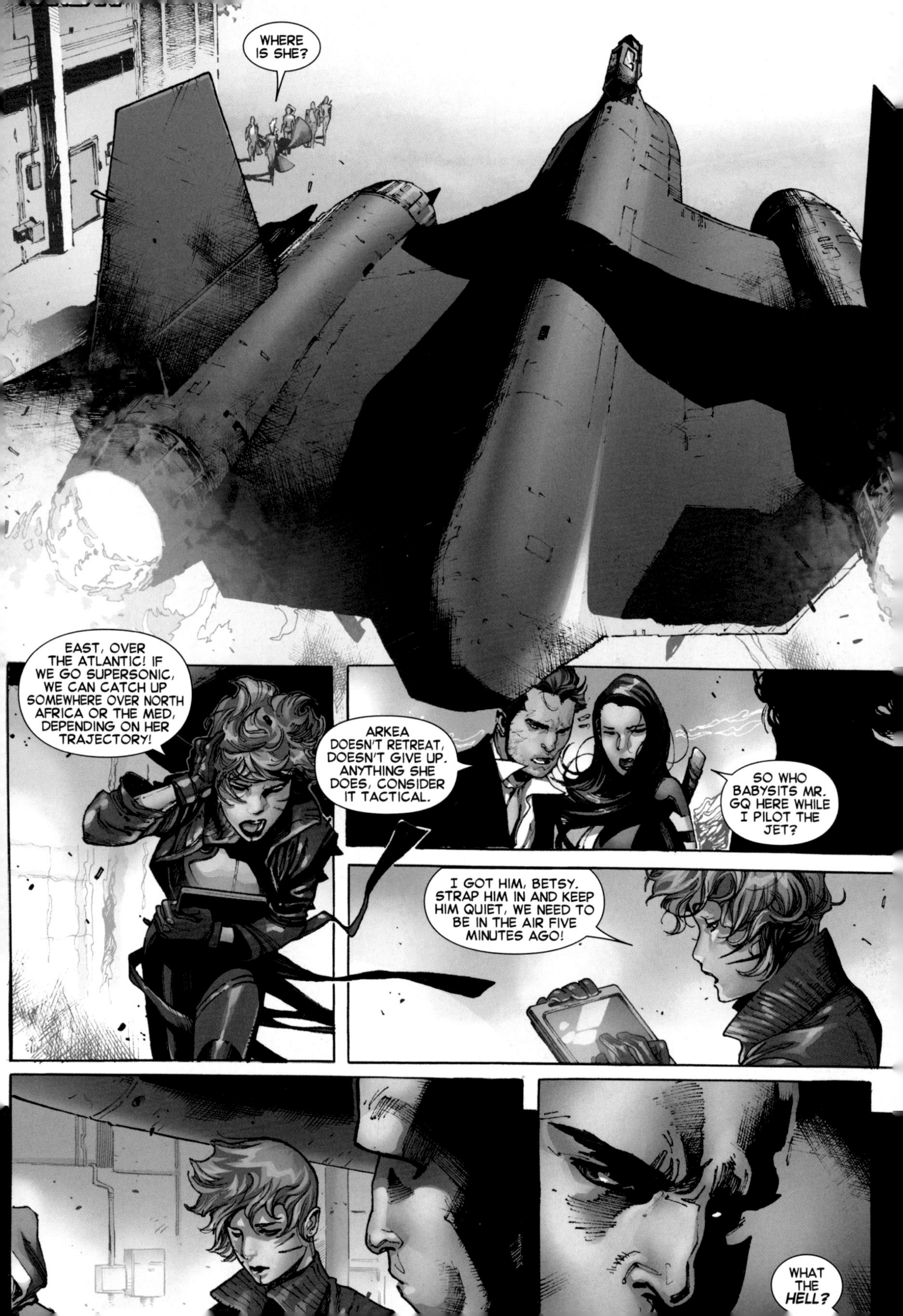
WHERE IS SHE?
EAST, OVER THE ATLANTIC! IF WE GO SUPERSONIC, WE CAN CATCH UP SOMEWHERE OVER NORTH AFRICA OR THE MED, DEPENDING ON HER TRAJECTORY!
ARKEA DOESN'T RETREAT, DOESN'T GIVE UP. ANYTHING SHE DOES, CONSIDER IT TACTICAL.
SO WHO BABYSITS MR. GQ HERE WHILE I PILOT THE JET?
I GOT HIM, BETSY. STRAP HIM IN AND KEEP HIM QUIET, WE NEED TO BE IN THE AIR FIVE MINUTES AGO!
WHAT THE *HELL?*

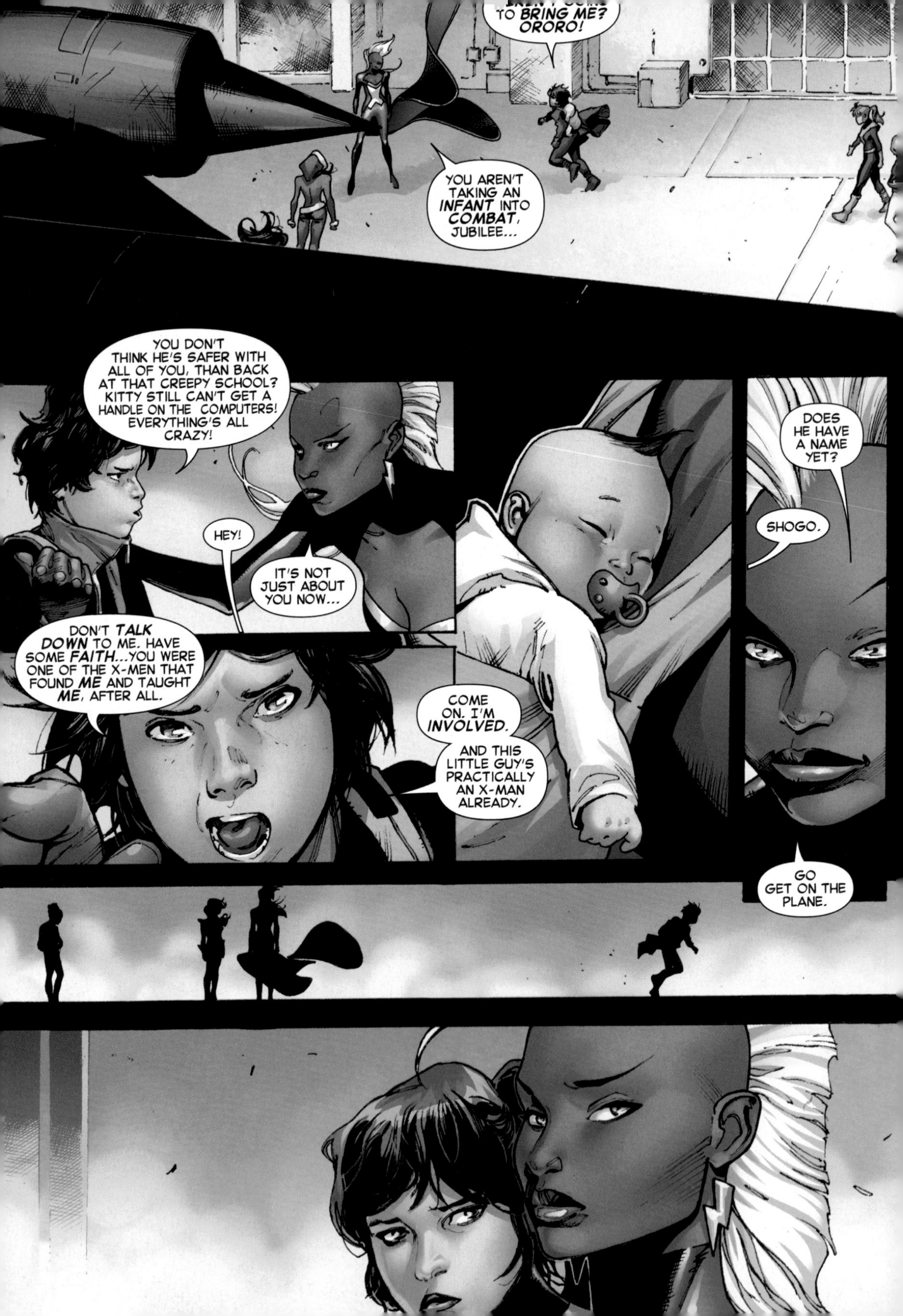
TO BRING ME? ORORO!
YOU AREN'T TAKING AN INFANT INTO COMBAT, JUBILEE...
YOU DON'T THINK HE'S SAFER WITH ALL OF YOU, THAN BACK AT THAT CREEPY SCHOOL? KITTY STILL CAN'T GET A HANDLE ON THE COMPUTERS! EVERYTHING'S ALL CRAZY!
HEY!
IT'S NOT JUST ABOUT YOU NOW...
DON'T TALK DOWN TO ME. HAVE SOME FAITH...YOU WERE ONE OF THE X-MEN THAT FOUND ME AND TAUGHT ME, AFTER ALL.
COME ON. I'M INVOLVED.
AND THIS LITTLE GUY'S PRACTICALLY AN X-MAN ALREADY.
DOES HE HAVE A NAME YET?
SHOGO.
GO GET ON THE PLANE.

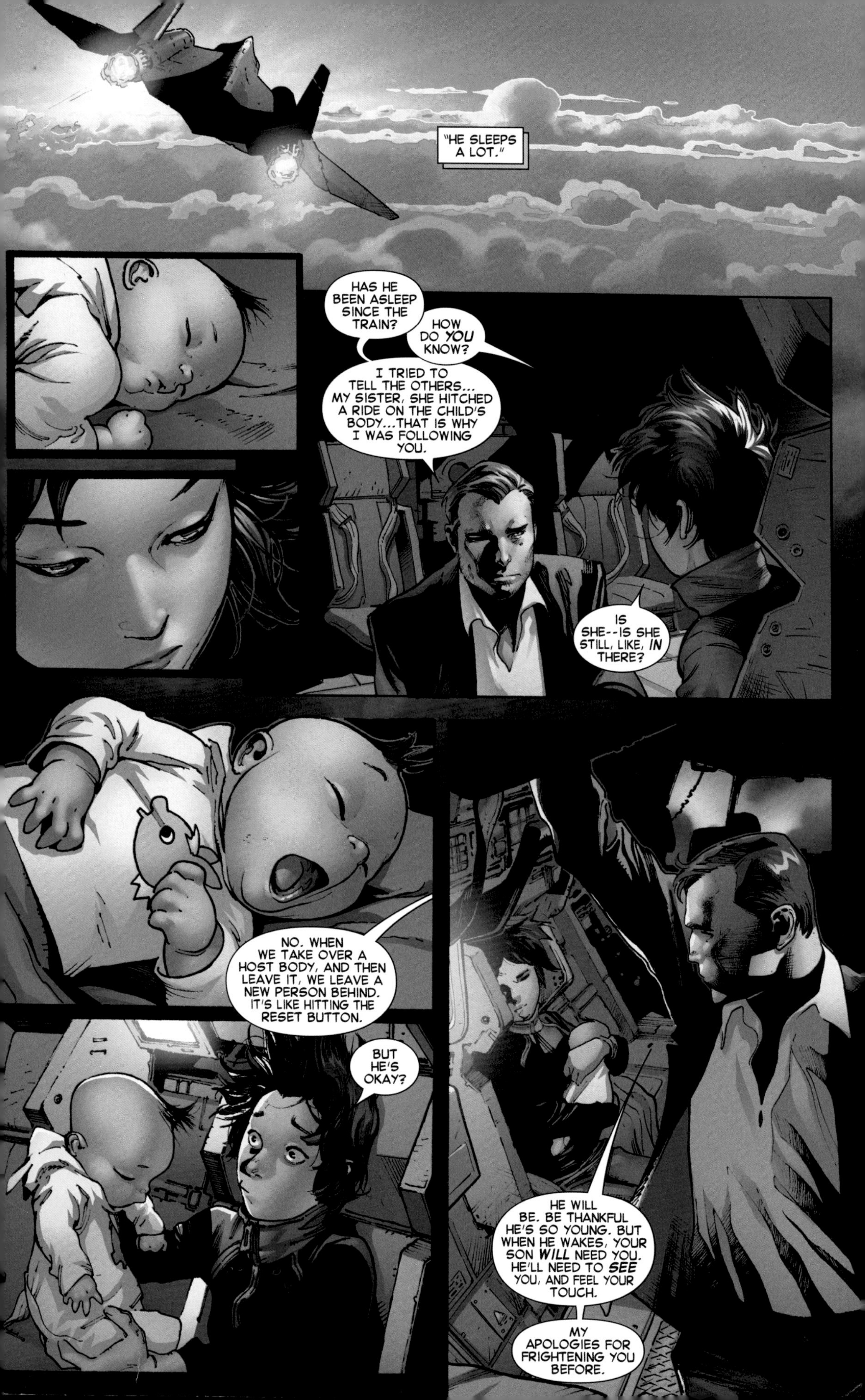
"HE SLEEPS A LOT."
HAS HE BEEN ASLEEP SINCE THE TRAIN?
HOW DO *YOU* KNOW?
I TRIED TO TELL THE OTHERS... MY SISTER, SHE HITCHED A RIDE ON THE CHILD'S BODY...THAT IS WHY I WAS FOLLOWING YOU.
IS SHE--IS SHE STILL, LIKE, *IN* THERE?
NO. WHEN WE TAKE OVER A HOST BODY, AND THEN LEAVE IT, WE LEAVE A NEW PERSON BEHIND. IT'S LIKE HITTING THE RESET BUTTON.
BUT HE'S OKAY?
HE WILL BE. BE THANKFUL HE'S SO YOUNG. BUT WHEN HE WAKES, YOUR SON *WILL* NEED YOU. HE'LL NEED TO *SEE* YOU, AND FEEL YOUR TOUCH.
MY APOLOGIES FOR FRIGHTENING YOU BEFORE.

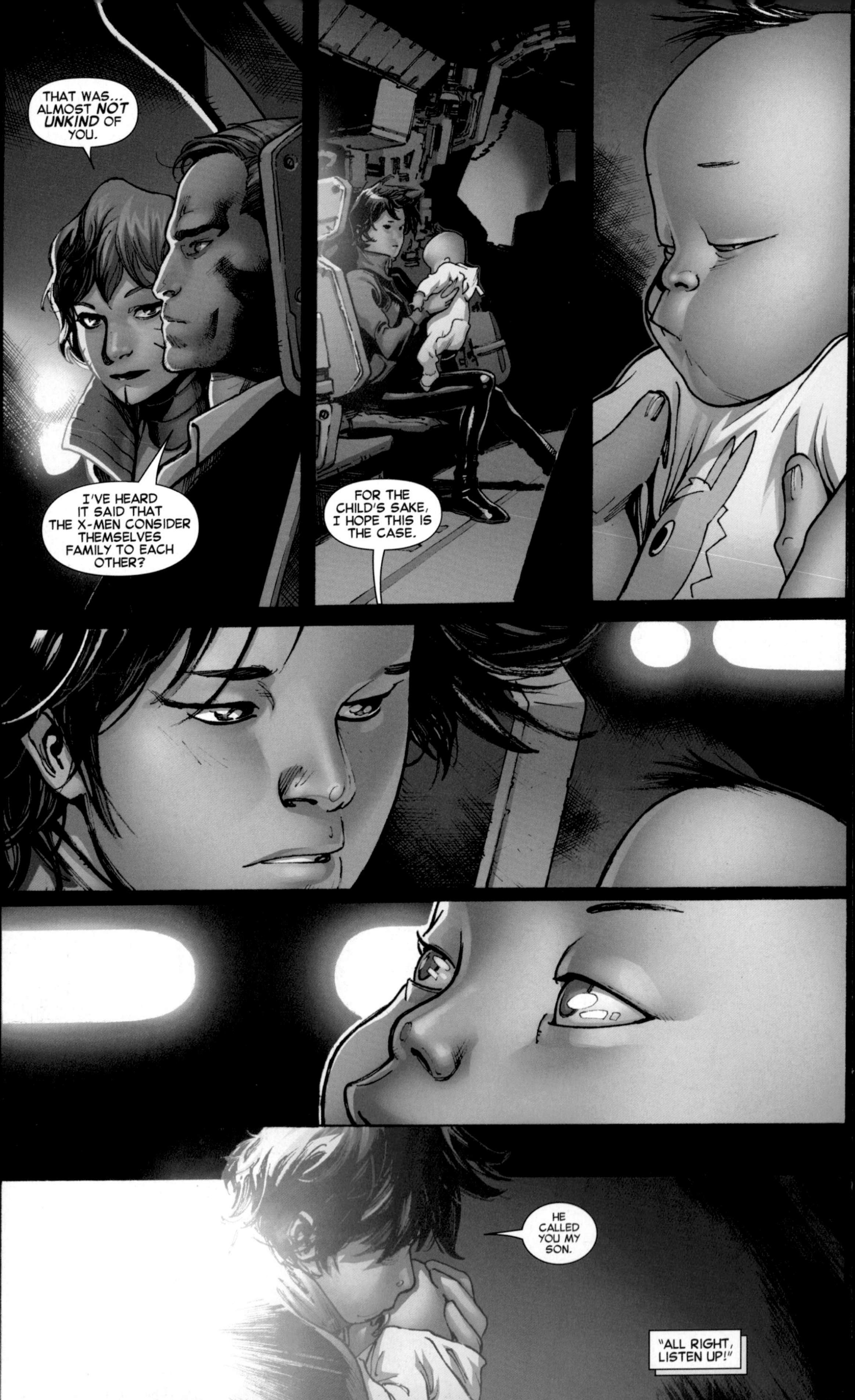
THAT WAS... ALMOST **NOT UNKIND** OF YOU.
I'VE HEARD IT SAID THAT THE X-MEN CONSIDER THEMSELVES FAMILY TO EACH OTHER?
FOR THE CHILD'S SAKE, I HOPE THIS IS THE CASE.
HE CALLED YOU MY SON.
"ALL RIGHT, LISTEN UP!"

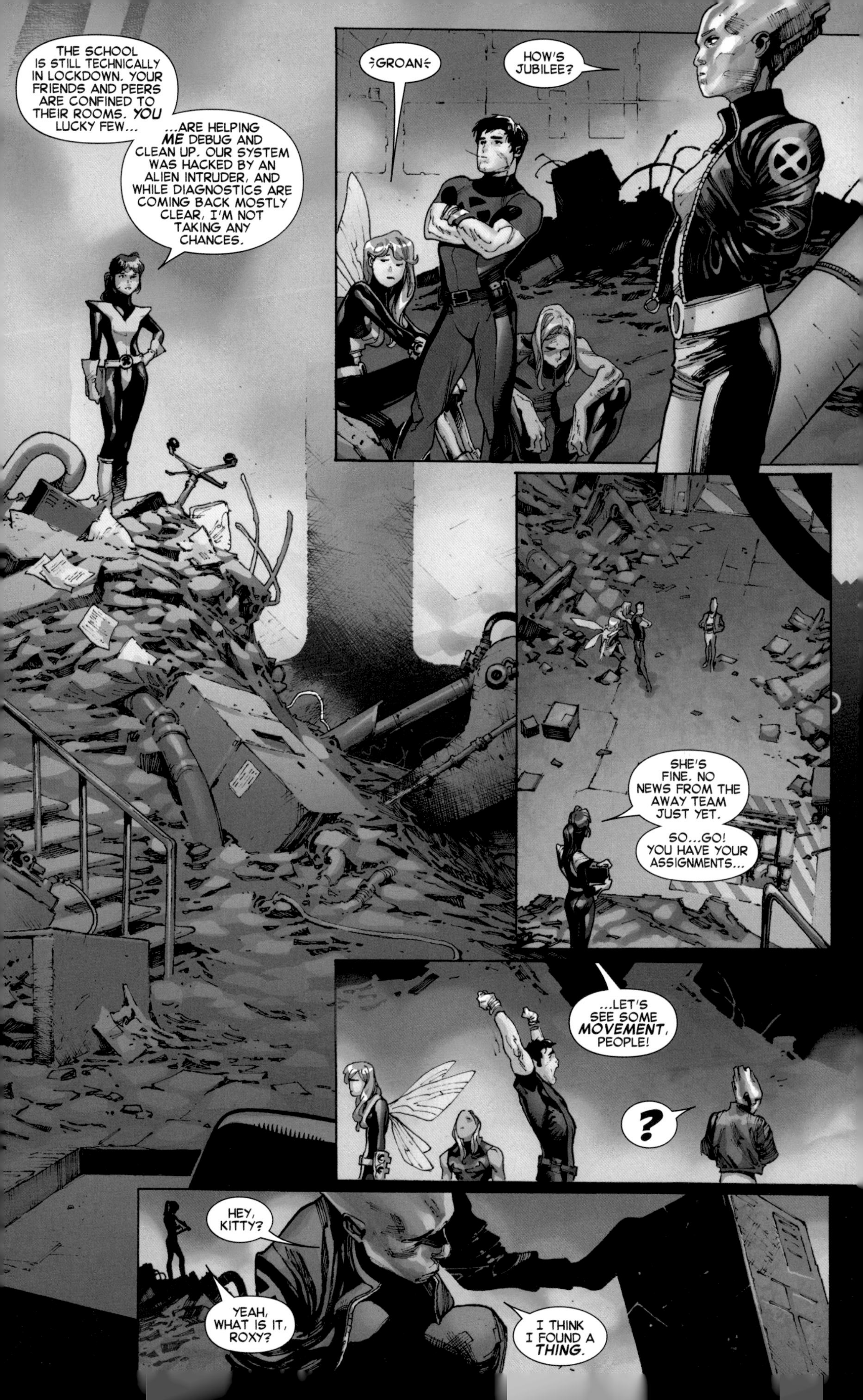
THE SCHOOL IS STILL TECHNICALLY IN LOCKDOWN. YOUR FRIENDS AND PEERS ARE CONFINED TO THEIR ROOMS. YOU LUCKY FEW...
...ARE HELPING ME DEBUG AND CLEAN UP. OUR SYSTEM WAS HACKED BY AN ALIEN INTRUDER, AND WHILE DIAGNOSTICS ARE COMING BACK MOSTLY CLEAR, I'M NOT TAKING ANY CHANCES.
GROAN
HOW'S JUBILEE?
SHE'S FINE. NO NEWS FROM THE AWAY TEAM JUST YET.
SO...GO! YOU HAVE YOUR ASSIGNMENTS...
...LET'S SEE SOME MOVEMENT, PEOPLE!
?
HEY, KITTY?
YEAH, WHAT IS IT, ROXY?
I THINK I FOUND A THING.

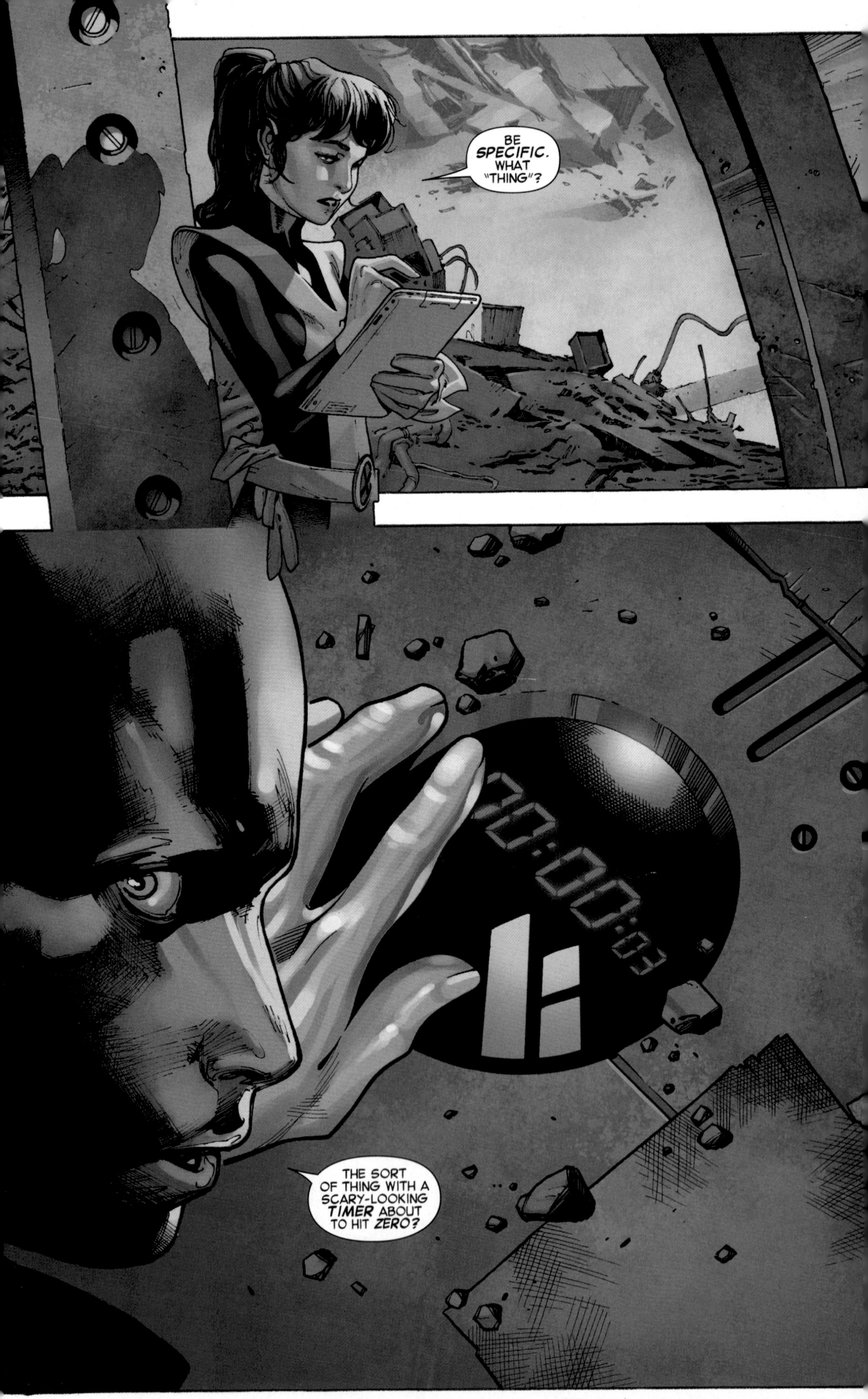
BE SPECIFIC. WHAT "THING"?
THE SORT OF THING WITH A SCARY-LOOKING TIMER ABOUT TO HIT ZERO?

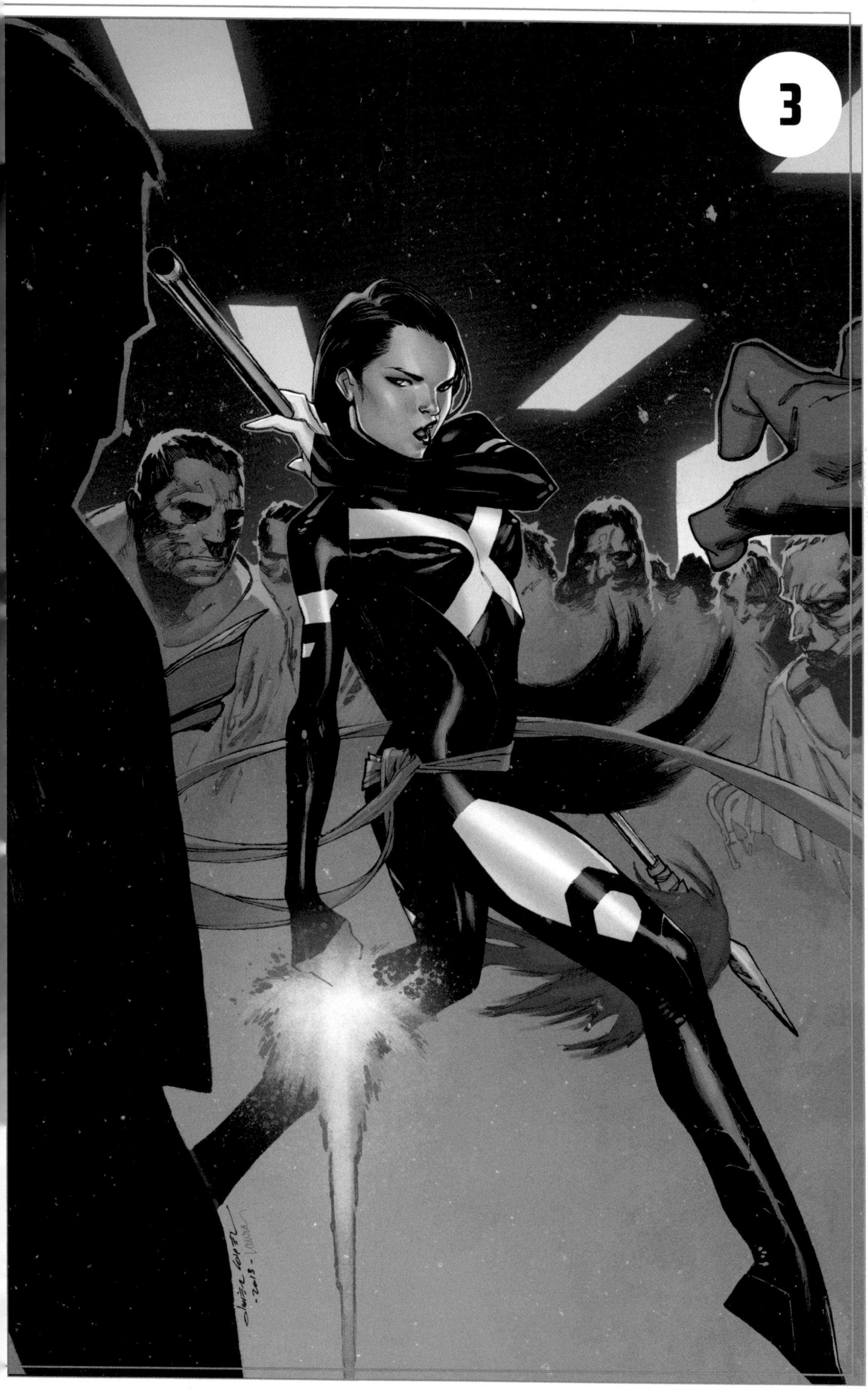
3

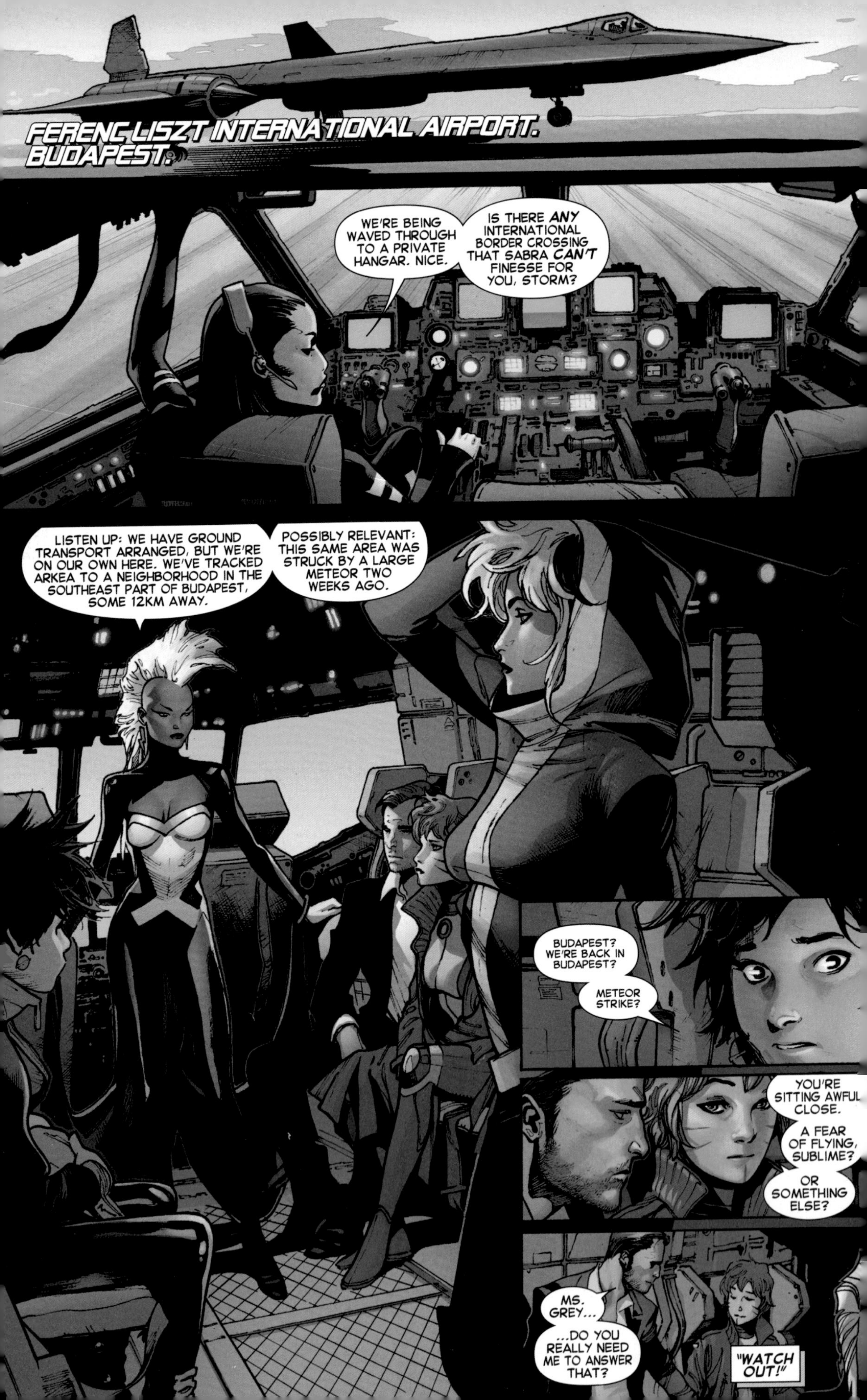
FERENC LISZT INTERNATIONAL AIRPORT. BUDAPEST.
WE'RE BEING WAVED THROUGH TO A PRIVATE HANGAR. NICE.
IS THERE ANY INTERNATIONAL BORDER CROSSING THAT SABRA CAN'T FINESSE FOR YOU, STORM?
LISTEN UP: WE HAVE GROUND TRANSPORT ARRANGED, BUT WE'RE ON OUR OWN HERE. WE'VE TRACKED ARKEA TO A NEIGHBORHOOD IN THE SOUTHEAST PART OF BUDAPEST, SOME 12KM AWAY.
POSSIBLY RELEVANT: THIS SAME AREA WAS STRUCK BY A LARGE METEOR TWO WEEKS AGO.
BUDAPEST? WE'RE BACK IN BUDAPEST?
METEOR STRIKE?
YOU'RE SITTING AWFUL CLOSE.
A FEAR OF FLYING, SUBLIME?
OR SOMETHING ELSE?
MS. GREY...
...DO YOU REALLY NEED ME TO ANSWER THAT?
"WATCH OUT!"

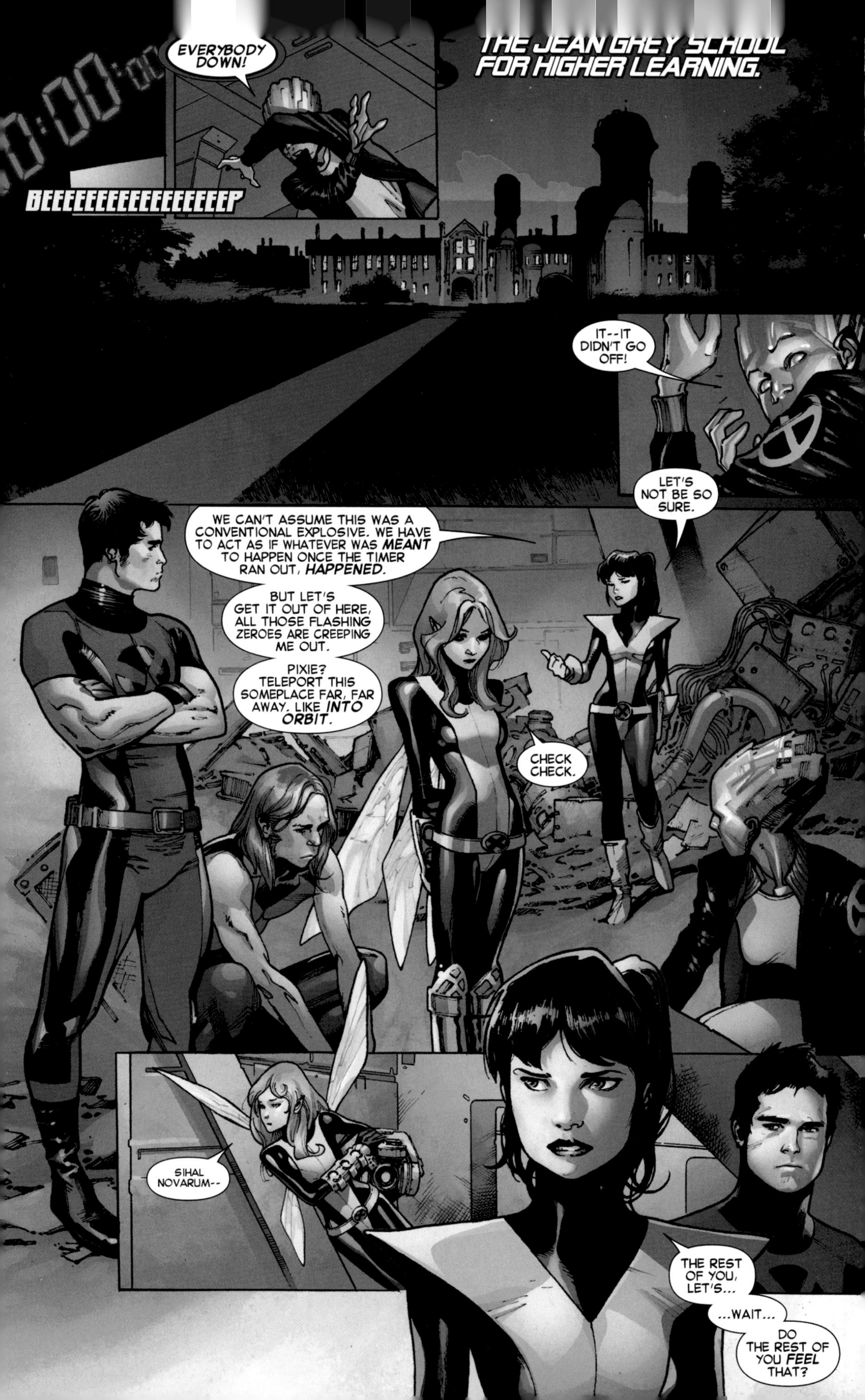
EVERYBODY DOWN!
THE JEAN GREY SCHOOL FOR HIGHER LEARNING.
BEEEEEEEEEEEEEEEEEEP
IT--IT DIDN'T GO OFF!
LET'S NOT BE SO SURE.
WE CAN'T ASSUME THIS WAS A CONVENTIONAL EXPLOSIVE. WE HAVE TO ACT AS IF WHATEVER WAS MEANT TO HAPPEN ONCE THE TIMER RAN OUT, HAPPENED.
BUT LET'S GET IT OUT OF HERE, ALL THOSE FLASHING ZEROES ARE CREEPING ME OUT.
PIXIE? TELEPORT THIS SOMEPLACE FAR, FAR AWAY. LIKE INTO ORBIT.
CHECK CHECK.
SIHAL NOVARUM--
THE REST OF YOU, LET'S...
...WAIT...
DO THE REST OF YOU FEEL THAT?

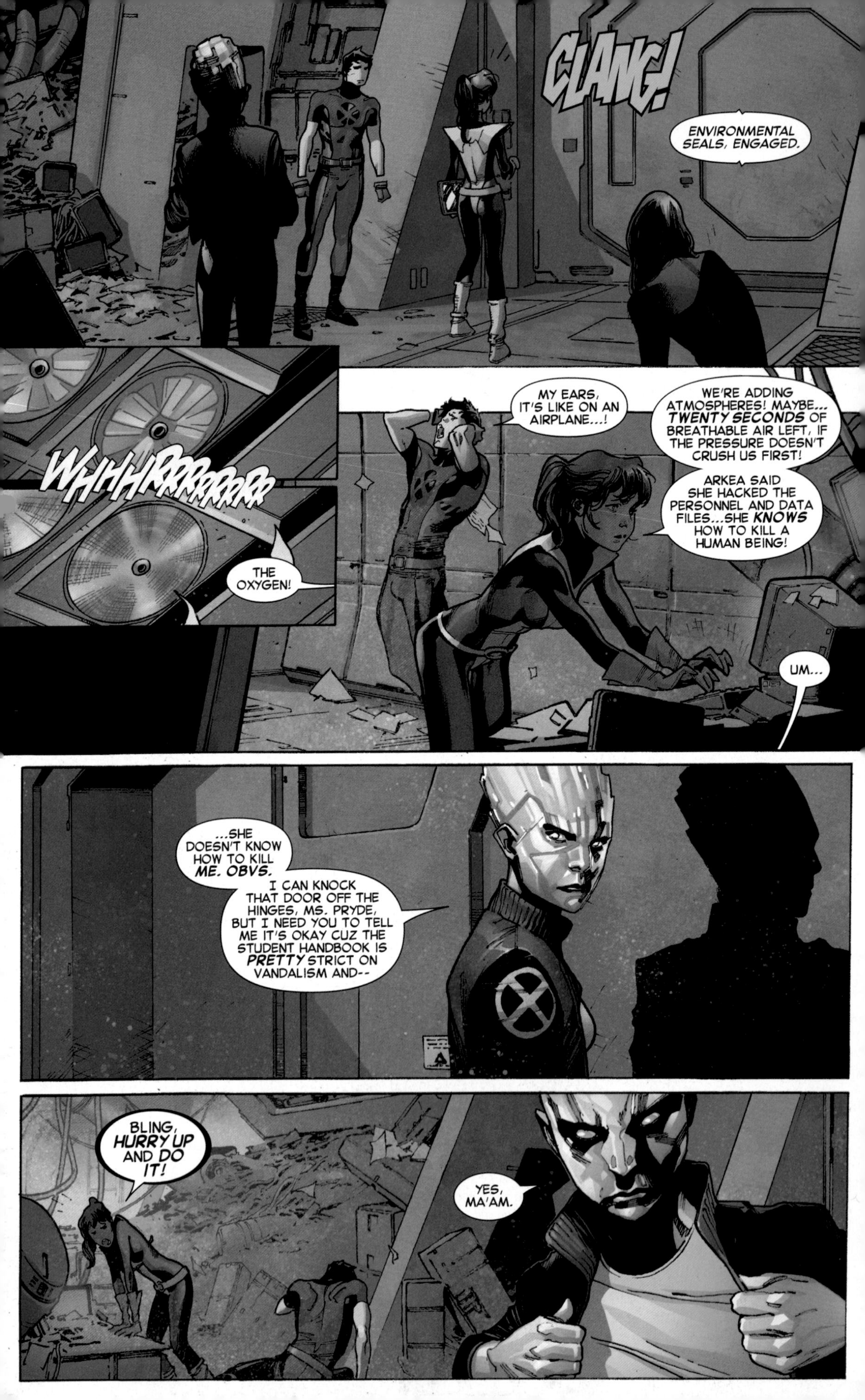
CLANG!
ENVIRONMENTAL SEALS, ENGAGED.
WHHHRRRRRRRRR
THE OXYGEN!
MY EARS, IT'S LIKE ON AN AIRPLANE...!
WE'RE ADDING ATMOSPHERES! MAYBE... TWENTY SECONDS OF BREATHABLE AIR LEFT, IF THE PRESSURE DOESN'T CRUSH US FIRST!
ARKEA SAID SHE HACKED THE PERSONNEL AND DATA FILES...SHE KNOWS HOW TO KILL A HUMAN BEING!
UM...
...SHE DOESN'T KNOW HOW TO KILL ME. OBVS.
I CAN KNOCK THAT DOOR OFF THE HINGES, MS. PRYDE, BUT I NEED YOU TO TELL ME IT'S OKAY CUZ THE STUDENT HANDBOOK IS PRETTY STRICT ON VANDALISM AND--
BLING, HURRY UP AND DO IT!
YES, MA'AM.

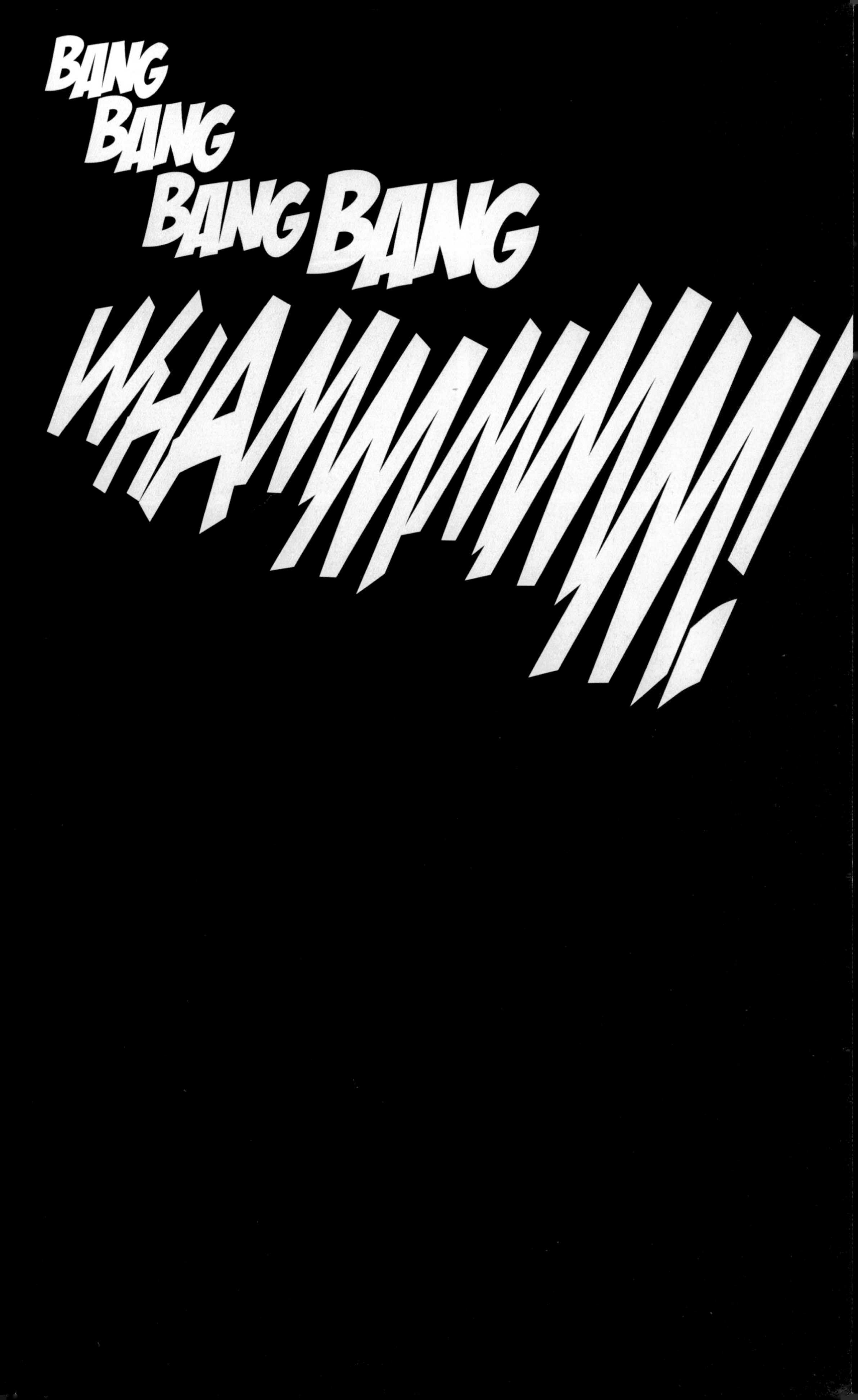
BANG
BANG
BANG BANG
WHAMMMM!!

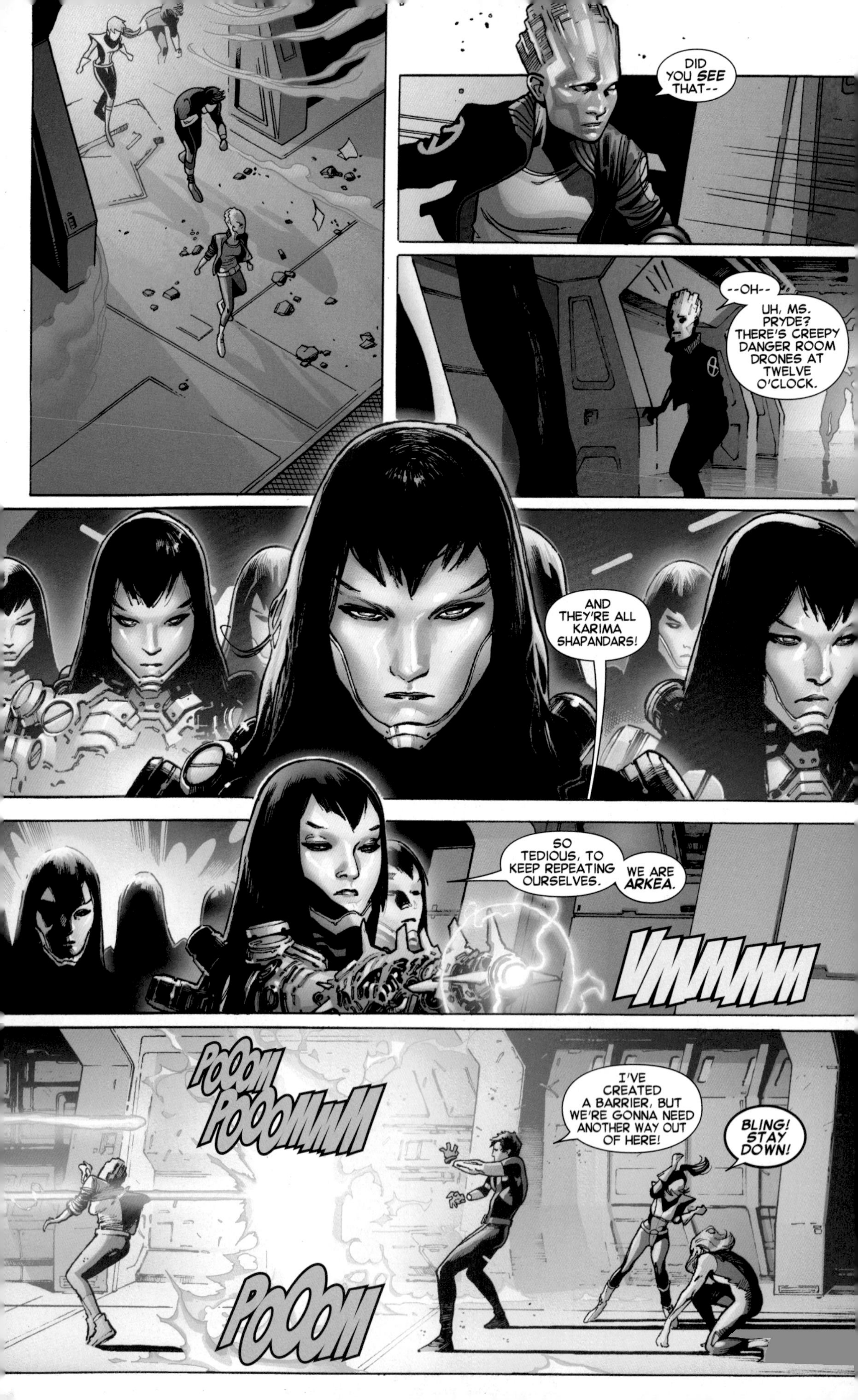
DID YOU SEE THAT--
--OH--
UH, MS. PRYDE? THERE'S CREEPY DANGER ROOM DRONES AT TWELVE O'CLOCK.
AND THEY'RE ALL KARIMA SHAPANDARS!
SO TEDIOUS, TO KEEP REPEATING OURSELVES.
WE ARE ARKEA.
VMMMMM
POOOM
POOOMMMM
I'VE CREATED A BARRIER, BUT WE'RE GONNA NEED ANOTHER WAY OUT OF HERE!
BLING! STAY DOWN!
POOOM

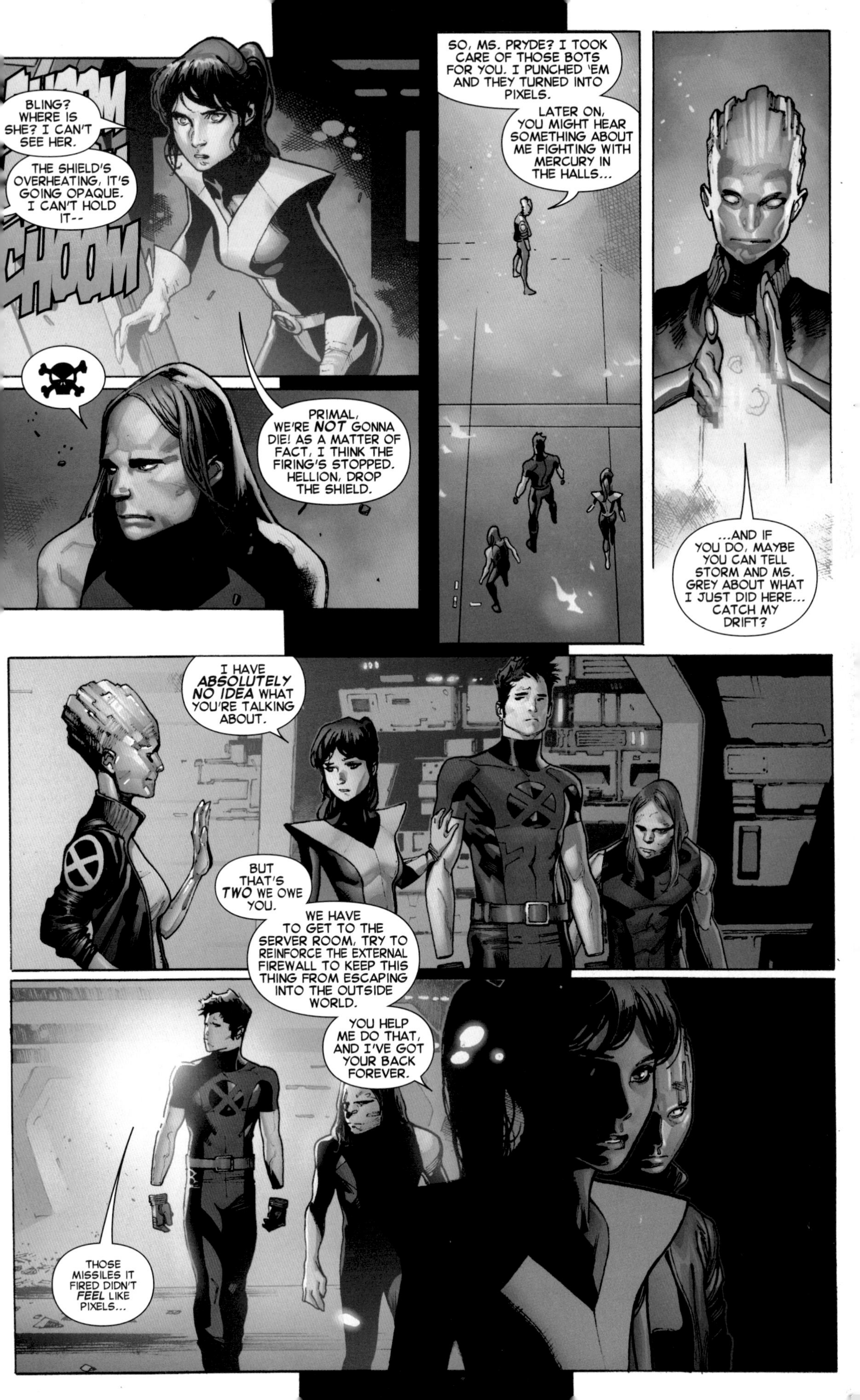
CHOOM
BLING? WHERE IS SHE? I CAN'T SEE HER.
THE SHIELD'S OVERHEATING, IT'S GOING OPAQUE. I CAN'T HOLD IT--
CHOOM
PRIMAL, WE'RE NOT GONNA DIE! AS A MATTER OF FACT, I THINK THE FIRING'S STOPPED. HELLION, DROP THE SHIELD.
SO, MS. PRYDE? I TOOK CARE OF THOSE BOTS FOR YOU. I PUNCHED 'EM AND THEY TURNED INTO PIXELS.
LATER ON, YOU MIGHT HEAR SOMETHING ABOUT ME FIGHTING WITH MERCURY IN THE HALLS...
...AND IF YOU DO, MAYBE YOU CAN TELL STORM AND MS. GREY ABOUT WHAT I JUST DID HERE... CATCH MY DRIFT?
I HAVE ABSOLUTELY NO IDEA WHAT YOU'RE TALKING ABOUT.
BUT THAT'S TWO WE OWE YOU.
WE HAVE TO GET TO THE SERVER ROOM, TRY TO REINFORCE THE EXTERNAL FIREWALL TO KEEP THIS THING FROM ESCAPING INTO THE OUTSIDE WORLD.
YOU HELP ME DO THAT, AND I'VE GOT YOUR BACK FOREVER.
THOSE MISSILES IT FIRED DIDN'T FEEL LIKE PIXELS...

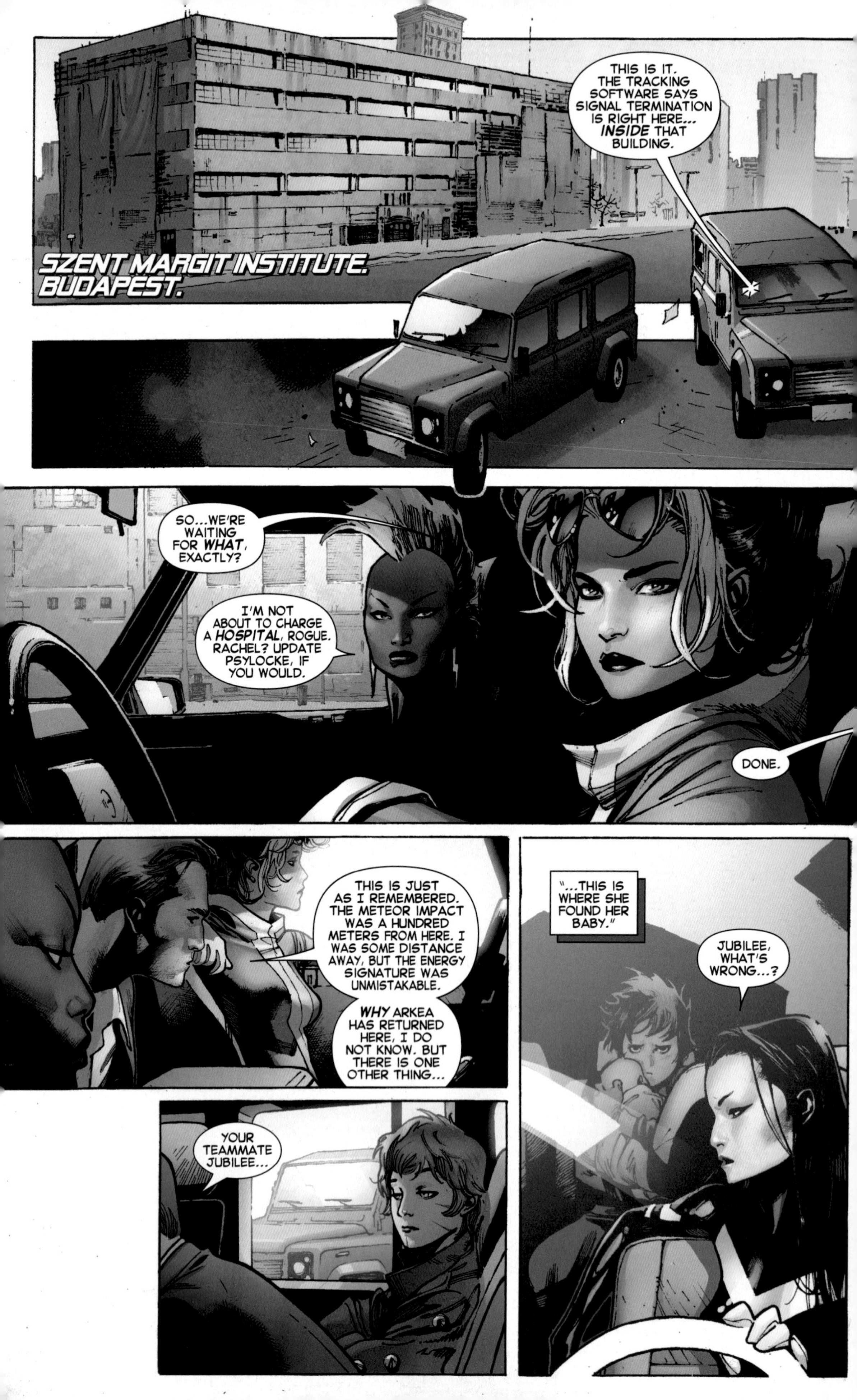
THIS IS IT. THE TRACKING SOFTWARE SAYS SIGNAL TERMINATION IS RIGHT HERE... INSIDE THAT BUILDING.
SZENT MARGIT INSTITUTE. BUDAPEST.
SO...WE'RE WAITING FOR WHAT, EXACTLY?
I'M NOT ABOUT TO CHARGE A HOSPITAL, ROGUE. RACHEL? UPDATE PSYLOCKE, IF YOU WOULD.
DONE.
THIS IS JUST AS I REMEMBERED. THE METEOR IMPACT WAS A HUNDRED METERS FROM HERE. I WAS SOME DISTANCE AWAY, BUT THE ENERGY SIGNATURE WAS UNMISTAKABLE.
WHY ARKEA HAS RETURNED HERE, I DO NOT KNOW. BUT THERE IS ONE OTHER THING...
YOUR TEAMMATE JUBILEE...
"...THIS IS WHERE SHE FOUND HER BABY."
JUBILEE, WHAT'S WRONG...?

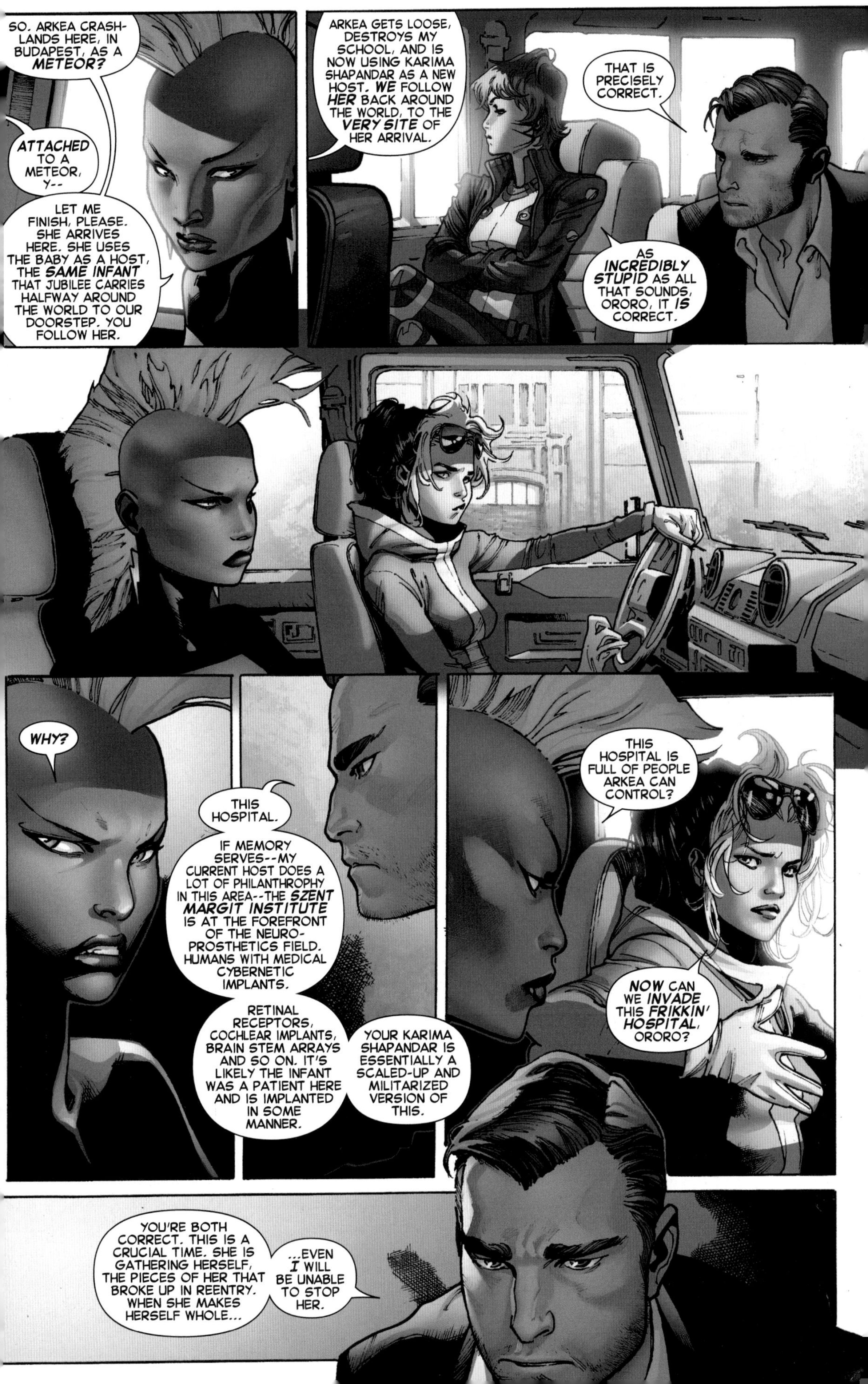
SO. ARKEA CRASH-LANDS HERE, IN BUDAPEST, AS A METEOR?
ATTACHED TO A METEOR, Y--
LET ME FINISH, PLEASE. SHE ARRIVES HERE. SHE USES THE BABY AS A HOST, THE SAME INFANT THAT JUBILEE CARRIES HALFWAY AROUND THE WORLD TO OUR DOORSTEP. YOU FOLLOW HER.
ARKEA GETS LOOSE, DESTROYS MY SCHOOL, AND IS NOW USING KARIMA SHAPANDAR AS A NEW HOST. WE FOLLOW HER BACK AROUND THE WORLD, TO THE VERY SITE OF HER ARRIVAL.
THAT IS PRECISELY CORRECT.
AS INCREDIBLY STUPID AS ALL THAT SOUNDS, ORORO, IT IS CORRECT.
WHY?
THIS HOSPITAL.
IF MEMORY SERVES--MY CURRENT HOST DOES A LOT OF PHILANTHROPHY IN THIS AREA--THE SZENT MARGIT INSTITUTE IS AT THE FOREFRONT OF THE NEURO-PROSTHETICS FIELD. HUMANS WITH MEDICAL CYBERNETIC IMPLANTS.
RETINAL RECEPTORS, COCHLEAR IMPLANTS, BRAIN STEM ARRAYS AND SO ON. IT'S LIKELY THE INFANT WAS A PATIENT HERE AND IS IMPLANTED IN SOME MANNER.
YOUR KARIMA SHAPANDAR IS ESSENTIALLY A SCALED-UP AND MILITARIZED VERSION OF THIS.
THIS HOSPITAL IS FULL OF PEOPLE ARKEA CAN CONTROL?
NOW CAN WE INVADE THIS FRIKKIN' HOSPITAL, ORORO?
YOU'RE BOTH CORRECT. THIS IS A CRUCIAL TIME. SHE IS GATHERING HERSELF, THE PIECES OF HER THAT BROKE UP IN REENTRY. WHEN SHE MAKES HERSELF WHOLE...
...EVEN I WILL BE UNABLE TO STOP HER.

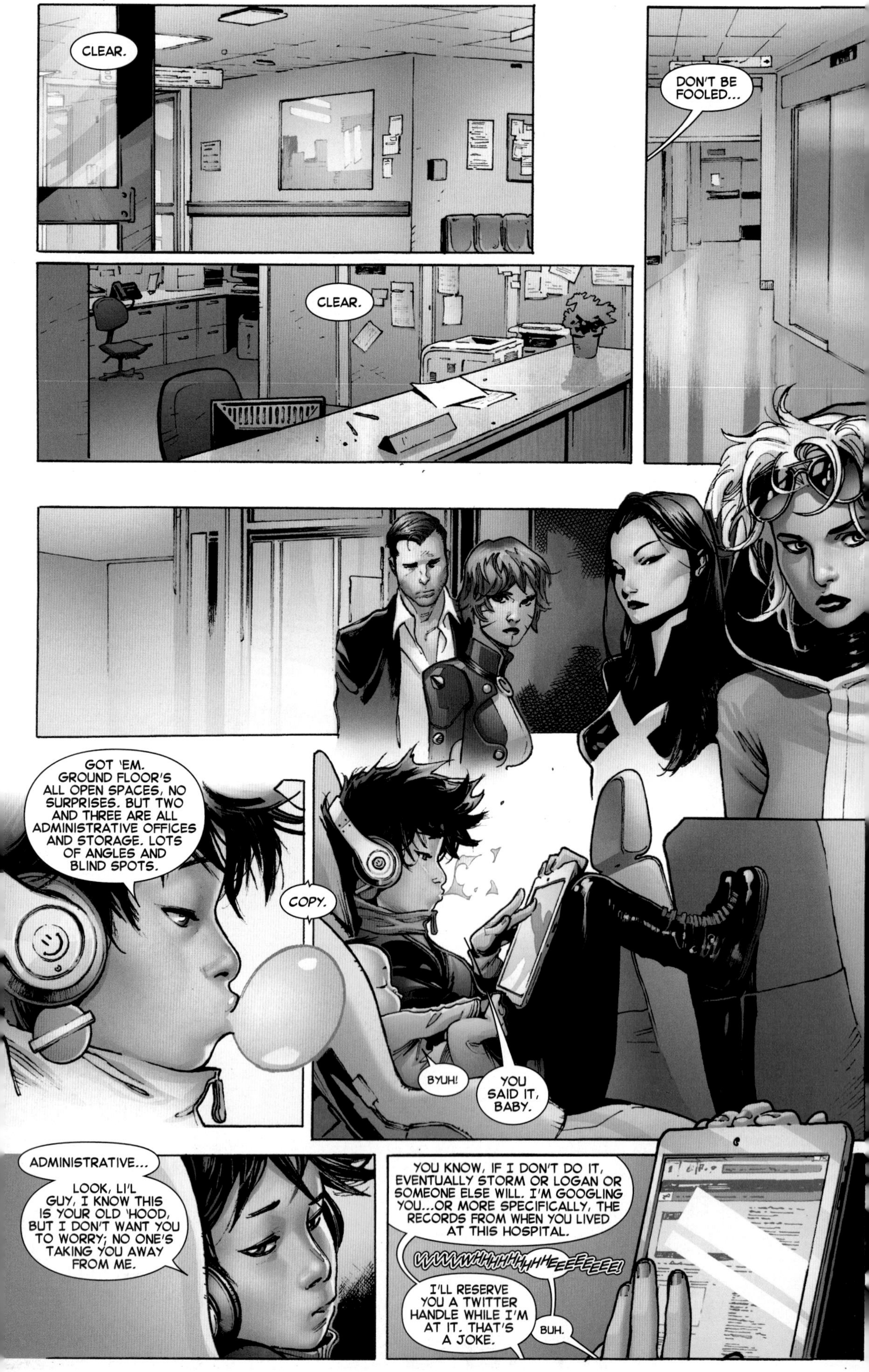
CLEAR.
DON'T BE FOOLED...
CLEAR.
GOT 'EM. GROUND FLOOR'S ALL OPEN SPACES, NO SURPRISES. BUT TWO AND THREE ARE ALL ADMINISTRATIVE OFFICES AND STORAGE. LOTS OF ANGLES AND BLIND SPOTS.
COPY.
BYUH!
YOU SAID IT, BABY.
ADMINISTRATIVE...
LOOK, LI'L GUY, I KNOW THIS IS YOUR OLD 'HOOD, BUT I DON'T WANT YOU TO WORRY; NO ONE'S TAKING YOU AWAY FROM ME.
YOU KNOW, IF I DON'T DO IT, EVENTUALLY STORM OR LOGAN OR SOMEONE ELSE WILL. I'M GOOGLING YOU...OR MORE SPECIFICALLY, THE RECORDS FROM WHEN YOU LIVED AT THIS HOSPITAL.
WWWWHHHHHHHEEEEEEEE!
I'LL RESERVE YOU A TWITTER HANDLE WHILE I'M AT IT. THAT'S A JOKE.
BUH.

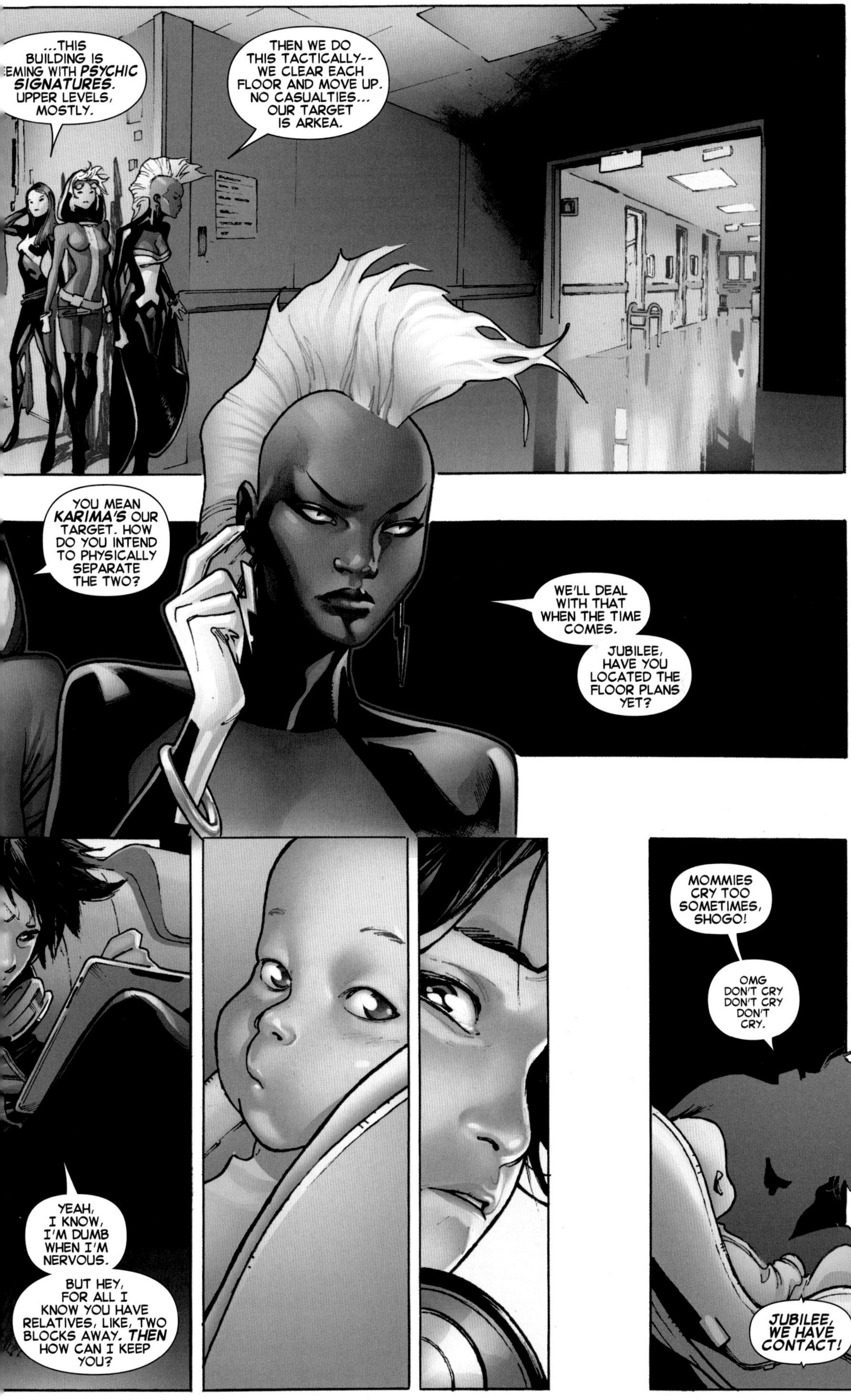
...THIS BUILDING IS EEMING WITH PSYCHIC SIGNATURES. UPPER LEVELS, MOSTLY.
THEN WE DO THIS TACTICALLY-- WE CLEAR EACH FLOOR AND MOVE UP. NO CASUALTIES... OUR TARGET IS ARKEA.
YOU MEAN KARIMA'S OUR TARGET. HOW DO YOU INTEND TO PHYSICALLY SEPARATE THE TWO?
WE'LL DEAL WITH THAT WHEN THE TIME COMES.
JUBILEE, HAVE YOU LOCATED THE FLOOR PLANS YET?
YEAH, I KNOW, I'M DUMB WHEN I'M NERVOUS.
BUT HEY, FOR ALL I KNOW YOU HAVE RELATIVES, LIKE, TWO BLOCKS AWAY. THEN HOW CAN I KEEP YOU?
MOMMIES CRY TOO SOMETIMES, SHOGO!
OMG DON'T CRY DON'T CRY DON'T CRY.
JUBILEE, WE HAVE CONTACT!

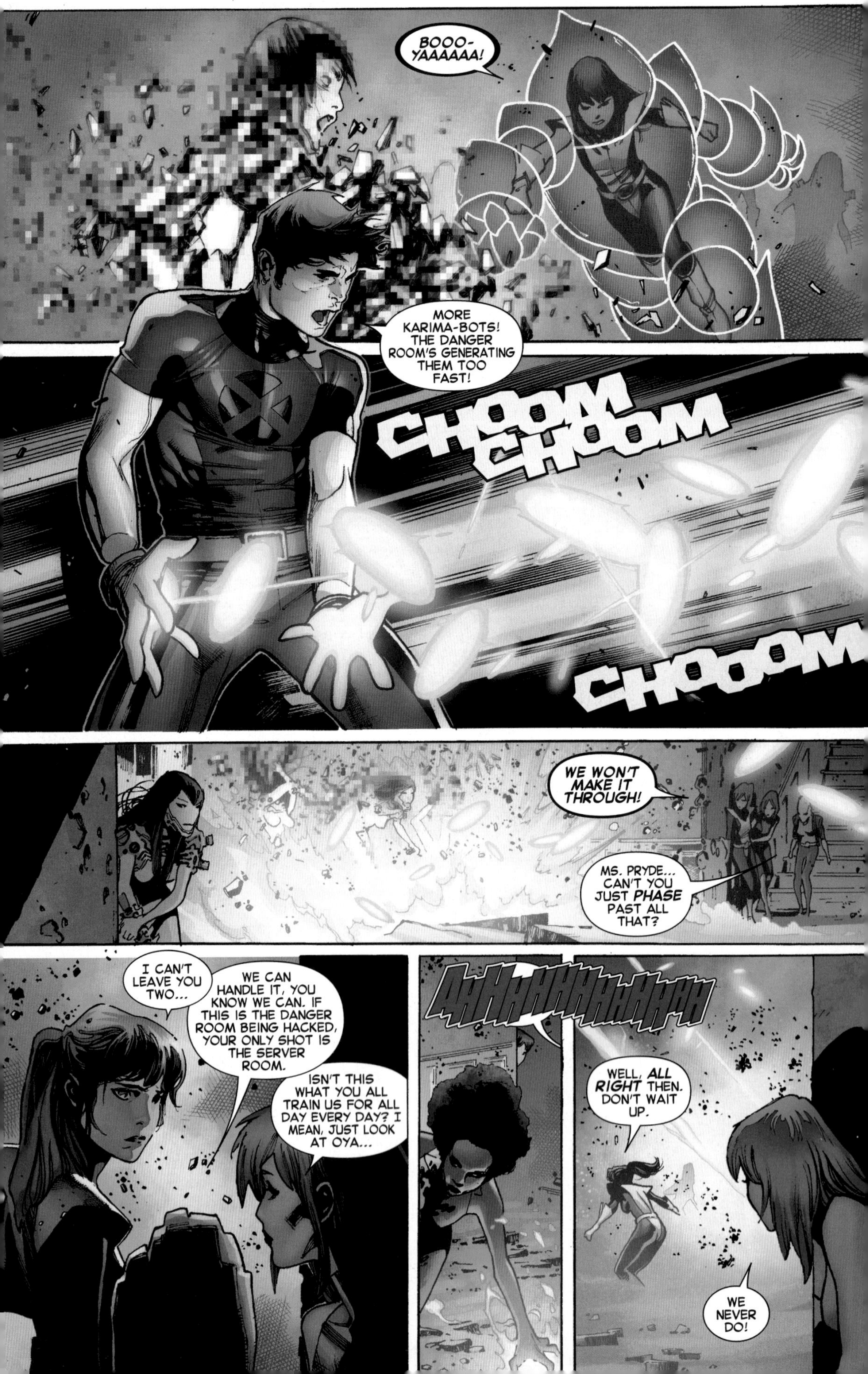
BOOO-YAAAAAA!
MORE KARIMA-BOTS! THE DANGER ROOM'S GENERATING THEM TOO FAST!
CHOOM CHOOM
CHOOOM
WE WON'T MAKE IT THROUGH!
MS. PRYDE... CAN'T YOU JUST PHASE PAST ALL THAT?
I CAN'T LEAVE YOU TWO...
WE CAN HANDLE IT, YOU KNOW WE CAN. IF THIS IS THE DANGER ROOM BEING HACKED, YOUR ONLY SHOT IS THE SERVER ROOM.
ISN'T THIS WHAT YOU ALL TRAIN US FOR ALL DAY EVERY DAY? I MEAN, JUST LOOK AT OYA...
AHHHHHHHHHHHHH
WELL, ALL RIGHT THEN. DON'T WAIT UP.
WE NEVER DO!

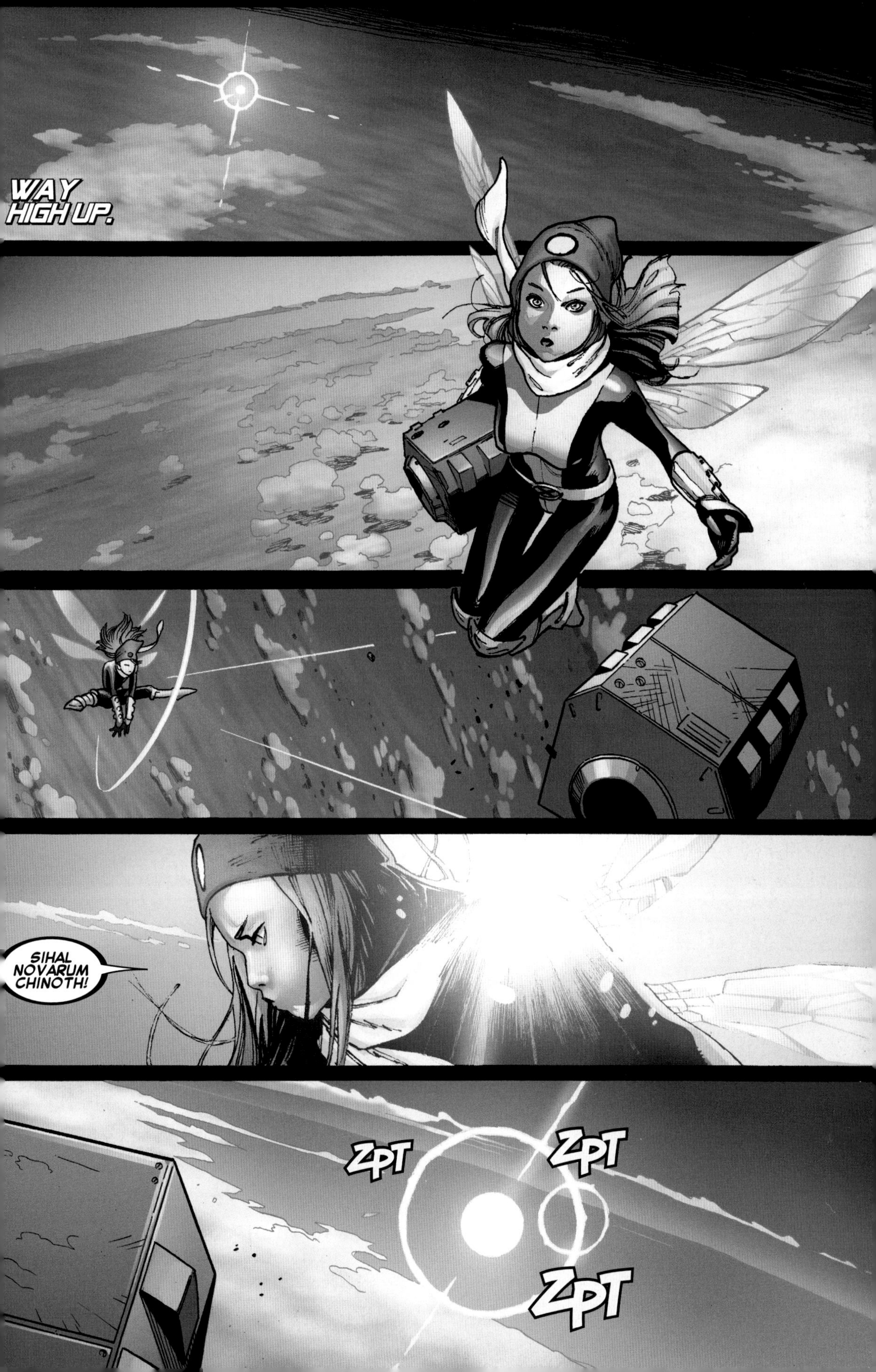
WAY HIGH UP.
SIHAL NOVARUM CHINOTH!
ZPT
ZPT
ZPT

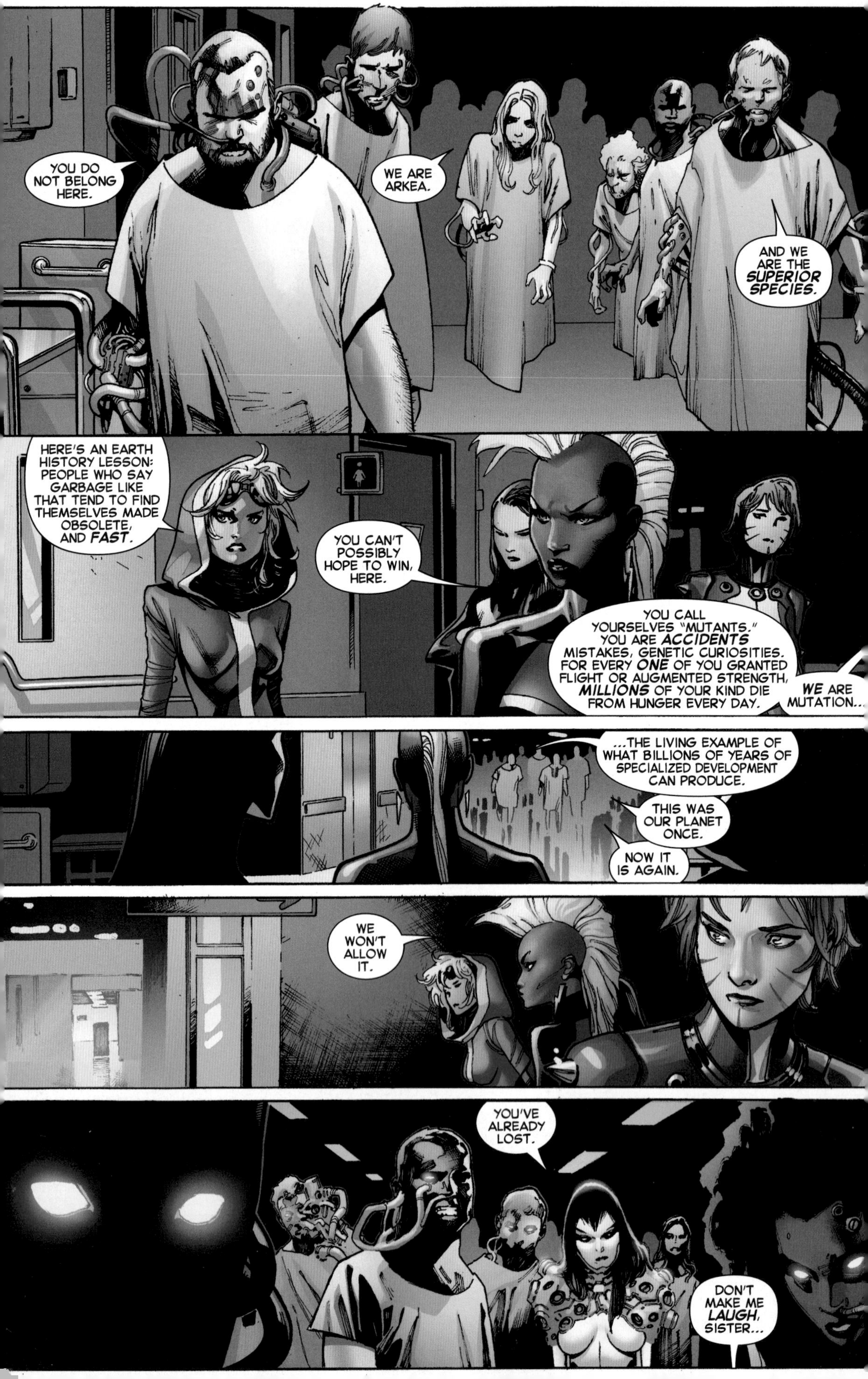

YOU DO NOT BELONG HERE.
WE ARE ARKEA.
AND WE ARE THE SUPERIOR SPECIES.
HERE'S AN EARTH HISTORY LESSON: PEOPLE WHO SAY GARBAGE LIKE THAT TEND TO FIND THEMSELVES MADE OBSOLETE, AND FAST.
YOU CAN'T POSSIBLY HOPE TO WIN, HERE.
YOU CALL YOURSELVES "MUTANTS." YOU ARE ACCIDENTS MISTAKES, GENETIC CURIOSITIES. FOR EVERY ONE OF YOU GRANTED FLIGHT OR AUGMENTED STRENGTH, MILLIONS OF YOUR KIND DIE FROM HUNGER EVERY DAY.
WE ARE MUTATION...
...THE LIVING EXAMPLE OF WHAT BILLIONS OF YEARS OF SPECIALIZED DEVELOPMENT CAN PRODUCE.
THIS WAS OUR PLANET ONCE.
NOW IT IS AGAIN.
WE WON'T ALLOW IT.
YOU'VE ALREADY LOST.
DON'T MAKE ME LAUGH, SISTER...

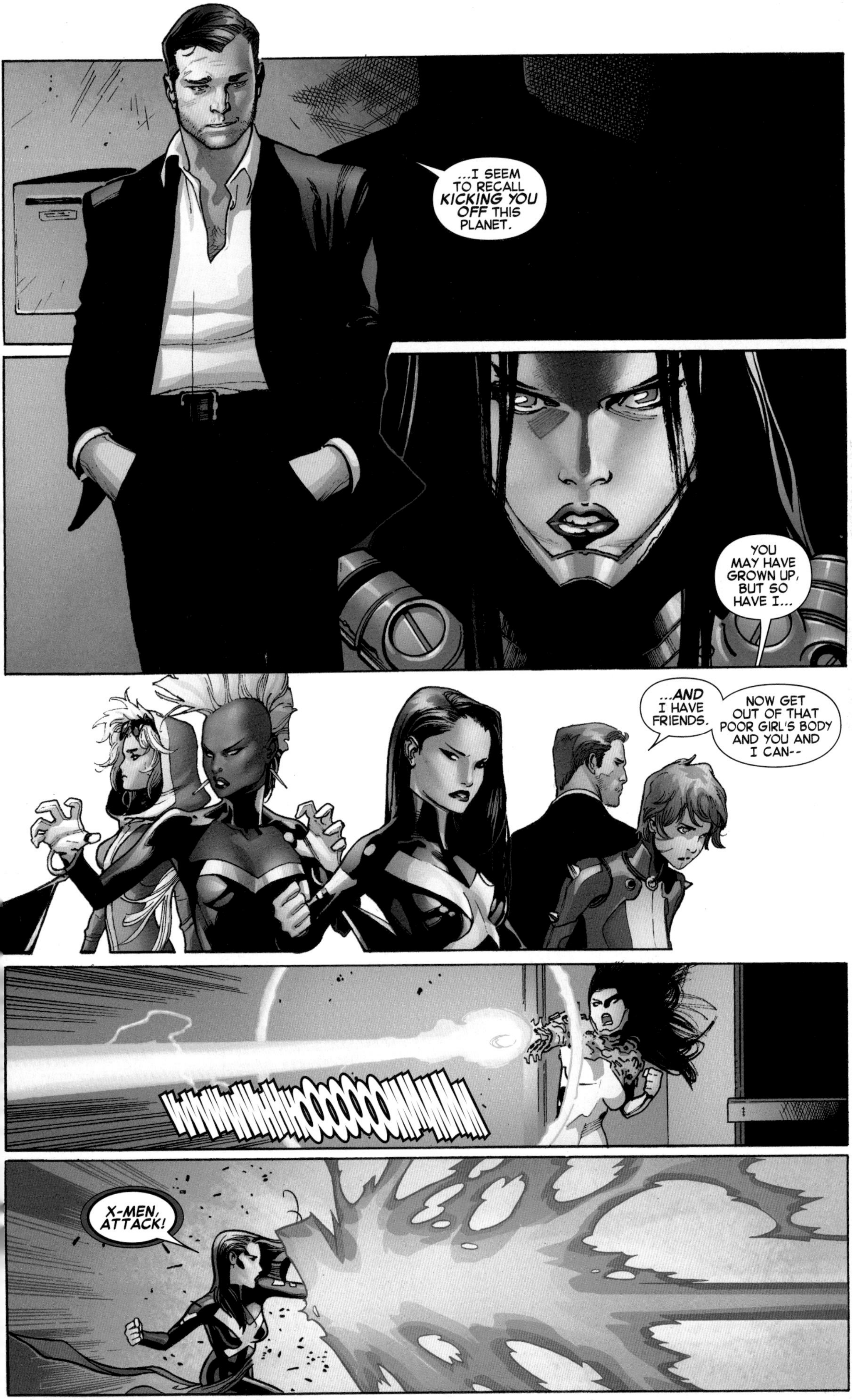
...I SEEM TO RECALL KICKING YOU OFF THIS PLANET.
YOU MAY HAVE GROWN UP, BUT SO HAVE I...
...AND I HAVE FRIENDS.
NOW GET OUT OF THAT POOR GIRL'S BODY AND YOU AND I CAN--
WHHHHHHHOOOOOOMMMMM
X-MEN, ATTACK!

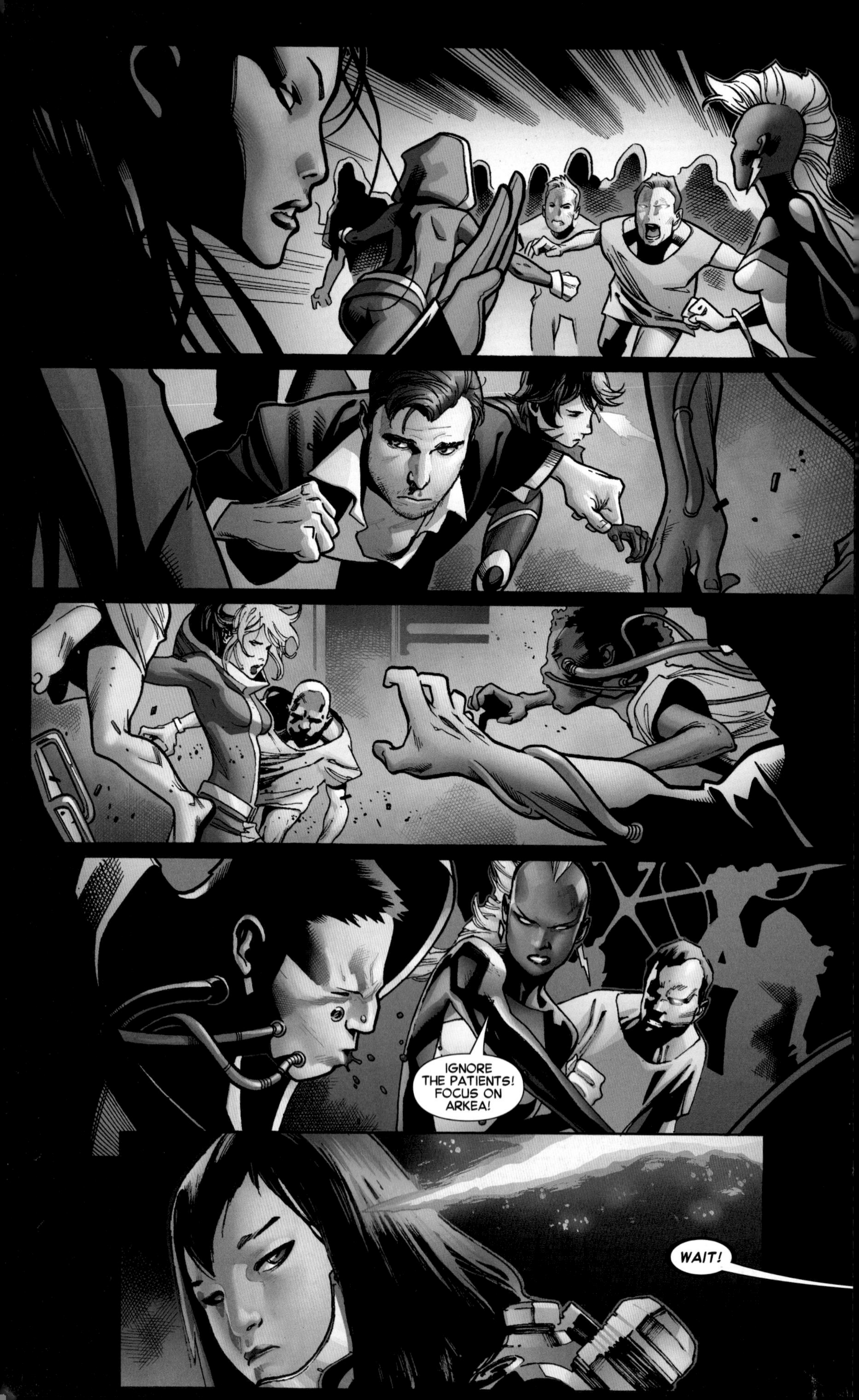
IGNORE THE PATIENTS! FOCUS ON ARKEA!
WAIT!

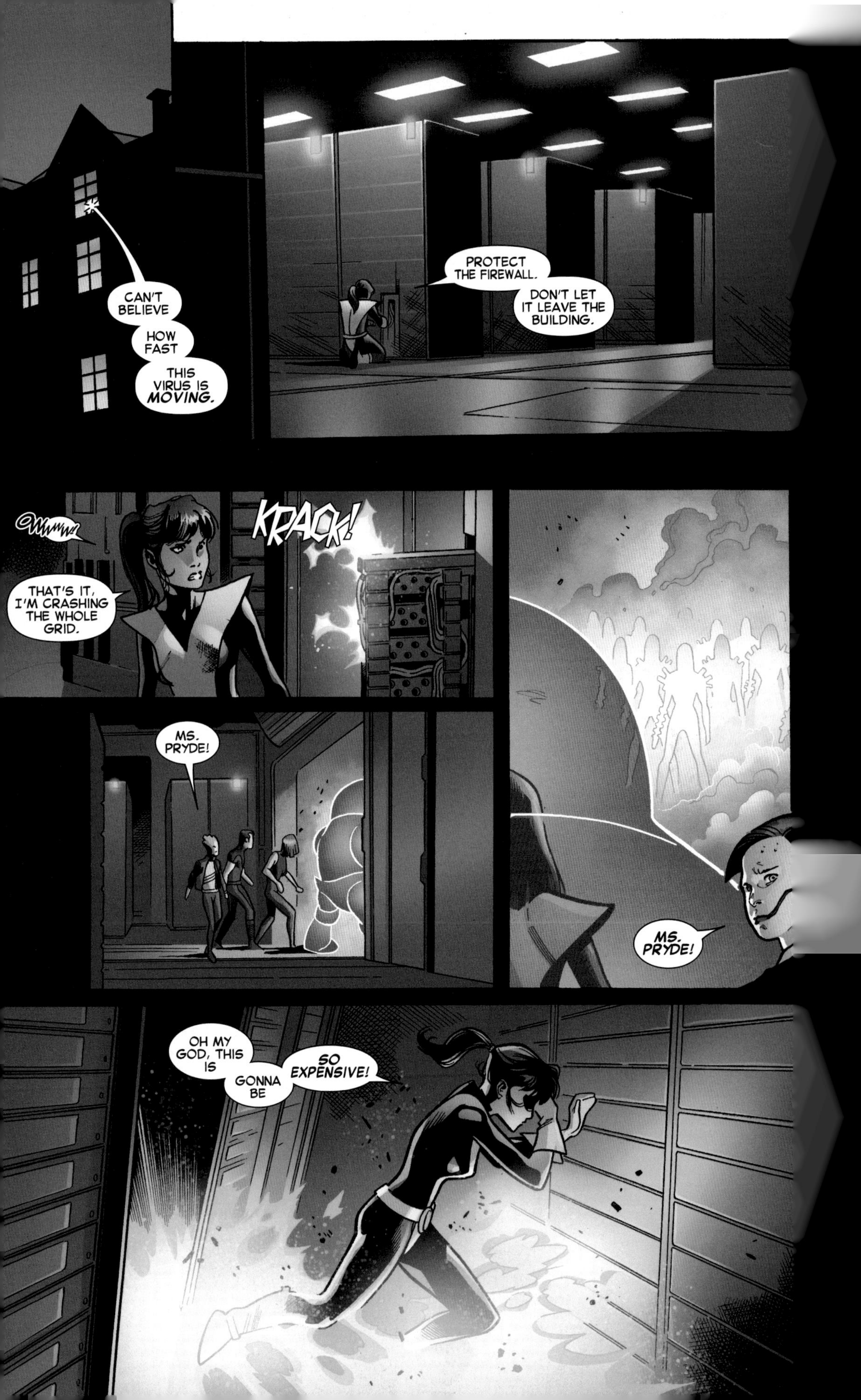
CAN'T BELIEVE
HOW FAST
THIS VIRUS IS MOVING.
PROTECT THE FIREWALL.
DON'T LET IT LEAVE THE BUILDING.
THAT'S IT, I'M CRASHING THE WHOLE GRID.
KRACK!
MS. PRYDE!
MS. PRYDE!
OH MY GOD, THIS IS
GONNA BE
SO EXPENSIVE!

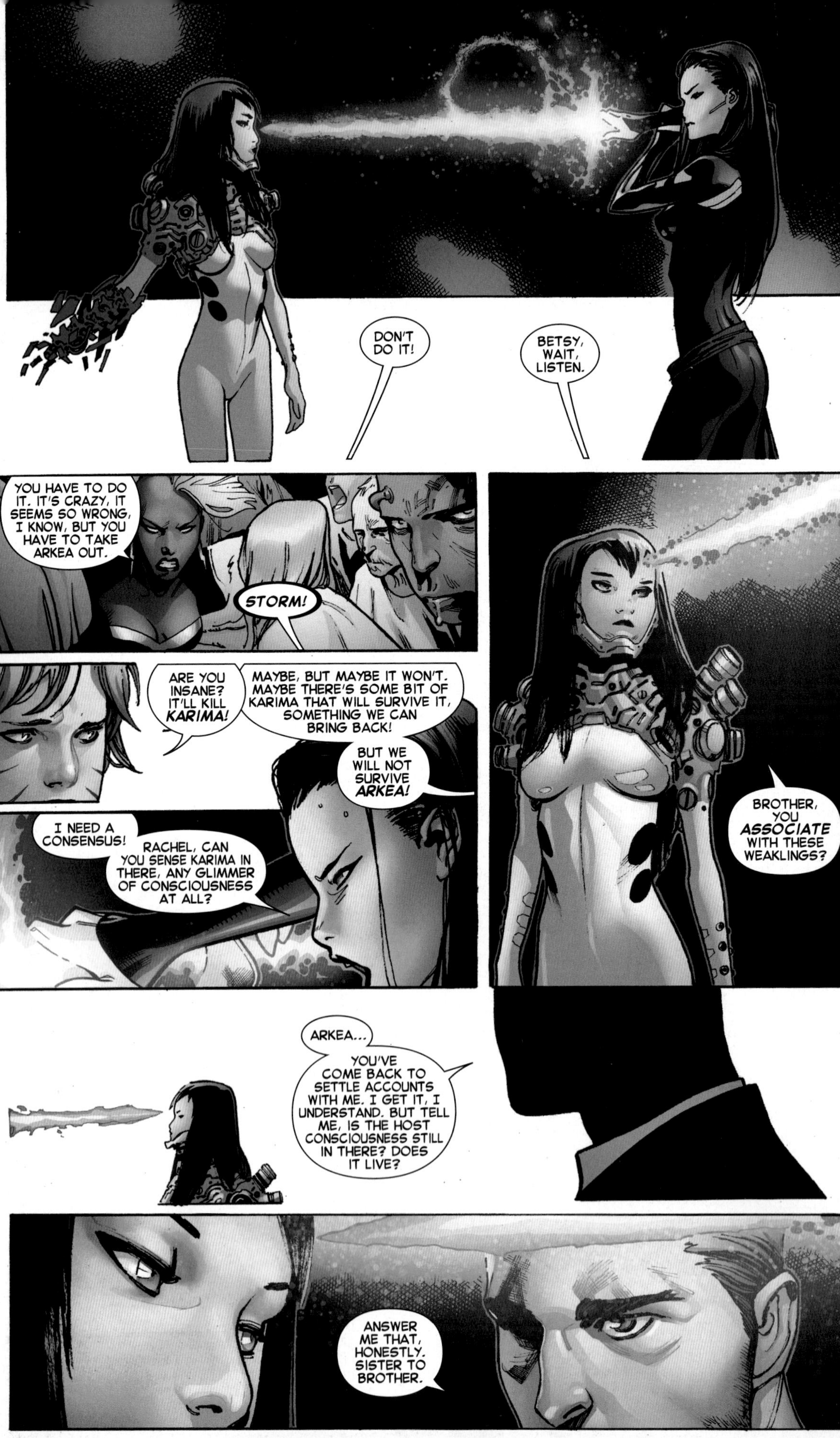
DON'T DO IT!
BETSY, WAIT, LISTEN.
YOU HAVE TO DO IT. IT'S CRAZY, IT SEEMS SO WRONG, I KNOW, BUT YOU HAVE TO TAKE ARKEA OUT.
STORM!
ARE YOU INSANE? IT'LL KILL KARIMA!
MAYBE, BUT MAYBE IT WON'T. MAYBE THERE'S SOME BIT OF KARIMA THAT WILL SURVIVE IT, SOMETHING WE CAN BRING BACK!
BUT WE WILL NOT SURVIVE ARKEA!
I NEED A CONSENSUS!
RACHEL, CAN YOU SENSE KARIMA IN THERE, ANY GLIMMER OF CONSCIOUSNESS AT ALL?
BROTHER, YOU ASSOCIATE WITH THESE WEAKLINGS?
ARKEA...
YOU'VE COME BACK TO SETTLE ACCOUNTS WITH ME. I GET IT, I UNDERSTAND. BUT TELL ME, IS THE HOST CONSCIOUSNESS STILL IN THERE? DOES IT LIVE?
ANSWER ME THAT, HONESTLY. SISTER TO BROTHER.

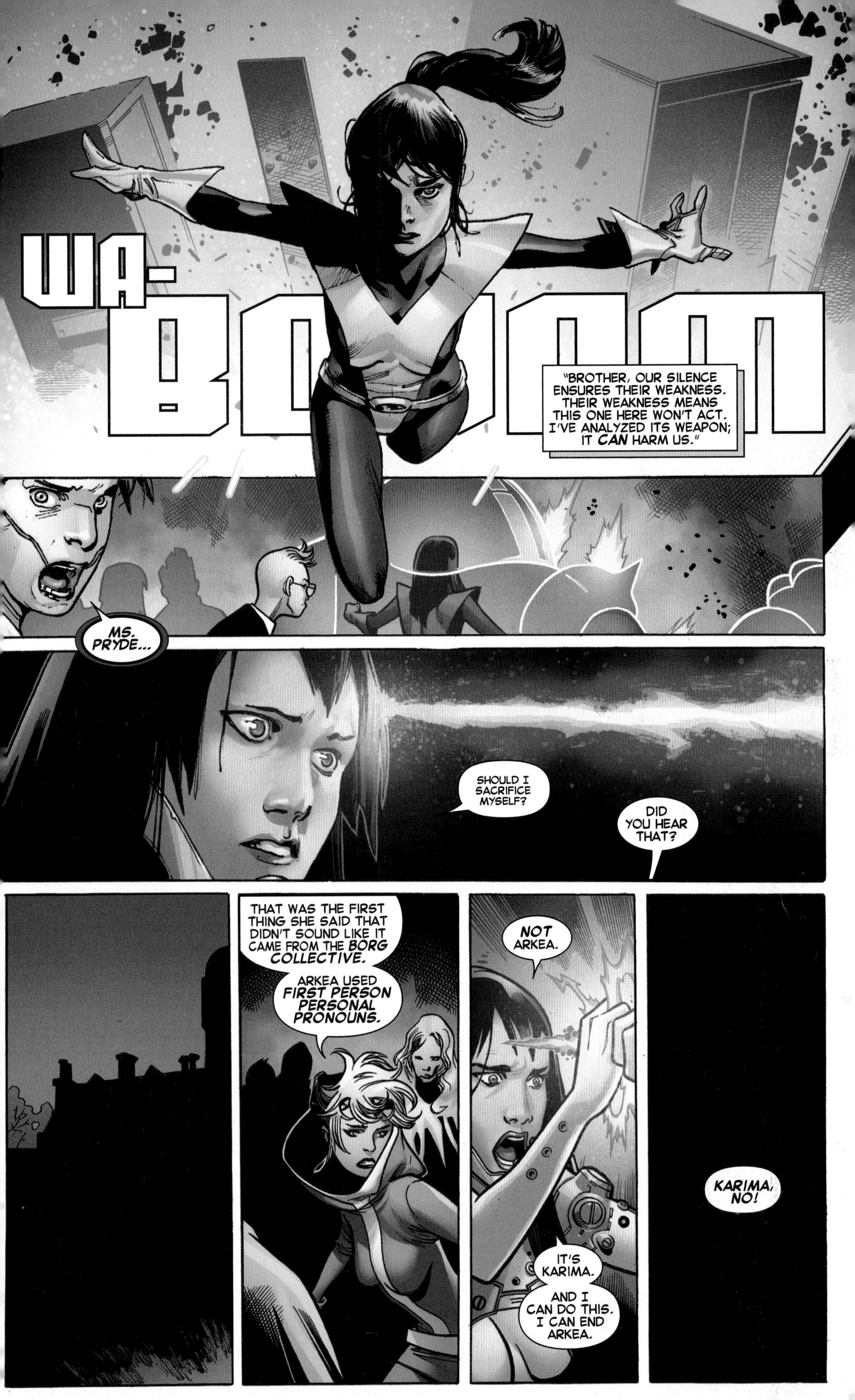
WA-BOOOM!
"BROTHER, OUR SILENCE ENSURES THEIR WEAKNESS. THEIR WEAKNESS MEANS THIS ONE HERE WON'T ACT. I'VE ANALYZED ITS WEAPON; IT CAN HARM US."
MS. PRYDE...
SHOULD I SACRIFICE MYSELF?
DID YOU HEAR THAT?
THAT WAS THE FIRST THING SHE SAID THAT DIDN'T SOUND LIKE IT CAME FROM THE BORG COLLECTIVE.
ARKEA USED FIRST PERSON PERSONAL PRONOUNS.
NOT ARKEA.
IT'S KARIMA.
AND I CAN DO THIS. I CAN END ARKEA.
KARIMA, NO!

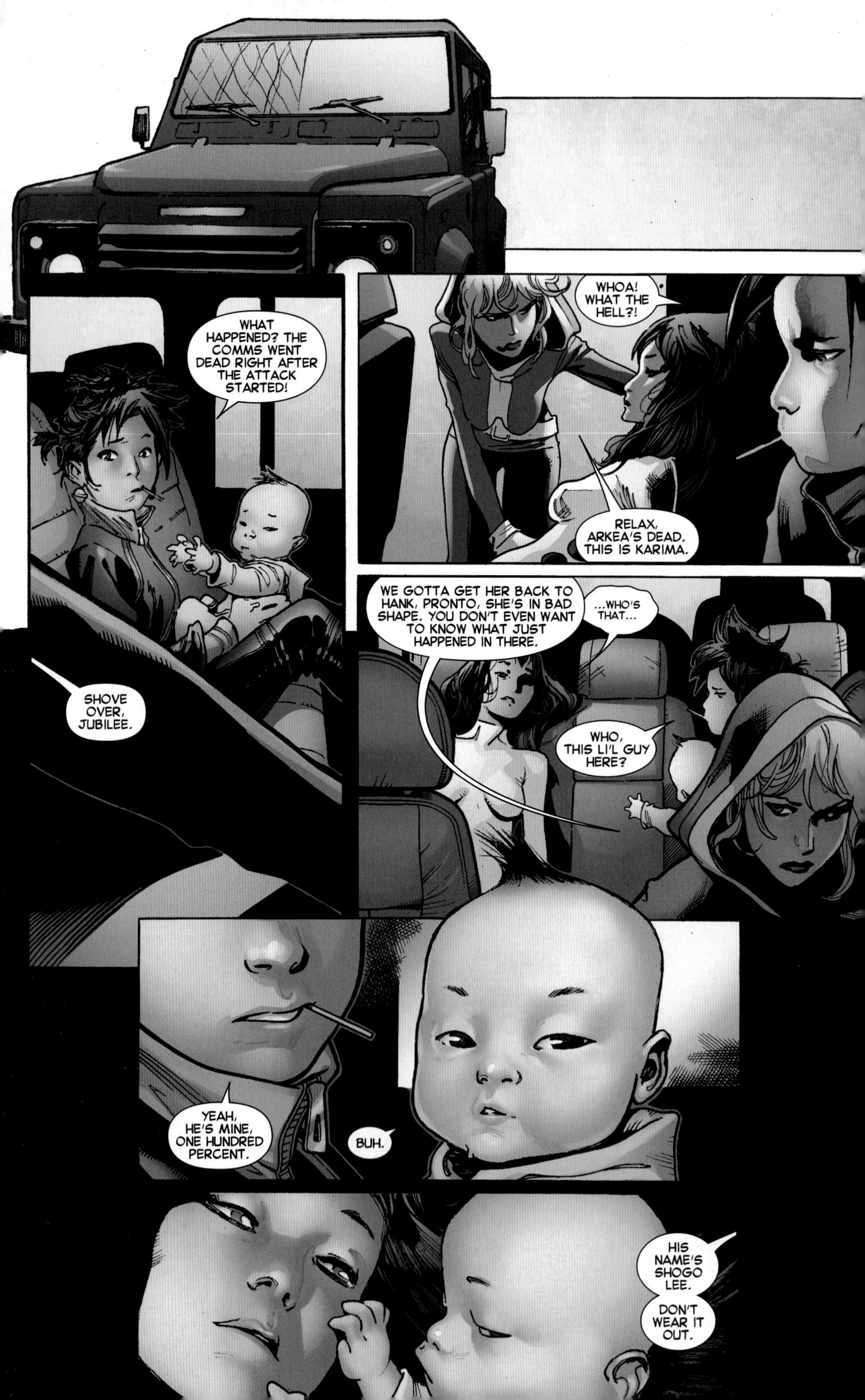

WHAT HAPPENED? THE COMMS WENT DEAD RIGHT AFTER THE ATTACK STARTED!
SHOVE OVER, JUBILEE.
WHOA! WHAT THE HELL?!
RELAX, ARKEA'S DEAD. THIS IS KARIMA.
WE GOTTA GET HER BACK TO HANK, PRONTO, SHE'S IN BAD SHAPE. YOU DON'T EVEN WANT TO KNOW WHAT JUST HAPPENED IN THERE.
...WHO'S THAT...
WHO, THIS LI'L GUY HERE?
YEAH, HE'S MINE, ONE HUNDRED PERCENT.
BUH.
HIS NAME'S SHOGO LEE.
DON'T WEAR IT OUT.

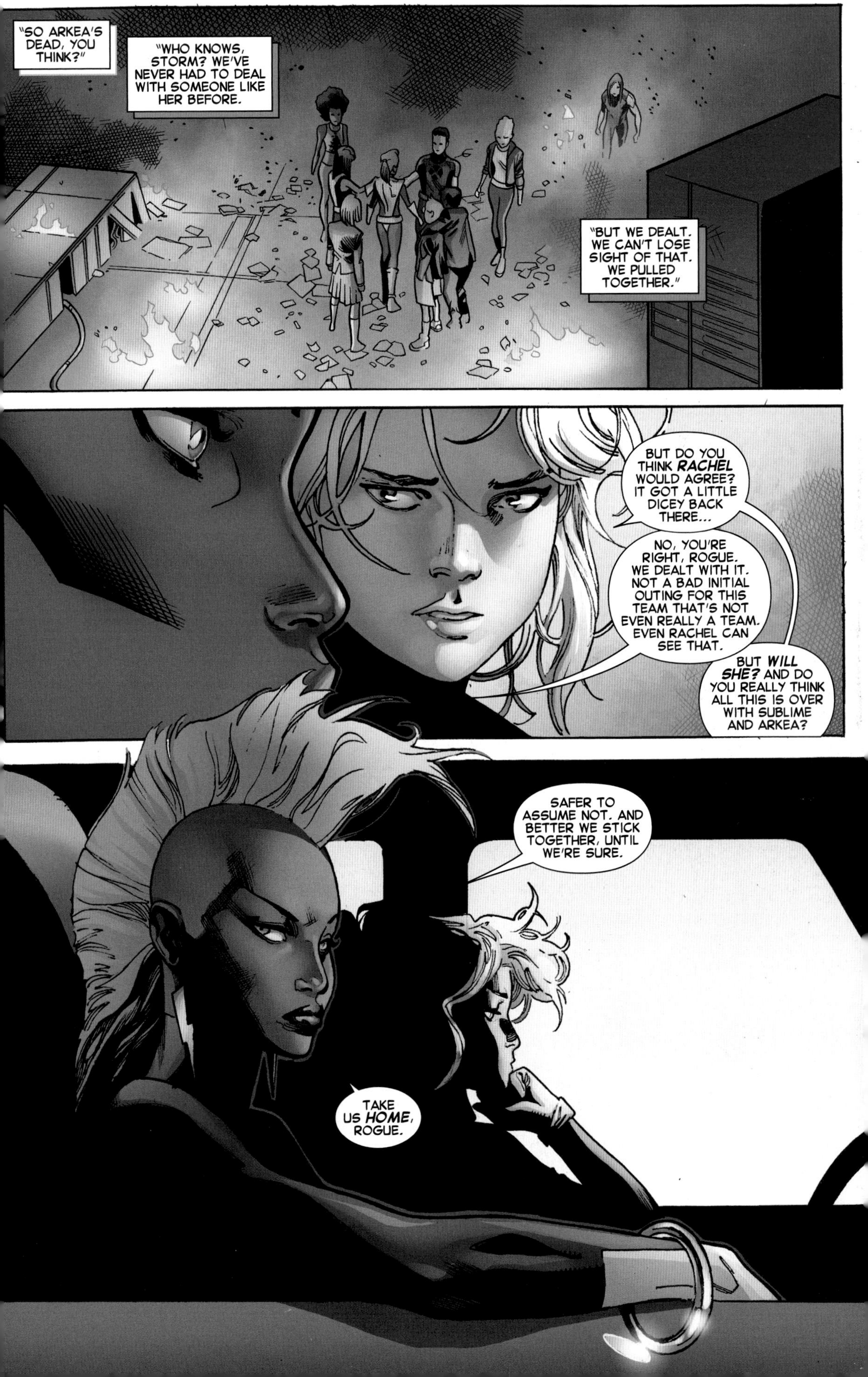
"SO ARKEA'S DEAD, YOU THINK?"
"WHO KNOWS, STORM? WE'VE NEVER HAD TO DEAL WITH SOMEONE LIKE HER BEFORE.
"BUT WE DEALT. WE CAN'T LOSE SIGHT OF THAT. WE PULLED TOGETHER."
BUT DO YOU THINK RACHEL WOULD AGREE? IT GOT A LITTLE DICEY BACK THERE...
NO, YOU'RE RIGHT, ROGUE. WE DEALT WITH IT. NOT A BAD INITIAL OUTING FOR THIS TEAM THAT'S NOT EVEN REALLY A TEAM. EVEN RACHEL CAN SEE THAT.
BUT WILL SHE? AND DO YOU REALLY THINK ALL THIS IS OVER WITH SUBLIME AND ARKEA?
SAFER TO ASSUME NOT. AND BETTER WE STICK TOGETHER, UNTIL WE'RE SURE.
TAKE US HOME, ROGUE.

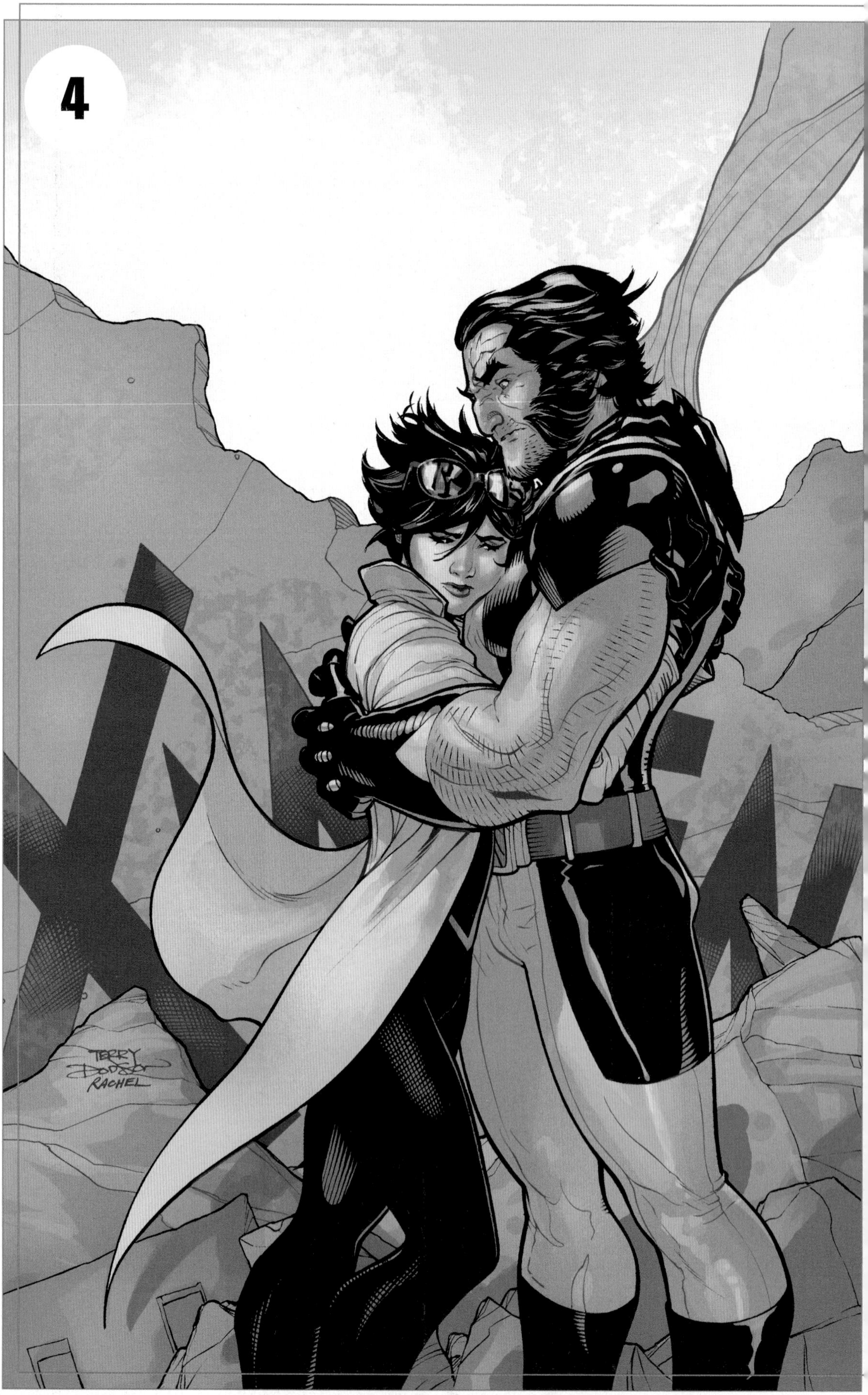
4
TERRY DODSON RACHEL

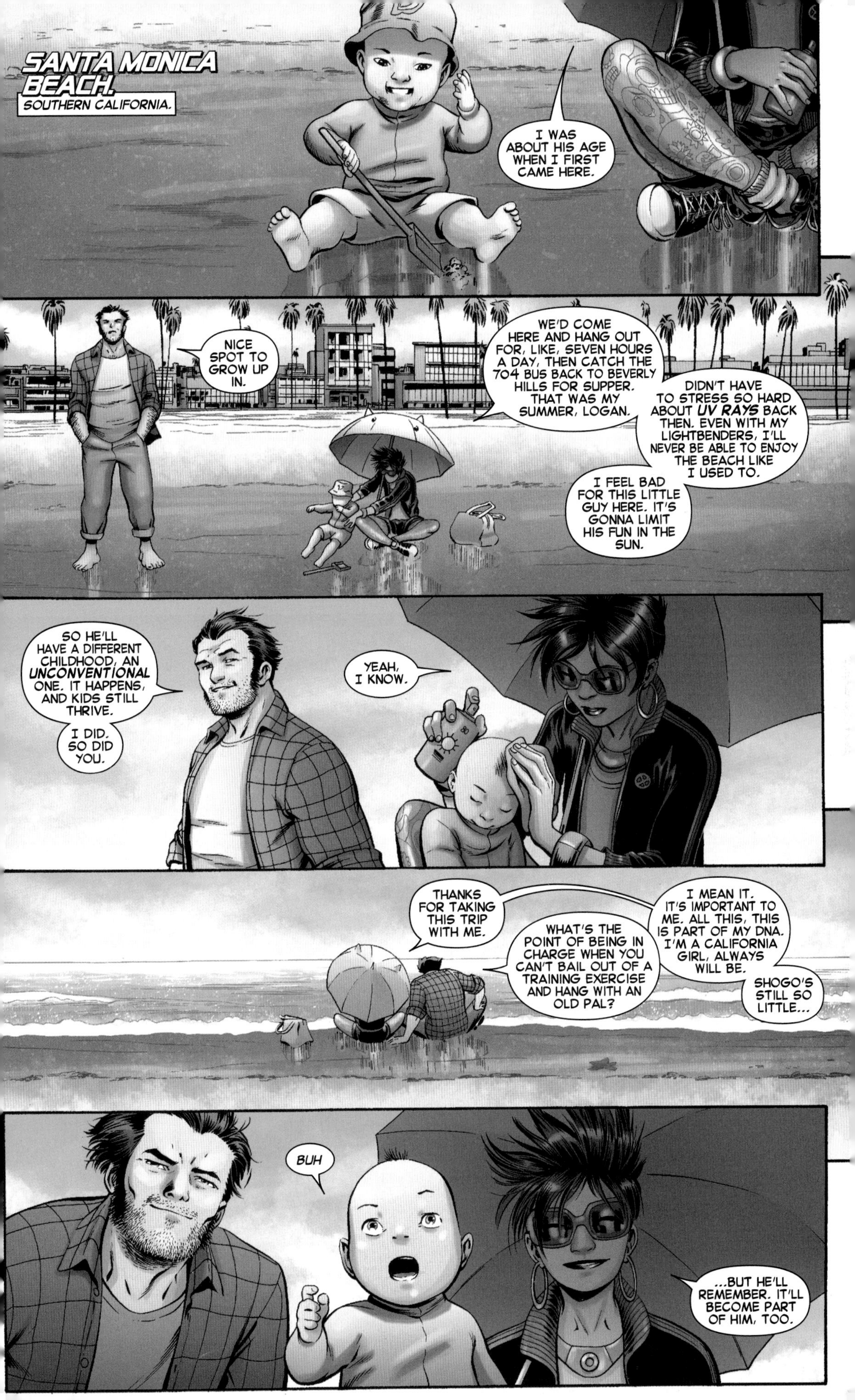
SANTA MONICA BEACH.
SOUTHERN CALIFORNIA.
I WAS ABOUT HIS AGE WHEN I FIRST CAME HERE.
NICE SPOT TO GROW UP IN.
WE'D COME HERE AND HANG OUT FOR, LIKE, SEVEN HOURS A DAY, THEN CATCH THE 704 BUS BACK TO BEVERLY HILLS FOR SUPPER. THAT WAS MY SUMMER, LOGAN.
DIDN'T HAVE TO STRESS SO HARD ABOUT UV RAYS BACK THEN. EVEN WITH MY LIGHTBENDERS, I'LL NEVER BE ABLE TO ENJOY THE BEACH LIKE I USED TO.
I FEEL BAD FOR THIS LITTLE GUY HERE. IT'S GONNA LIMIT HIS FUN IN THE SUN.
SO HE'LL HAVE A DIFFERENT CHILDHOOD, AN UNCONVENTIONAL ONE. IT HAPPENS, AND KIDS STILL THRIVE.
I DID. SO DID YOU.
YEAH, I KNOW.
THANKS FOR TAKING THIS TRIP WITH ME.
WHAT'S THE POINT OF BEING IN CHARGE WHEN YOU CAN'T BAIL OUT OF A TRAINING EXERCISE AND HANG WITH AN OLD PAL?
I MEAN IT. IT'S IMPORTANT TO ME. ALL THIS, THIS IS PART OF MY DNA. I'M A CALIFORNIA GIRL, ALWAYS WILL BE.
SHOGO'S STILL SO LITTLE...
BUH
...BUT HE'LL REMEMBER. IT'LL BECOME PART OF HIM, TOO.

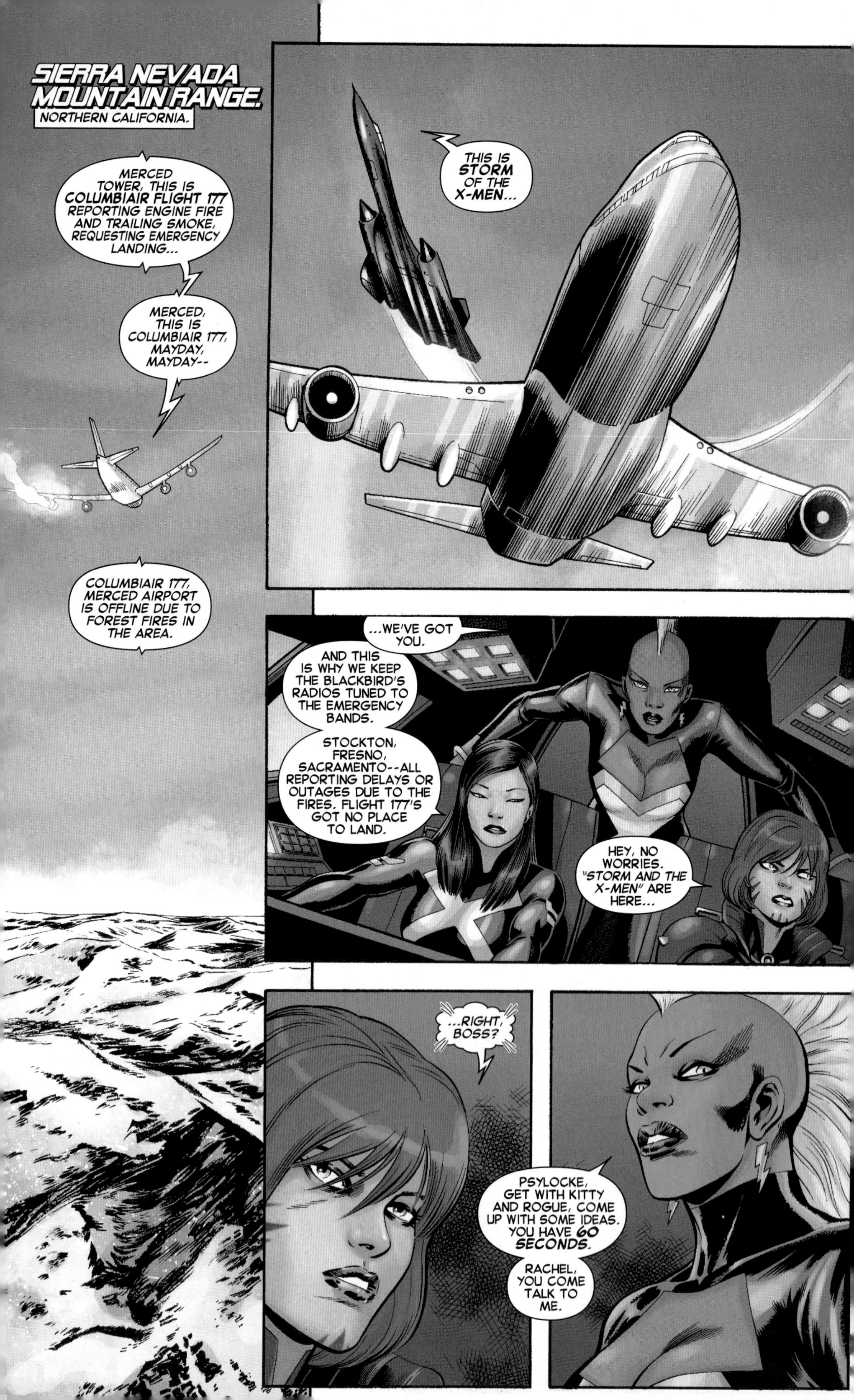
SIERRA NEVADA MOUNTAIN RANGE.
NORTHERN CALIFORNIA.
MERCED TOWER, THIS IS COLUMBIAIR FLIGHT 177 REPORTING ENGINE FIRE AND TRAILING SMOKE, REQUESTING EMERGENCY LANDING...
MERCED, THIS IS COLUMBIAIR 177, MAYDAY, MAYDAY--
COLUMBIAIR 177, MERCED AIRPORT IS OFFLINE DUE TO FOREST FIRES IN THE AREA.
THIS IS STORM OF THE X-MEN...
...WE'VE GOT YOU.
AND THIS IS WHY WE KEEP THE BLACKBIRD'S RADIOS TUNED TO THE EMERGENCY BANDS.
STOCKTON, FRESNO, SACRAMENTO--ALL REPORTING DELAYS OR OUTAGES DUE TO THE FIRES. FLIGHT 177'S GOT NO PLACE TO LAND.
HEY, NO WORRIES. "STORM AND THE X-MEN" ARE HERE...
...RIGHT, BOSS?
PSYLOCKE, GET WITH KITTY AND ROGUE, COME UP WITH SOME IDEAS. YOU HAVE 60 SECONDS.
RACHEL, YOU COME TALK TO ME.

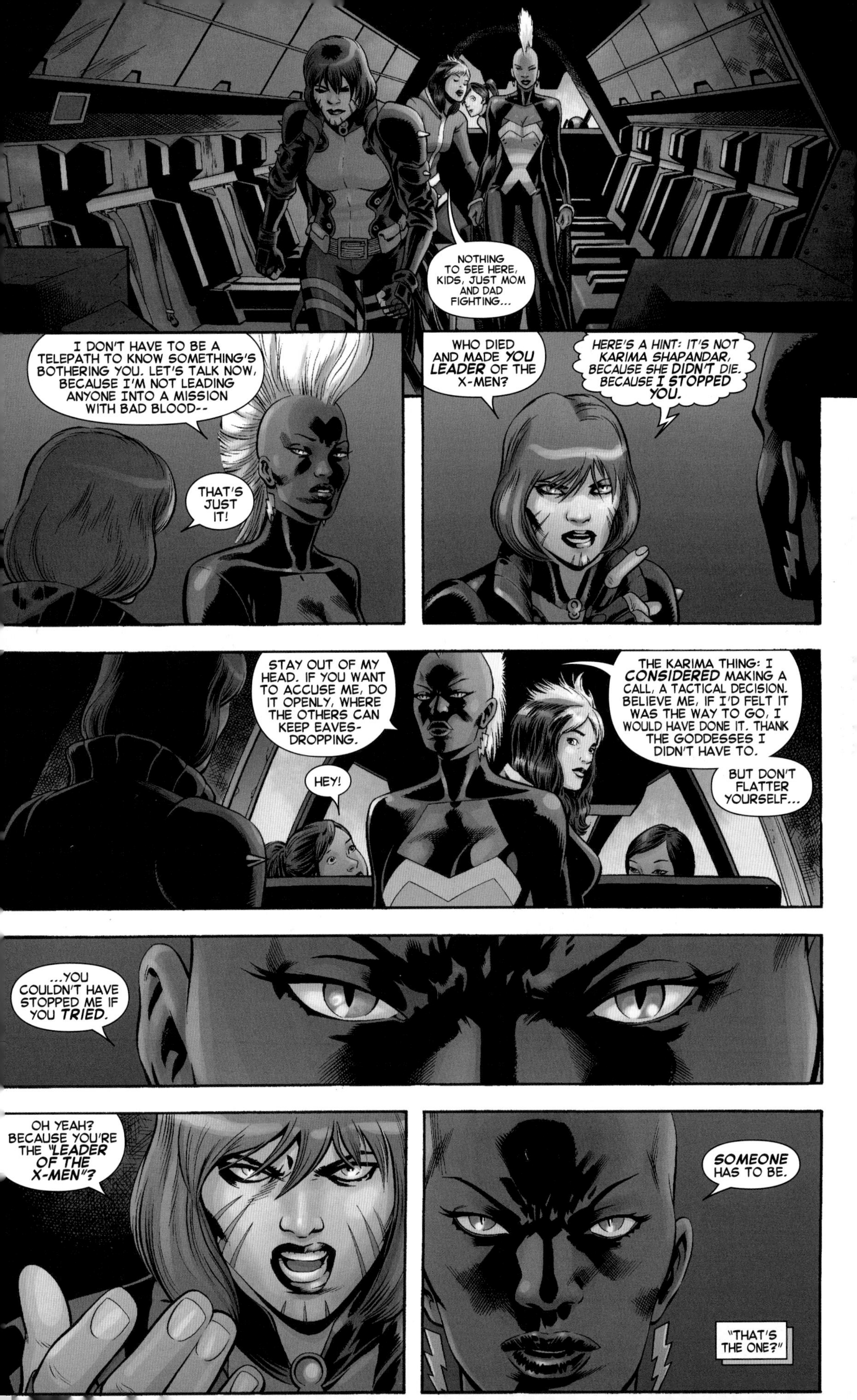
NOTHING TO SEE HERE, KIDS, JUST MOM AND DAD FIGHTING...
I DON'T HAVE TO BE A TELEPATH TO KNOW SOMETHING'S BOTHERING YOU. LET'S TALK NOW, BECAUSE I'M NOT LEADING ANYONE INTO A MISSION WITH BAD BLOOD--
THAT'S JUST IT!
WHO DIED AND MADE YOU LEADER OF THE X-MEN?
HERE'S A HINT: IT'S NOT KARIMA SHAPANDAR, BECAUSE SHE DIDN'T DIE. BECAUSE I STOPPED YOU.
STAY OUT OF MY HEAD. IF YOU WANT TO ACCUSE ME, DO IT OPENLY, WHERE THE OTHERS CAN KEEP EAVES-DROPPING.
HEY!
THE KARIMA THING: I CONSIDERED MAKING A CALL, A TACTICAL DECISION. BELIEVE ME, IF I'D FELT IT WAS THE WAY TO GO, I WOULD HAVE DONE IT. THANK THE GODDESSES I DIDN'T HAVE TO.
BUT DON'T FLATTER YOURSELF...
...YOU COULDN'T HAVE STOPPED ME IF YOU TRIED.
OH YEAH? BECAUSE YOU'RE THE "LEADER OF THE X-MEN"?
SOMEONE HAS TO BE.
"THAT'S THE ONE?"

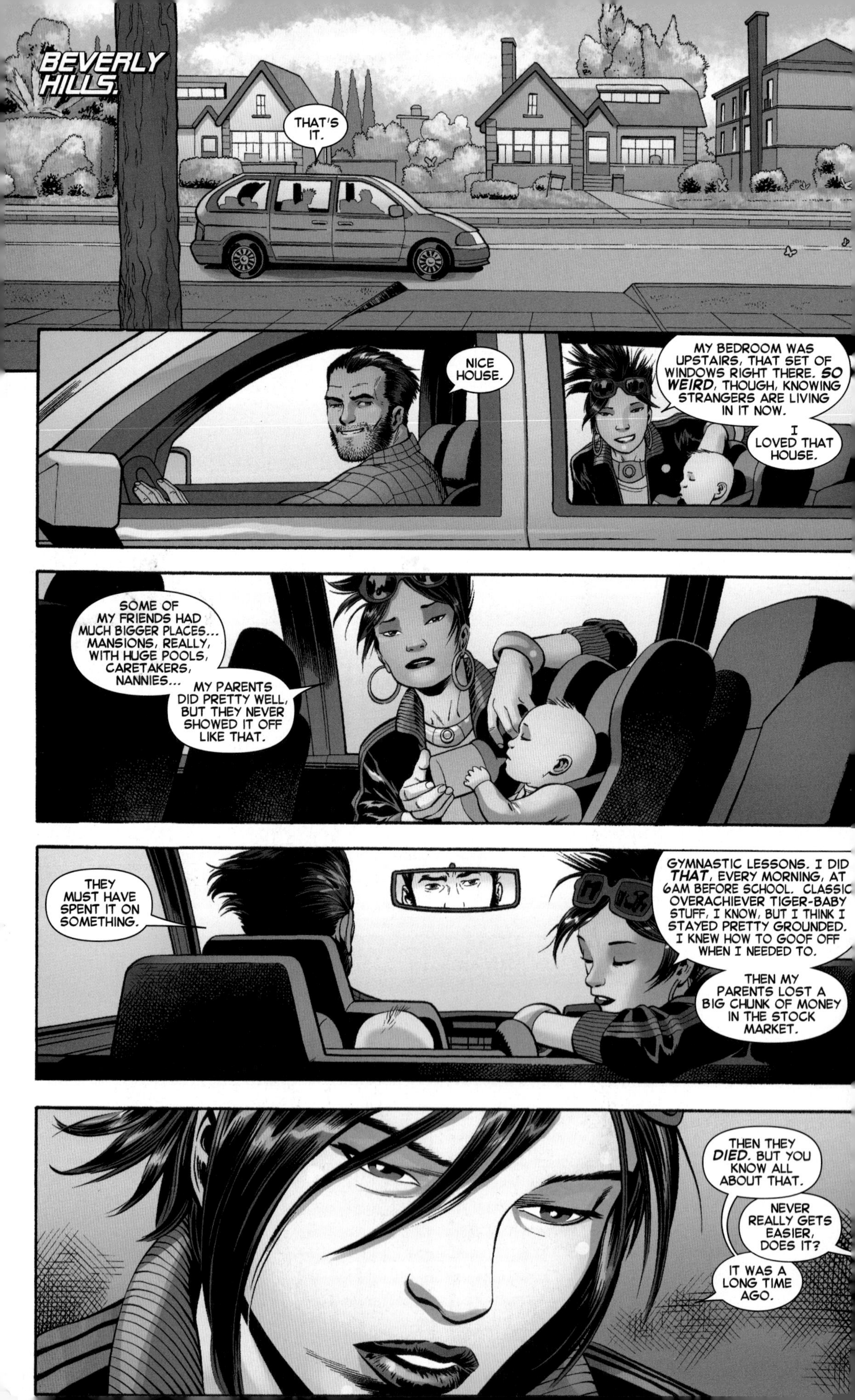
BEVERLY HILLS.
THAT'S IT.
NICE HOUSE.
MY BEDROOM WAS UPSTAIRS, THAT SET OF WINDOWS RIGHT THERE. SO WEIRD, THOUGH, KNOWING STRANGERS ARE LIVING IN IT NOW.
I LOVED THAT HOUSE.
SOME OF MY FRIENDS HAD MUCH BIGGER PLACES... MANSIONS, REALLY, WITH HUGE POOLS, CARETAKERS, NANNIES...
MY PARENTS DID PRETTY WELL, BUT THEY NEVER SHOWED IT OFF LIKE THAT.
THEY MUST HAVE SPENT IT ON SOMETHING.
GYMNASTIC LESSONS. I DID THAT, EVERY MORNING, AT 6AM BEFORE SCHOOL. CLASSIC OVERACHIEVER TIGER-BABY STUFF, I KNOW, BUT I THINK I STAYED PRETTY GROUNDED. I KNEW HOW TO GOOF OFF WHEN I NEEDED TO.
THEN MY PARENTS LOST A BIG CHUNK OF MONEY IN THE STOCK MARKET.
THEN THEY DIED. BUT YOU KNOW ALL ABOUT THAT.
NEVER REALLY GETS EASIER, DOES IT?
IT WAS A LONG TIME AGO.

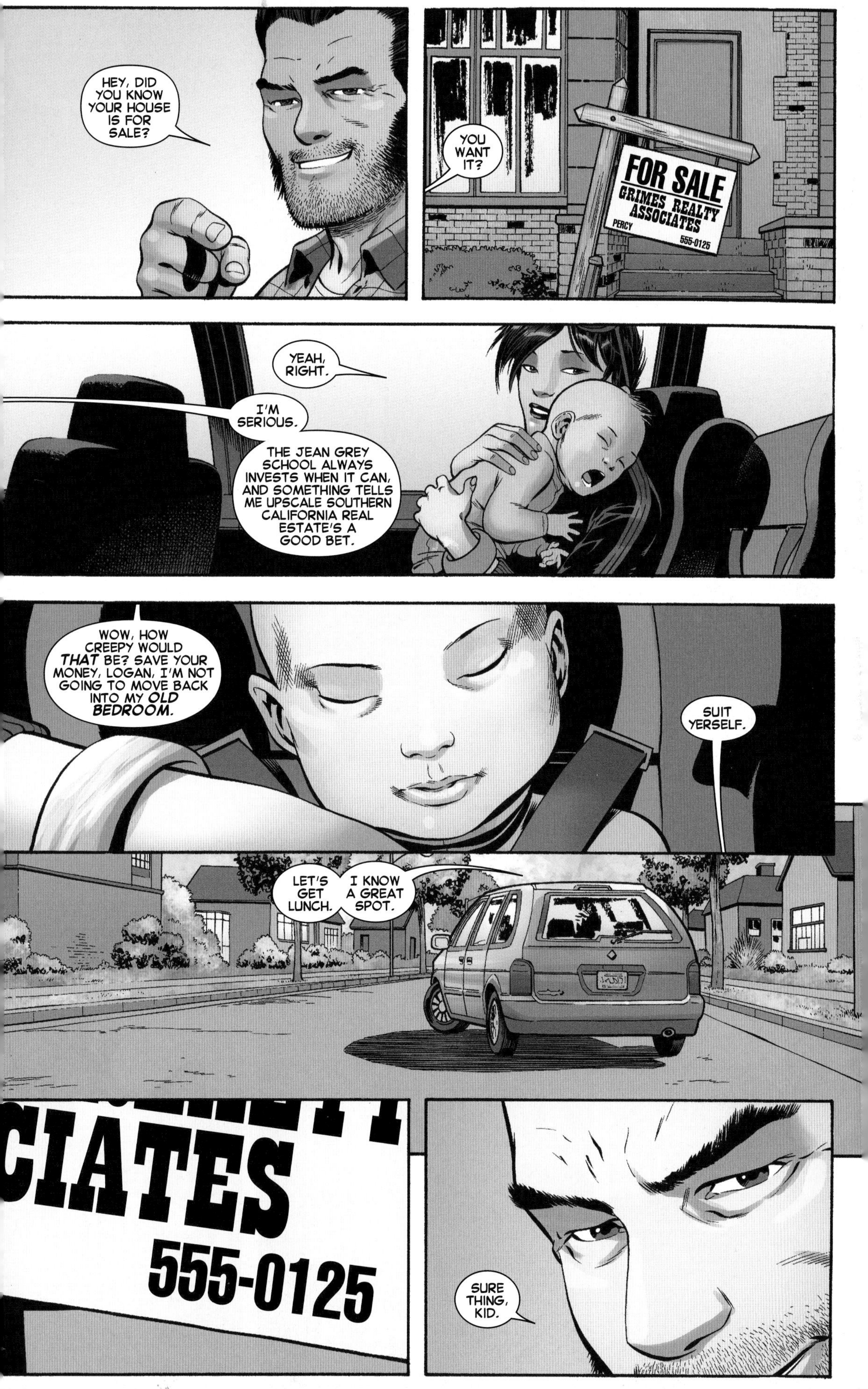
HEY, DID YOU KNOW YOUR HOUSE IS FOR SALE?
YOU WANT IT?
FOR SALE
GRIMES REALTY ASSOCIATES
PERCY
555-0125
YEAH, RIGHT.
I'M SERIOUS.
THE JEAN GREY SCHOOL ALWAYS INVESTS WHEN IT CAN, AND SOMETHING TELLS ME UPSCALE SOUTHERN CALIFORNIA REAL ESTATE'S A GOOD BET.
WOW, HOW CREEPY WOULD THAT BE? SAVE YOUR MONEY, LOGAN, I'M NOT GOING TO MOVE BACK INTO MY OLD BEDROOM.
SUIT YERSELF.
LET'S GET LUNCH.
I KNOW A GREAT SPOT.
CIATES
555-0125
SURE THING, KID.

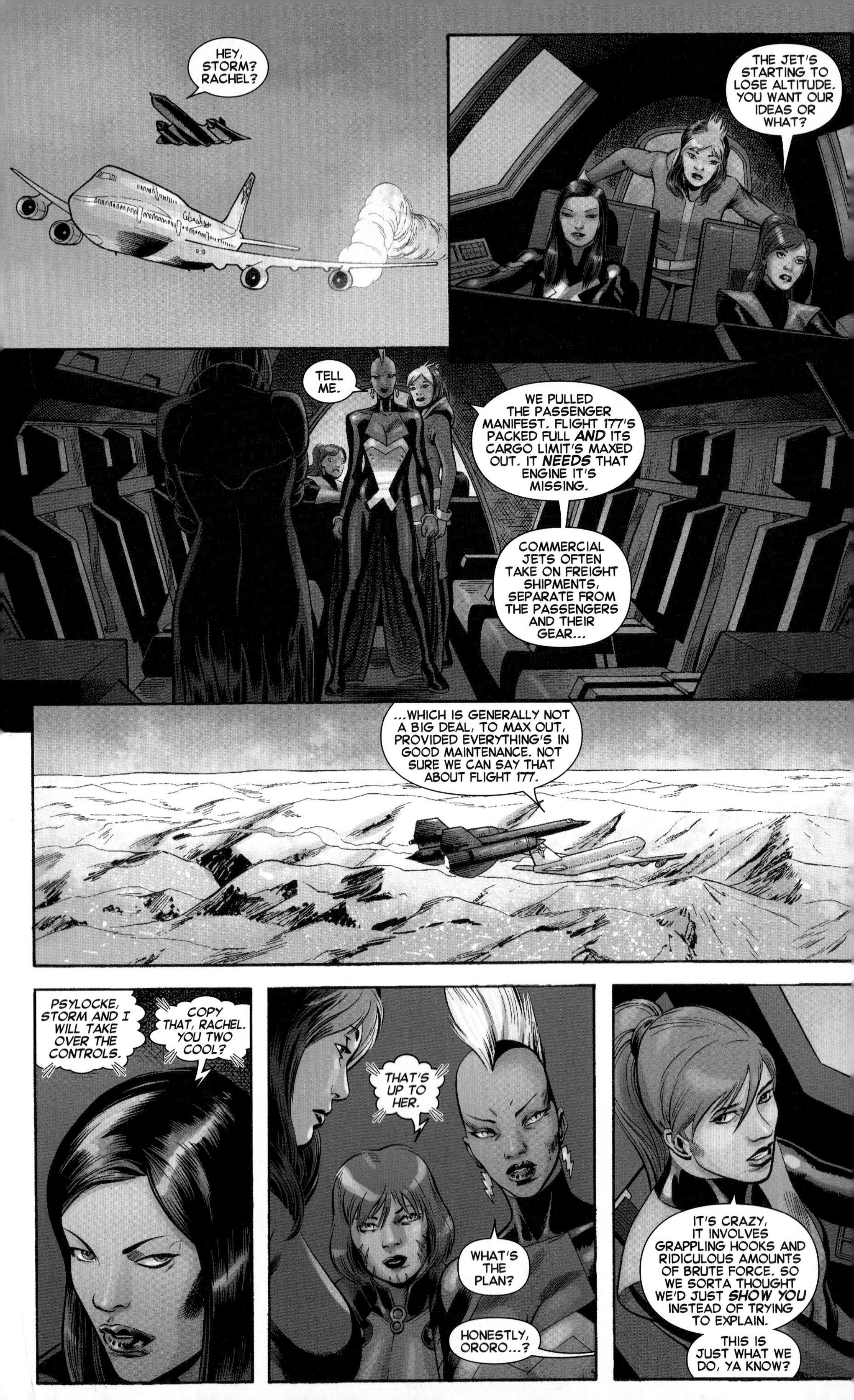
HEY, STORM? RACHEL?
THE JET'S STARTING TO LOSE ALTITUDE. YOU WANT OUR IDEAS OR WHAT?
TELL ME.
WE PULLED THE PASSENGER MANIFEST. FLIGHT 177'S PACKED FULL AND ITS CARGO LIMIT'S MAXED OUT. IT NEEDS THAT ENGINE IT'S MISSING.
COMMERCIAL JETS OFTEN TAKE ON FREIGHT SHIPMENTS, SEPARATE FROM THE PASSENGERS AND THEIR GEAR...
...WHICH IS GENERALLY NOT A BIG DEAL, TO MAX OUT, PROVIDED EVERYTHING'S IN GOOD MAINTENANCE. NOT SURE WE CAN SAY THAT ABOUT FLIGHT 177.
PSYLOCKE, STORM AND I WILL TAKE OVER THE CONTROLS.
COPY THAT, RACHEL. YOU TWO COOL?
THAT'S UP TO HER.
WHAT'S THE PLAN?
HONESTLY, ORORO...?
IT'S CRAZY, IT INVOLVES GRAPPLING HOOKS AND RIDICULOUS AMOUNTS OF BRUTE FORCE. SO WE SORTA THOUGHT WE'D JUST SHOW YOU INSTEAD OF TRYING TO EXPLAIN.
THIS IS JUST WHAT WE DO, YA KNOW?

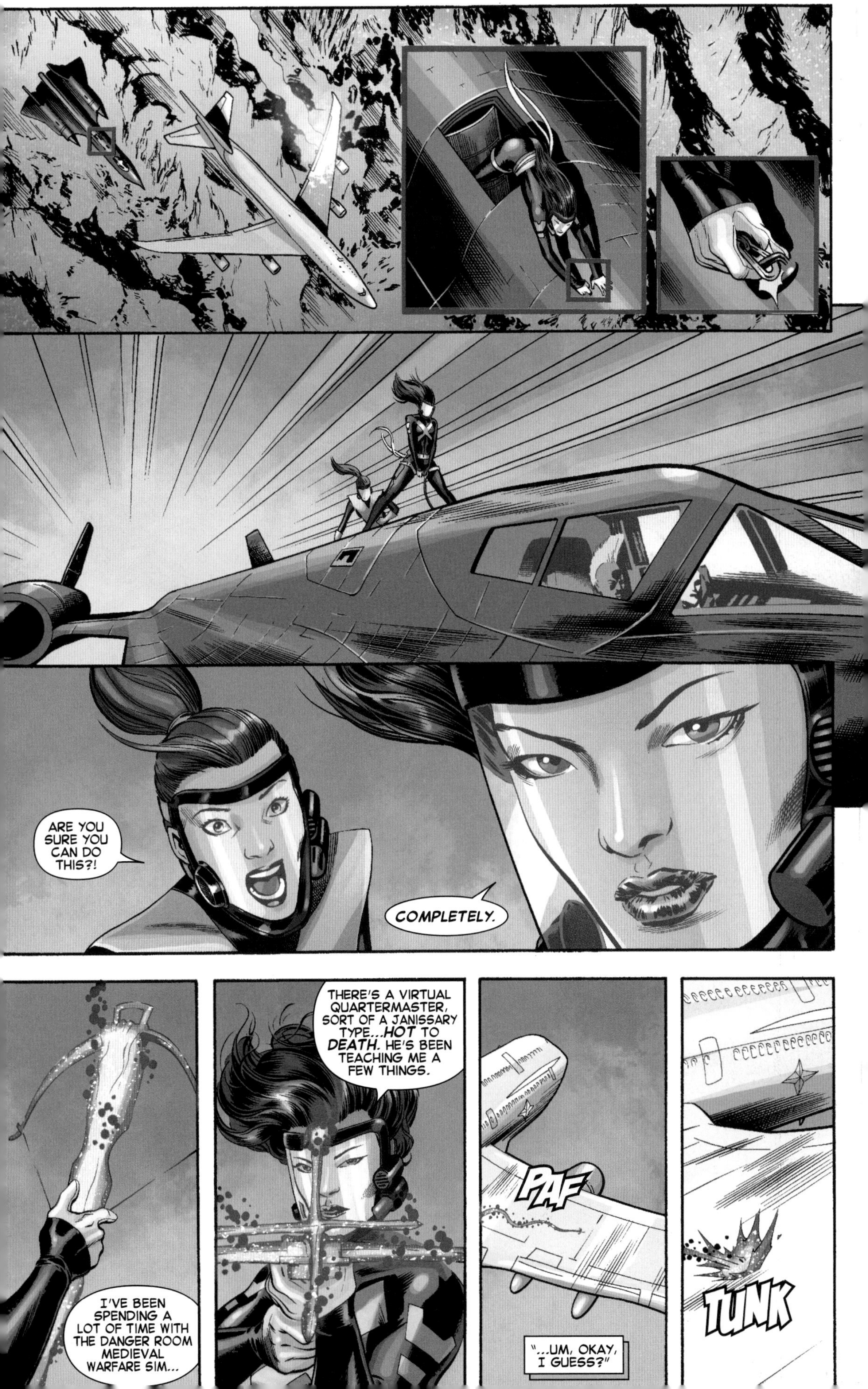
ARE YOU SURE YOU CAN DO THIS?!
COMPLETELY.
I'VE BEEN SPENDING A LOT OF TIME WITH THE DANGER ROOM MEDIEVAL WARFARE SIM...
THERE'S A VIRTUAL QUARTERMASTER, SORT OF A JANISSARY TYPE...HOT TO DEATH. HE'S BEEN TEACHING ME A FEW THINGS.
PAF
"...UM, OKAY, I GUESS?"
TUNK

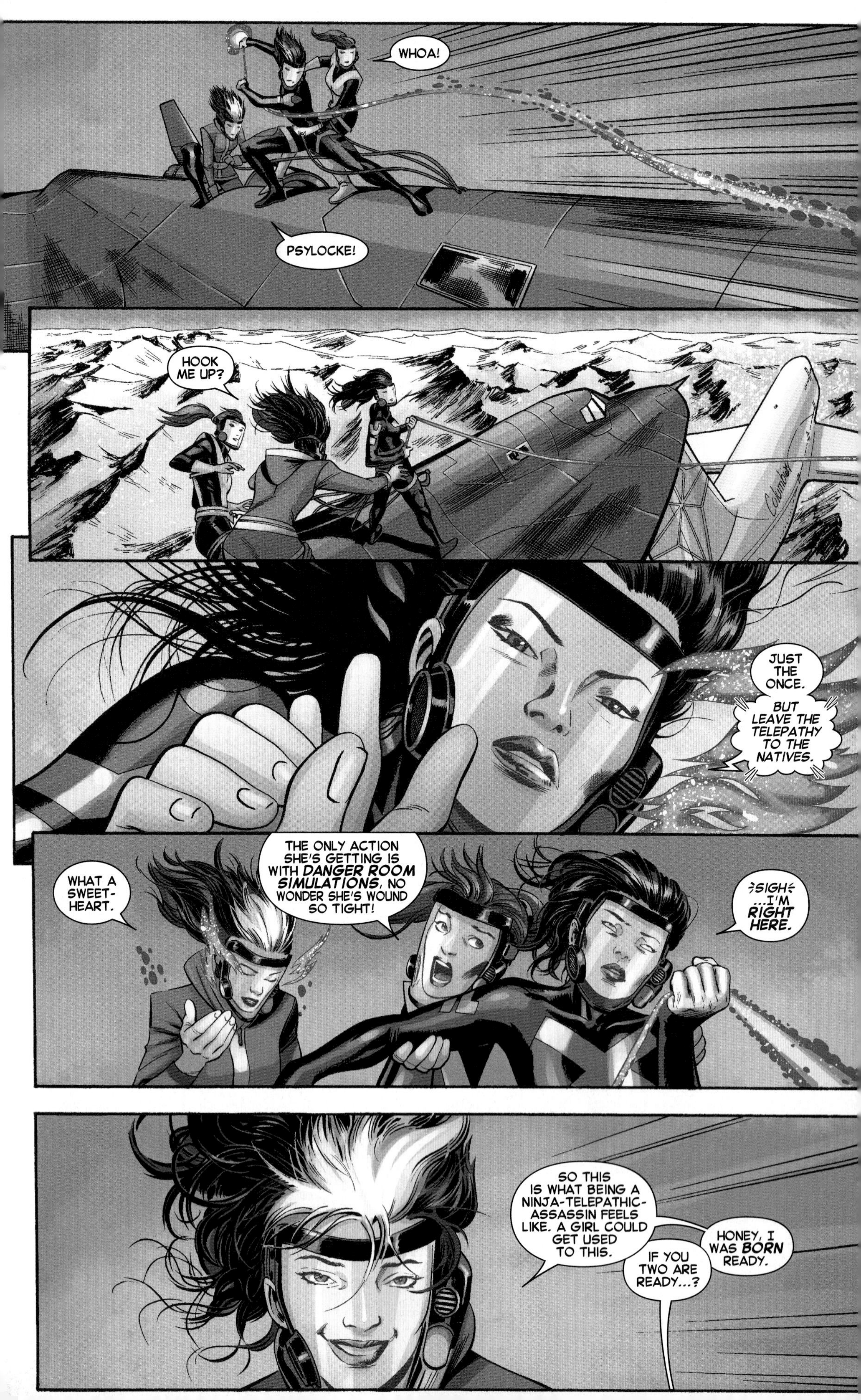
WHOA!
PSYLOCKE!
HOOK ME UP?
JUST THE ONCE.
BUT LEAVE THE TELEPATHY TO THE NATIVES.
WHAT A SWEET-HEART.
THE ONLY ACTION SHE'S GETTING IS WITH DANGER ROOM SIMULATIONS, NO WONDER SHE'S WOUND SO TIGHT!
SIGH ...I'M RIGHT HERE.
SO THIS IS WHAT BEING A NINJA-TELEPATHIC-ASSASSIN FEELS LIKE. A GIRL COULD GET USED TO THIS.
HONEY, I WAS BORN READY.
IF YOU TWO ARE READY...?

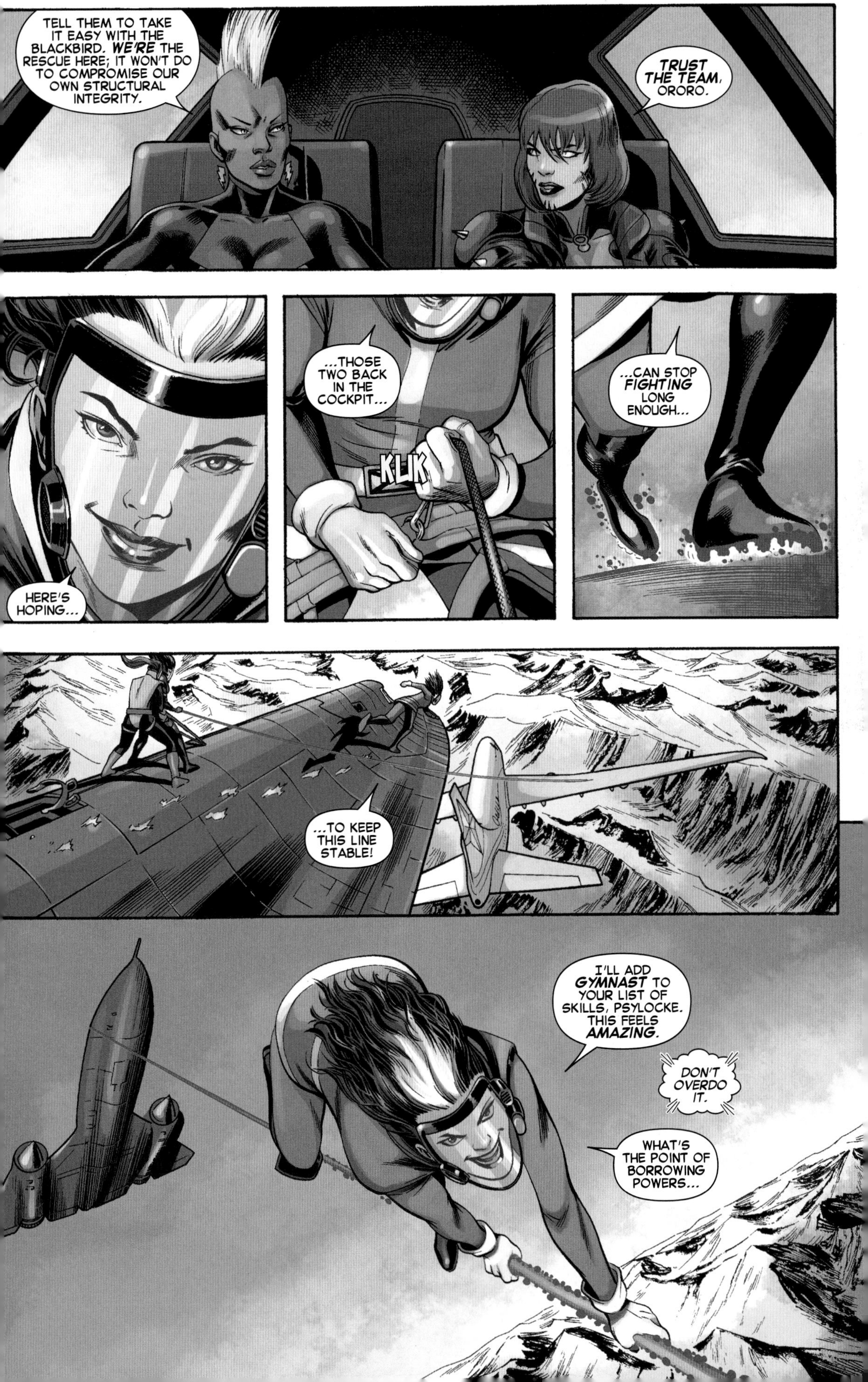
TELL THEM TO TAKE IT EASY WITH THE BLACKBIRD. WE'RE THE RESCUE HERE; IT WON'T DO TO COMPROMISE OUR OWN STRUCTURAL INTEGRITY.
TRUST THE TEAM, ORORO.
HERE'S HOPING...
...THOSE TWO BACK IN THE COCKPIT...
KLIK
...CAN STOP FIGHTING LONG ENOUGH...
...TO KEEP THIS LINE STABLE!
I'LL ADD GYMNAST TO YOUR LIST OF SKILLS, PSYLOCKE. THIS FEELS AMAZING.
DON'T OVERDO IT.
WHAT'S THE POINT OF BORROWING POWERS...

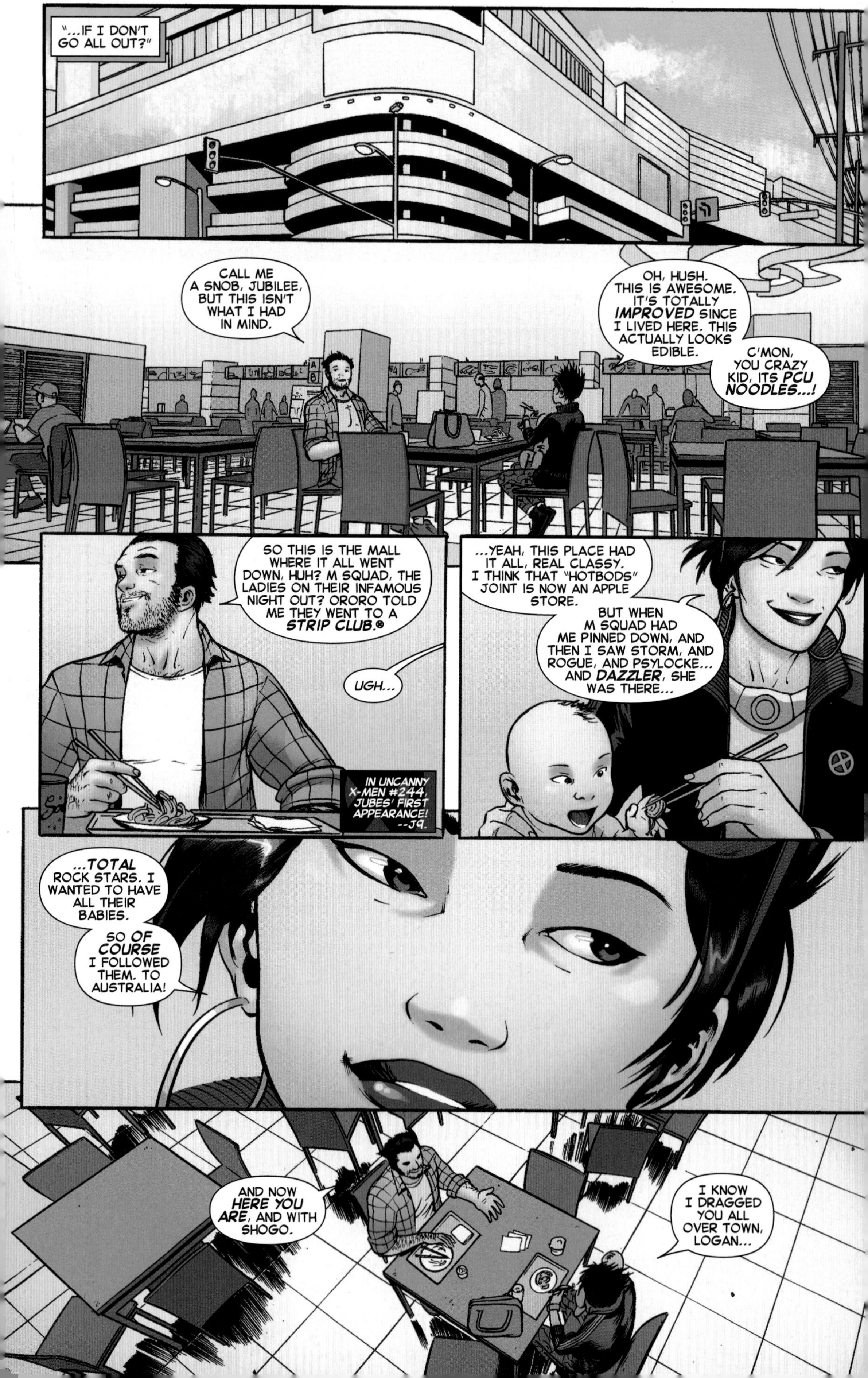
"...IF I DON'T GO ALL OUT?"
CALL ME A SNOB, JUBILEE, BUT THIS ISN'T WHAT I HAD IN MIND.
OH, HUSH. THIS IS AWESOME. IT'S TOTALLY IMPROVED SINCE I LIVED HERE. THIS ACTUALLY LOOKS EDIBLE.
C'MON, YOU CRAZY KID, ITS PCU NOODLES...!
SO THIS IS THE MALL WHERE IT ALL WENT DOWN, HUH? M SQUAD, THE LADIES ON THEIR INFAMOUS NIGHT OUT? ORORO TOLD ME THEY WENT TO A STRIP CLUB.
UGH...
IN UNCANNY X-MEN #244, JUBES' FIRST APPEARANCE! --JQ.
...YEAH, THIS PLACE HAD IT ALL, REAL CLASSY. I THINK THAT "HOTBODS" JOINT IS NOW AN APPLE STORE.
BUT WHEN M SQUAD HAD ME PINNED DOWN, AND THEN I SAW STORM, AND ROGUE, AND PSYLOCKE... AND DAZZLER, SHE WAS THERE...
...TOTAL ROCK STARS. I WANTED TO HAVE ALL THEIR BABIES.
SO OF COURSE I FOLLOWED THEM. TO AUSTRALIA!
AND NOW HERE YOU ARE, AND WITH SHOGO.
I KNOW I DRAGGED YOU ALL OVER TOWN, LOGAN...

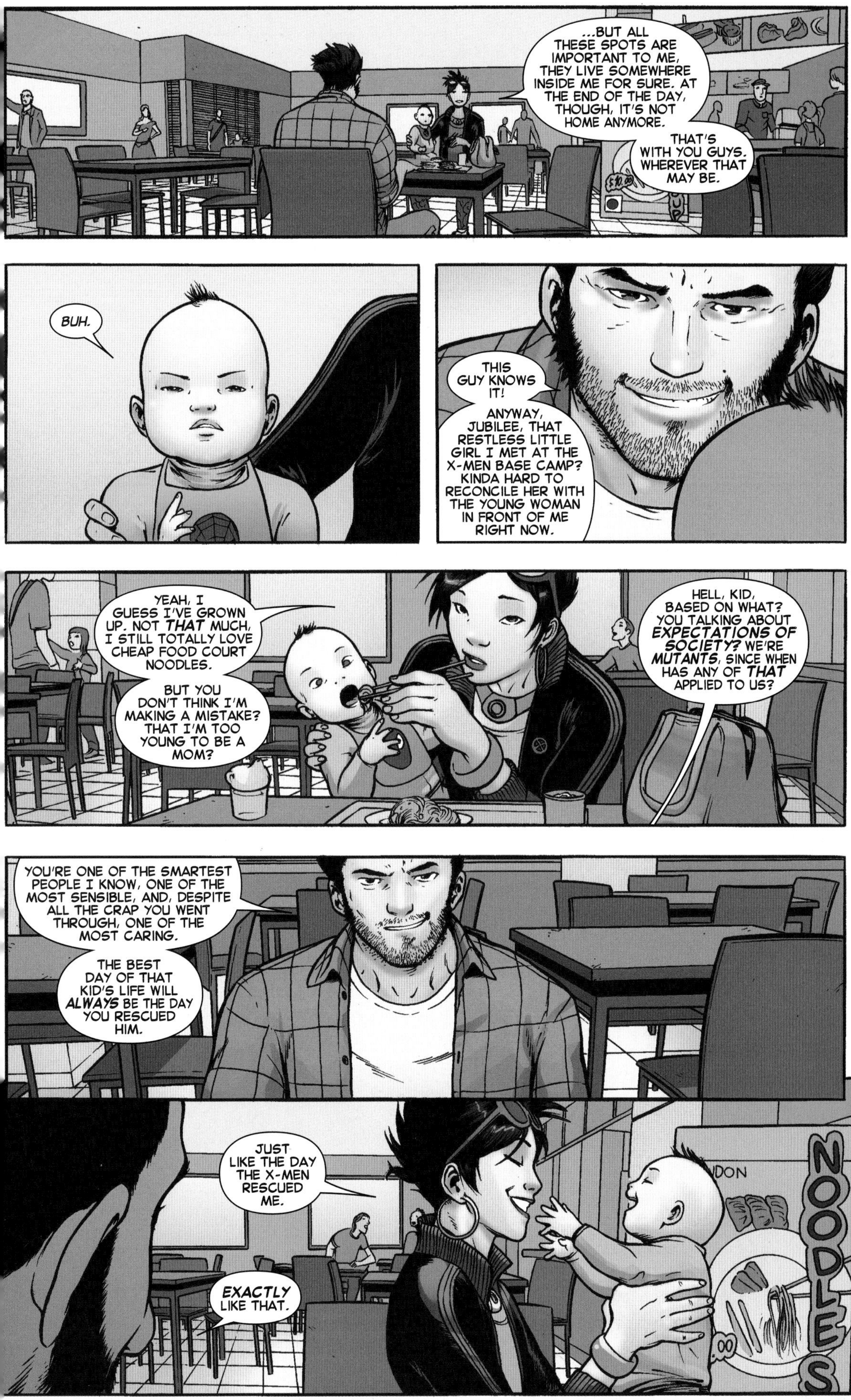
...BUT ALL THESE SPOTS ARE IMPORTANT TO ME, THEY LIVE SOMEWHERE INSIDE ME FOR SURE. AT THE END OF THE DAY, THOUGH, IT'S NOT HOME ANYMORE.
THAT'S WITH YOU GUYS. WHEREVER THAT MAY BE.
$10.00
BUH.
THIS GUY KNOWS IT!
ANYWAY, JUBILEE, THAT RESTLESS LITTLE GIRL I MET AT THE X-MEN BASE CAMP? KINDA HARD TO RECONCILE HER WITH THE YOUNG WOMAN IN FRONT OF ME RIGHT NOW.
YEAH, I GUESS I'VE GROWN UP. NOT THAT MUCH, I STILL TOTALLY LOVE CHEAP FOOD COURT NOODLES.
BUT YOU DON'T THINK I'M MAKING A MISTAKE? THAT I'M TOO YOUNG TO BE A MOM?
HELL, KID, BASED ON WHAT? YOU TALKING ABOUT EXPECTATIONS OF SOCIETY? WE'RE MUTANTS, SINCE WHEN HAS ANY OF THAT APPLIED TO US?
YOU'RE ONE OF THE SMARTEST PEOPLE I KNOW, ONE OF THE MOST SENSIBLE, AND, DESPITE ALL THE CRAP YOU WENT THROUGH, ONE OF THE MOST CARING.
THE BEST DAY OF THAT KID'S LIFE WILL ALWAYS BE THE DAY YOU RESCUED HIM.
JUST LIKE THE DAY THE X-MEN RESCUED ME.
UDON
NOODLES
EXACTLY LIKE THAT.

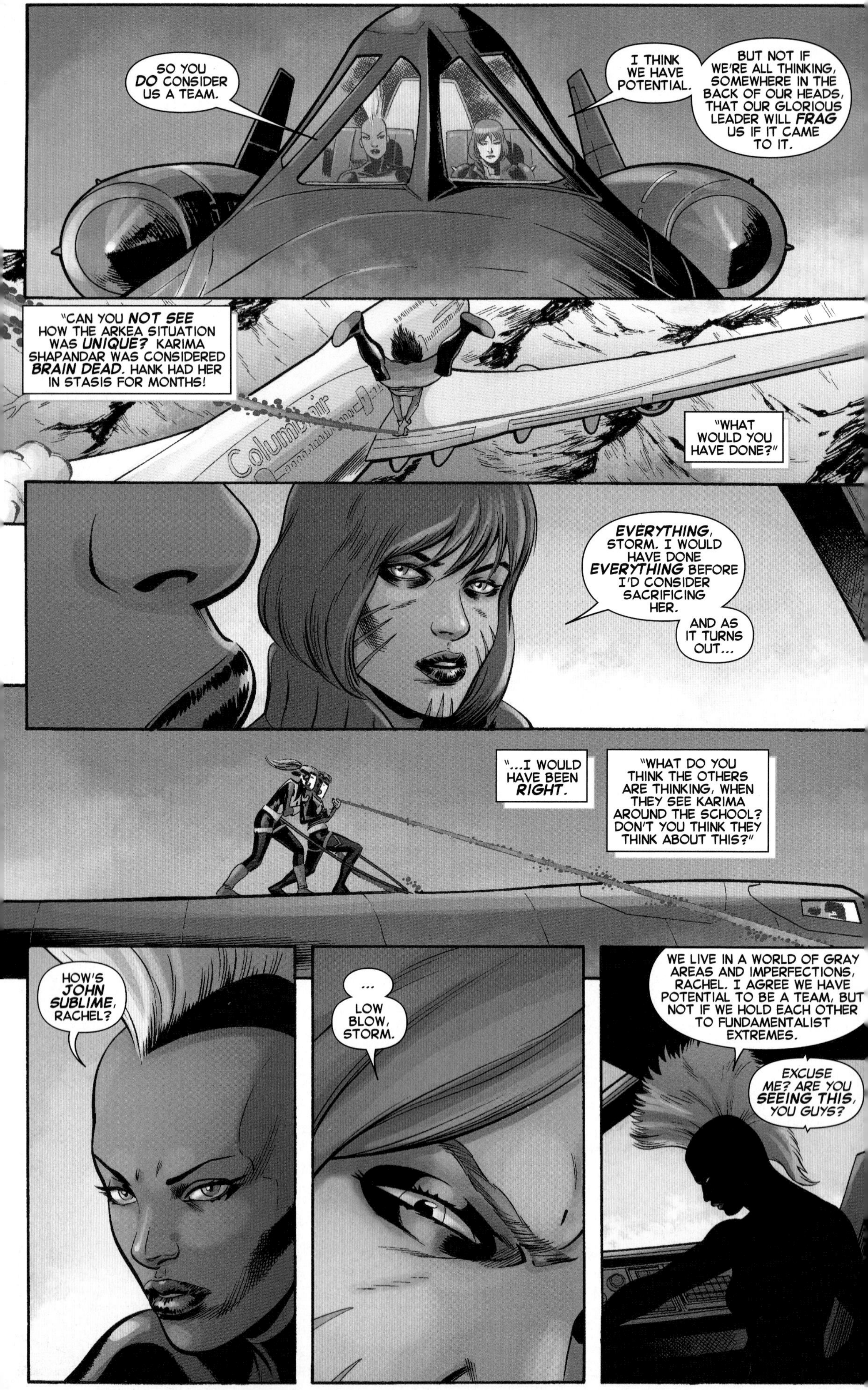
SO YOU DO CONSIDER US A TEAM.
I THINK WE HAVE POTENTIAL.
BUT NOT IF WE'RE ALL THINKING, SOMEWHERE IN THE BACK OF OUR HEADS, THAT OUR GLORIOUS LEADER WILL FRAG US IF IT CAME TO IT.
"CAN YOU NOT SEE HOW THE ARKEA SITUATION WAS UNIQUE? KARIMA SHAPANDAR WAS CONSIDERED BRAIN DEAD. HANK HAD HER IN STASIS FOR MONTHS!
"WHAT WOULD YOU HAVE DONE?"
EVERYTHING, STORM. I WOULD HAVE DONE EVERYTHING BEFORE I'D CONSIDER SACRIFICING HER.
AND AS IT TURNS OUT...
"...I WOULD HAVE BEEN RIGHT.
"WHAT DO YOU THINK THE OTHERS ARE THINKING, WHEN THEY SEE KARIMA AROUND THE SCHOOL? DON'T YOU THINK THEY THINK ABOUT THIS?"
HOW'S JOHN SUBLIME, RACHEL?
...
LOW BLOW, STORM.
WE LIVE IN A WORLD OF GRAY AREAS AND IMPERFECTIONS, RACHEL. I AGREE WE HAVE POTENTIAL TO BE A TEAM, BUT NOT IF WE HOLD EACH OTHER TO FUNDAMENTALIST EXTREMES.
EXCUSE ME? ARE YOU SEEING THIS, YOU GUYS?

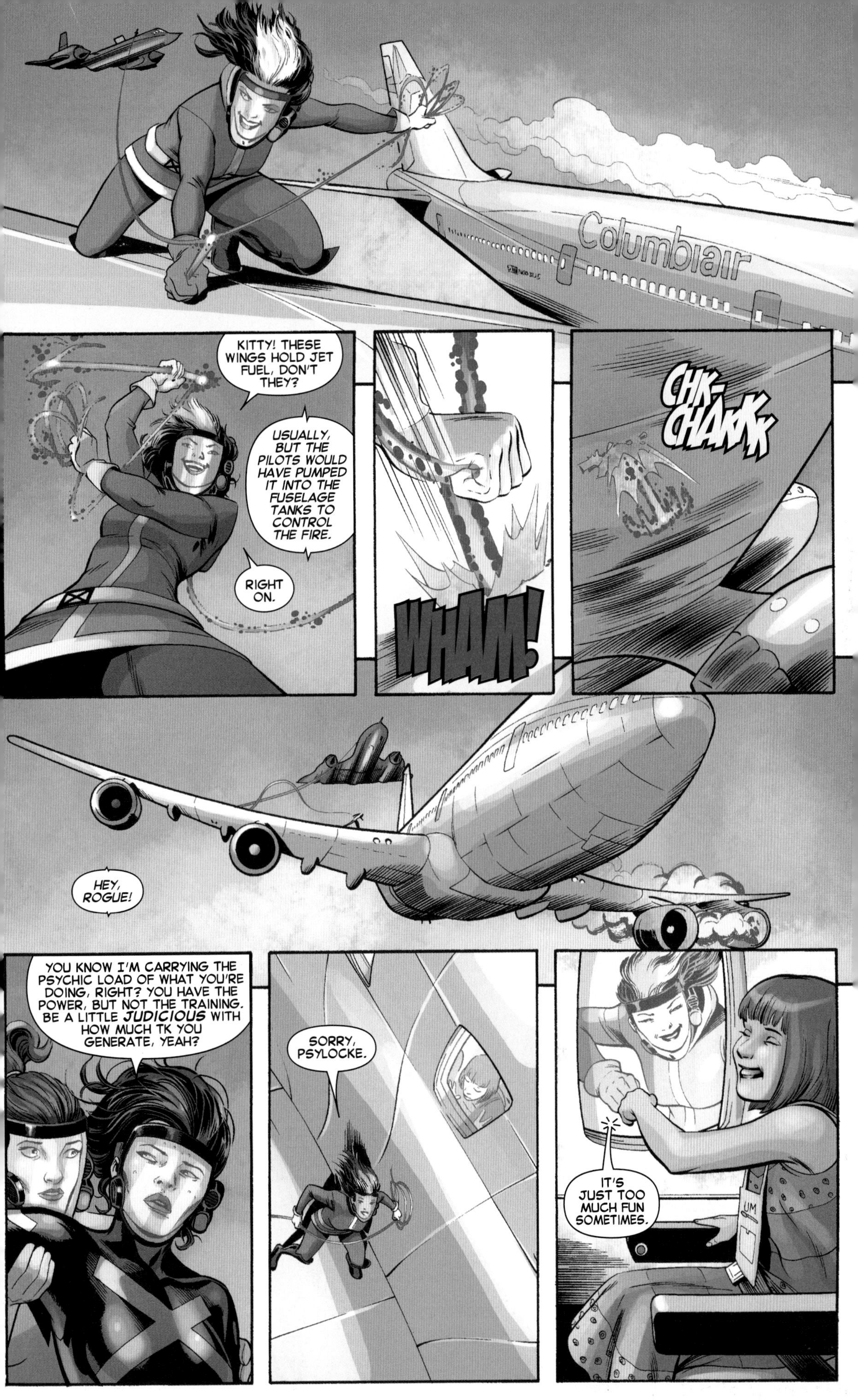
Columbiair
KITTY! THESE WINGS HOLD JET FUEL, DON'T THEY?
USUALLY, BUT THE PILOTS WOULD HAVE PUMPED IT INTO THE FUSELAGE TANKS TO CONTROL THE FIRE.
RIGHT ON.
WHAM!
CHK-CHARKK
HEY, ROGUE!
YOU KNOW I'M CARRYING THE PSYCHIC LOAD OF WHAT YOU'RE DOING, RIGHT? YOU HAVE THE POWER, BUT NOT THE TRAINING. BE A LITTLE JUDICIOUS WITH HOW MUCH TK YOU GENERATE, YEAH?
SORRY, PSYLOCKE.
IT'S JUST TOO MUCH FUN SOMETIMES.

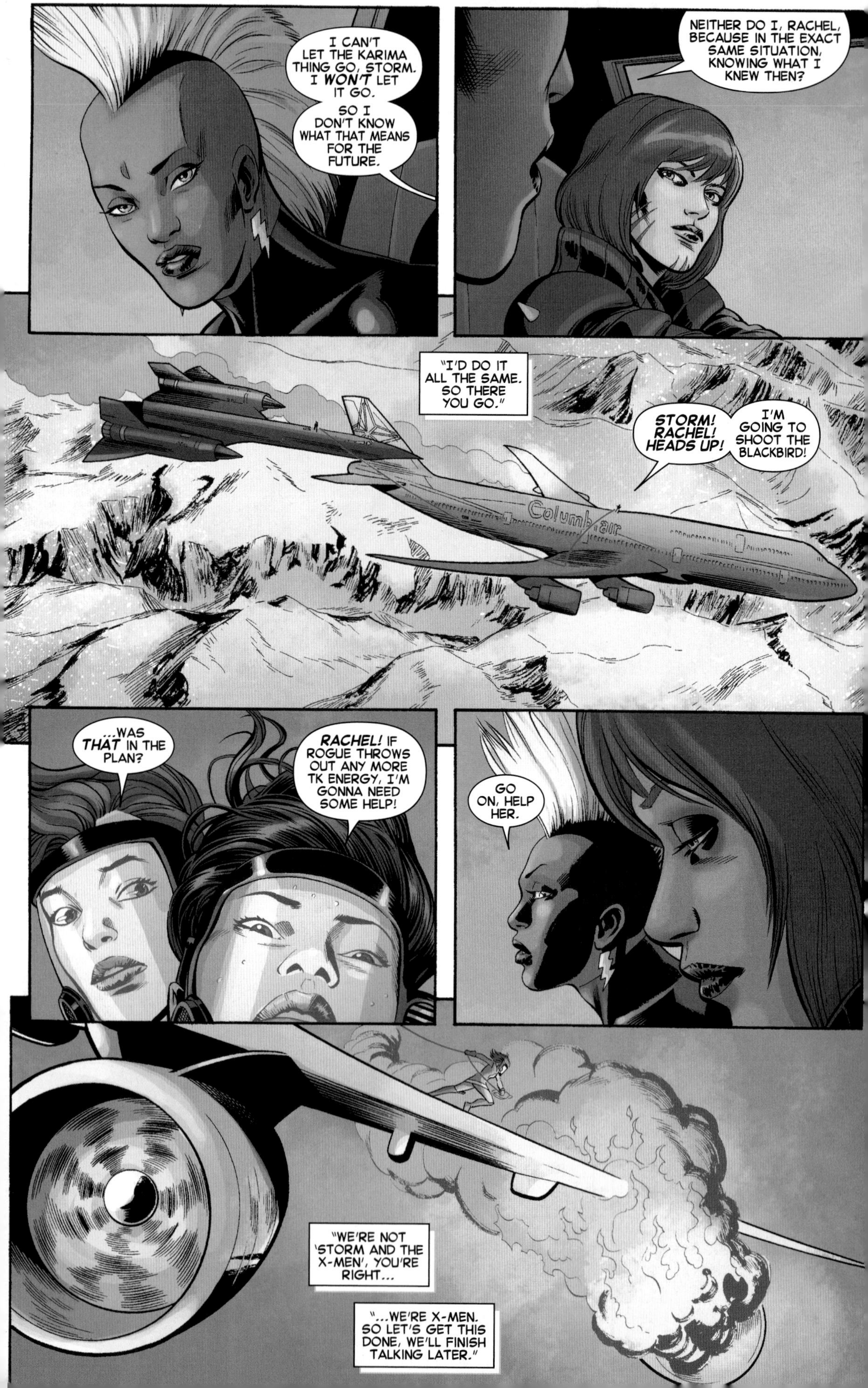
I CAN'T LET THE KARIMA THING GO, STORM. I *WON'T* LET IT GO.
SO I DON'T KNOW WHAT THAT MEANS FOR THE FUTURE.
NEITHER DO I, RACHEL, BECAUSE IN THE EXACT SAME SITUATION, KNOWING WHAT I KNEW THEN?
"I'D DO IT ALL THE SAME. SO THERE YOU GO."
STORM! RACHEL! HEADS UP!
I'M GOING TO SHOOT THE BLACKBIRD!
Columbair
...WAS *THAT* IN THE PLAN?
RACHEL! IF ROGUE THROWS OUT ANY MORE TK ENERGY, I'M GONNA NEED SOME HELP!
GO ON, HELP HER.
"WE'RE NOT 'STORM AND THE X-MEN', YOU'RE RIGHT...
"...WE'RE X-MEN. SO LET'S GET THIS DONE, WE'LL FINISH TALKING LATER."

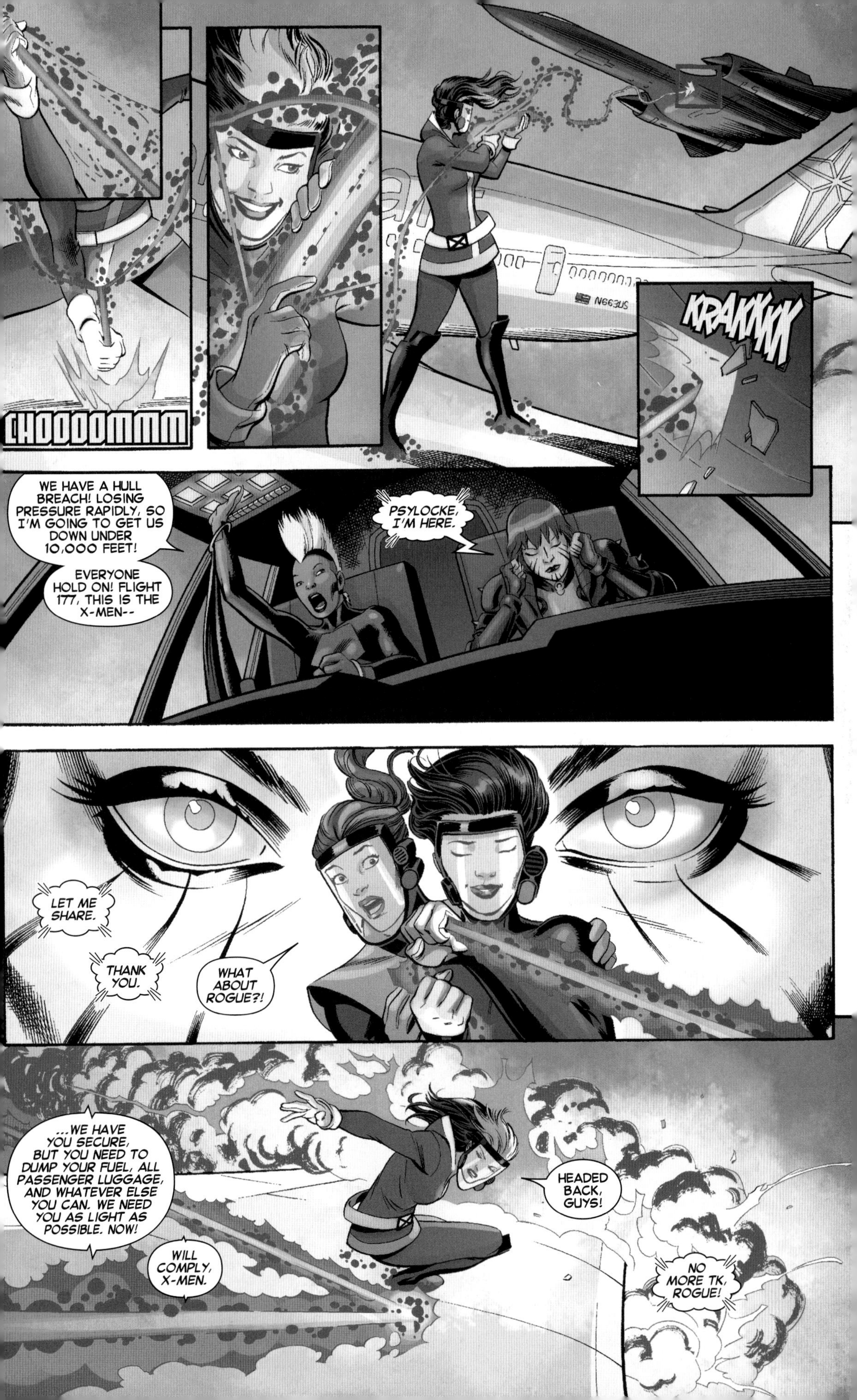
CHOOOOMMM
N663US
KRAKKKK
WE HAVE A HULL BREACH! LOSING PRESSURE RAPIDLY, SO I'M GOING TO GET US DOWN UNDER 10,000 FEET!
EVERYONE HOLD ON! FLIGHT 177, THIS IS THE X-MEN--
PSYLOCKE, I'M HERE.
LET ME SHARE.
THANK YOU.
WHAT ABOUT ROGUE?!
...WE HAVE YOU SECURE, BUT YOU NEED TO DUMP YOUR FUEL, ALL PASSENGER LUGGAGE, AND WHATEVER ELSE YOU CAN. WE NEED YOU AS LIGHT AS POSSIBLE. NOW!
WILL COMPLY, X-MEN.
HEADED BACK, GUYS!
NO MORE TK, ROGUE!

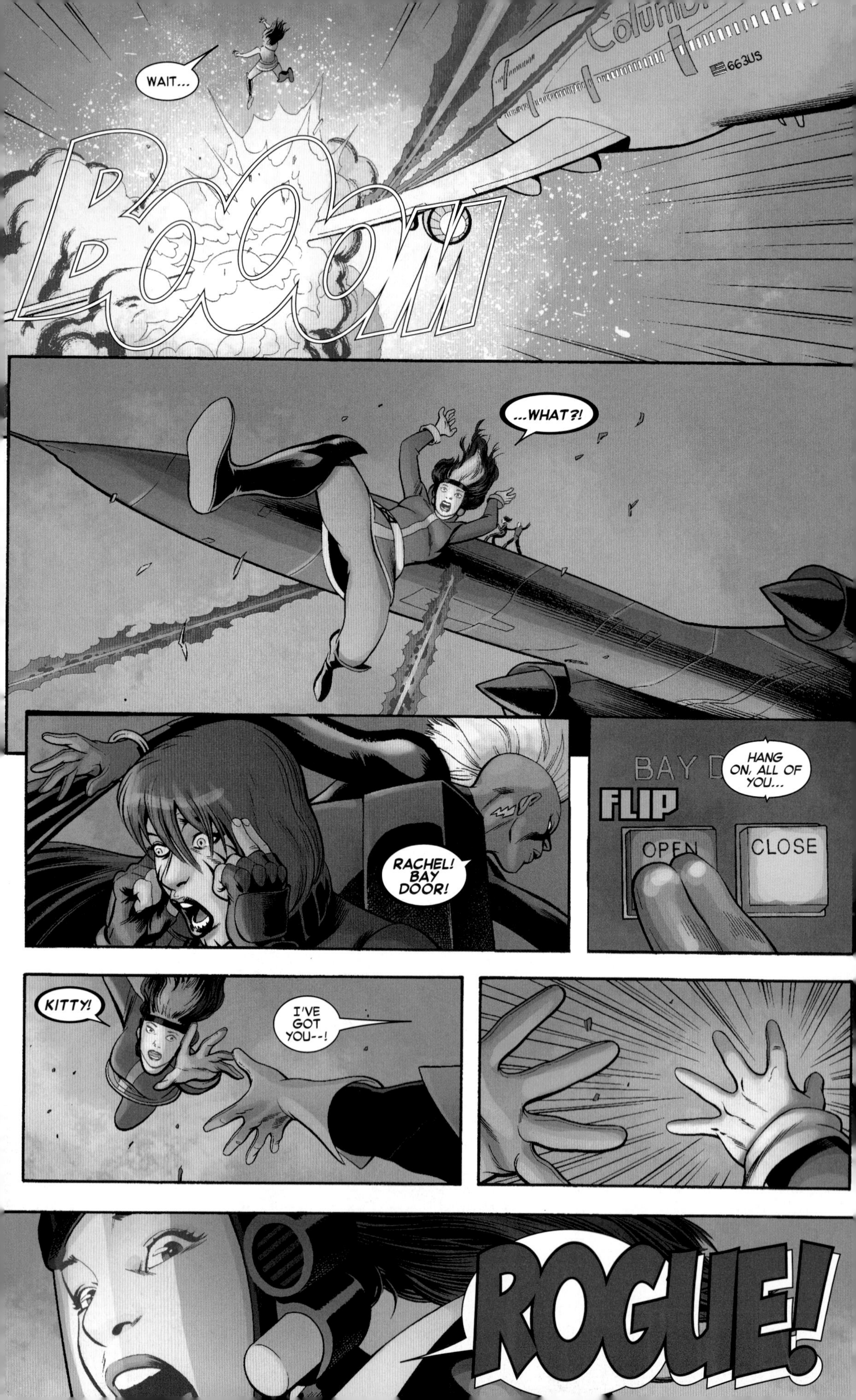
WAIT...
BOOOM!
...WHAT?!
RACHEL! BAY DOOR!
BAY D
FLIP
HANG ON, ALL OF YOU...
OPEN
CLOSE
KITTY!
I'VE GOT YOU--!
ROGUE!

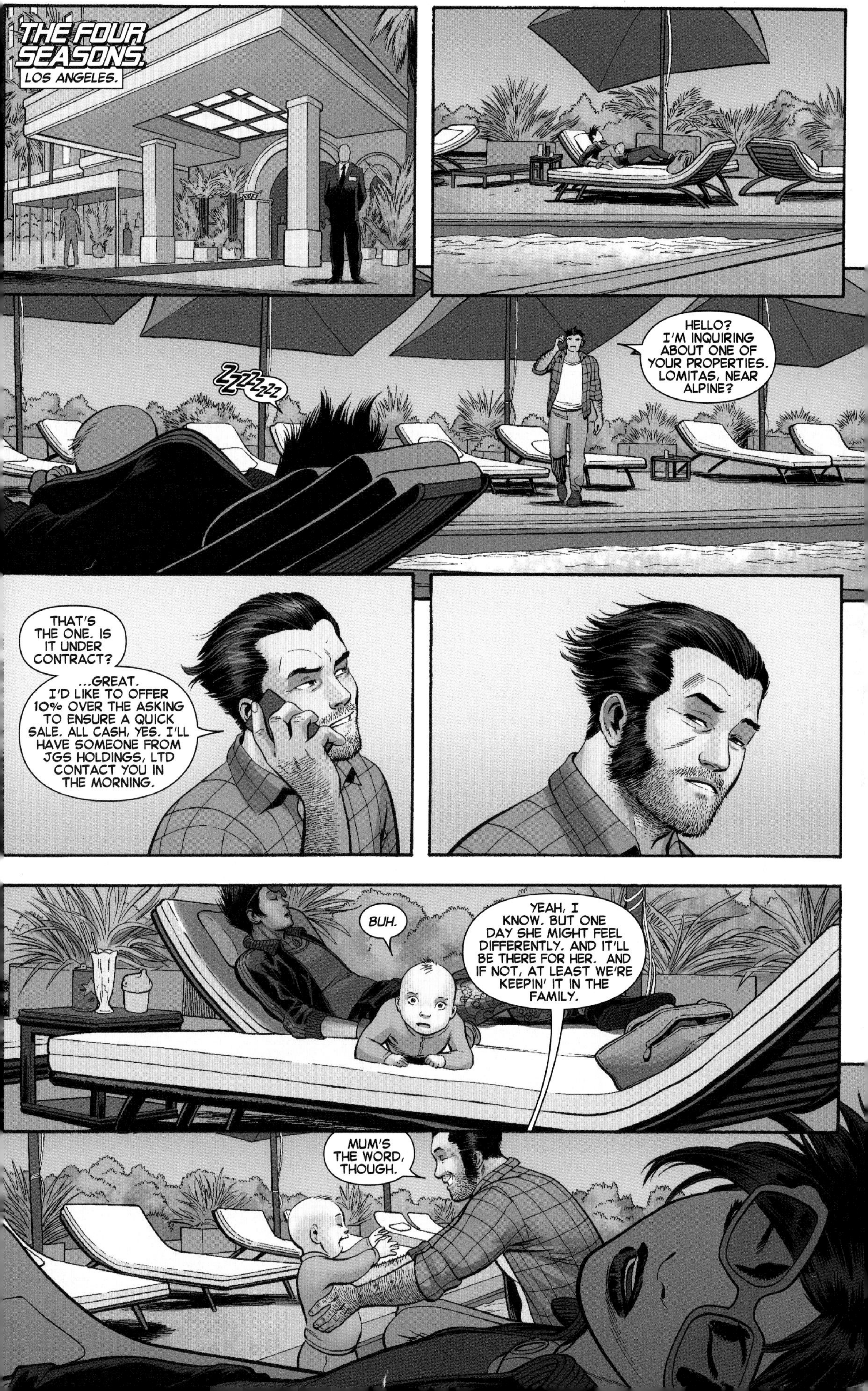
THE FOUR SEASONS.
LOS ANGELES.
ZZZZZZZZ
HELLO? I'M INQUIRING ABOUT ONE OF YOUR PROPERTIES. LOMITAS, NEAR ALPINE?
THAT'S THE ONE. IS IT UNDER CONTRACT?
...GREAT. I'D LIKE TO OFFER 10% OVER THE ASKING TO ENSURE A QUICK SALE. ALL CASH, YES. I'LL HAVE SOMEONE FROM JGS HOLDINGS, LTD CONTACT YOU IN THE MORNING.
BUH.
YEAH, I KNOW. BUT ONE DAY SHE MIGHT FEEL DIFFERENTLY. AND IT'LL BE THERE FOR HER. AND IF NOT, AT LEAST WE'RE KEEPIN' IT IN THE FAMILY.
MUM'S THE WORD, THOUGH.

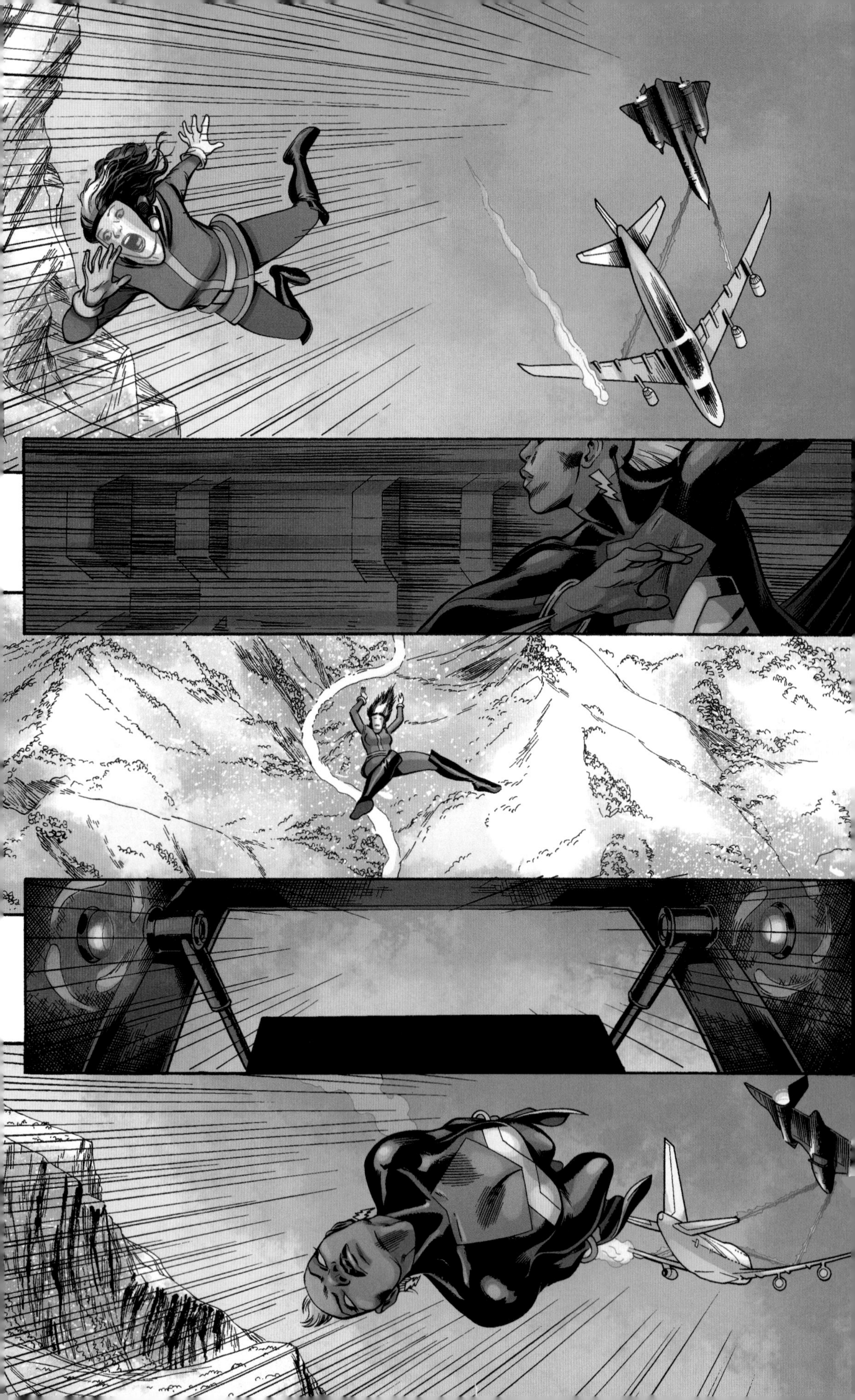

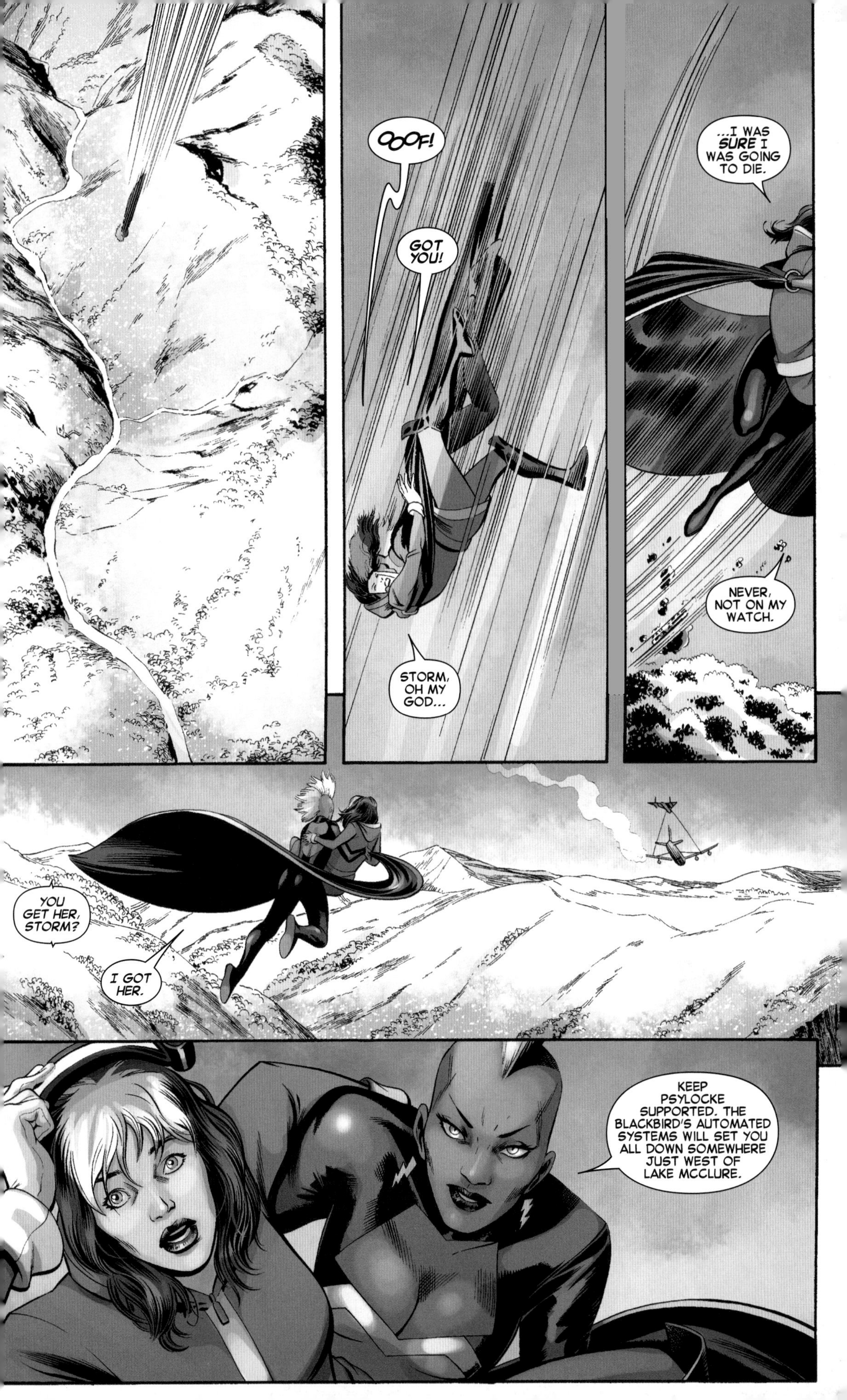
OOOF!
GOT YOU!
STORM, OH MY GOD...
...I WAS SURE I WAS GOING TO DIE.
NEVER, NOT ON MY WATCH.
YOU GET HER, STORM?
I GOT HER.
KEEP PSYLOCKE SUPPORTED. THE BLACKBIRD'S AUTOMATED SYSTEMS WILL SET YOU ALL DOWN SOMEWHERE JUST WEST OF LAKE MCCLURE.

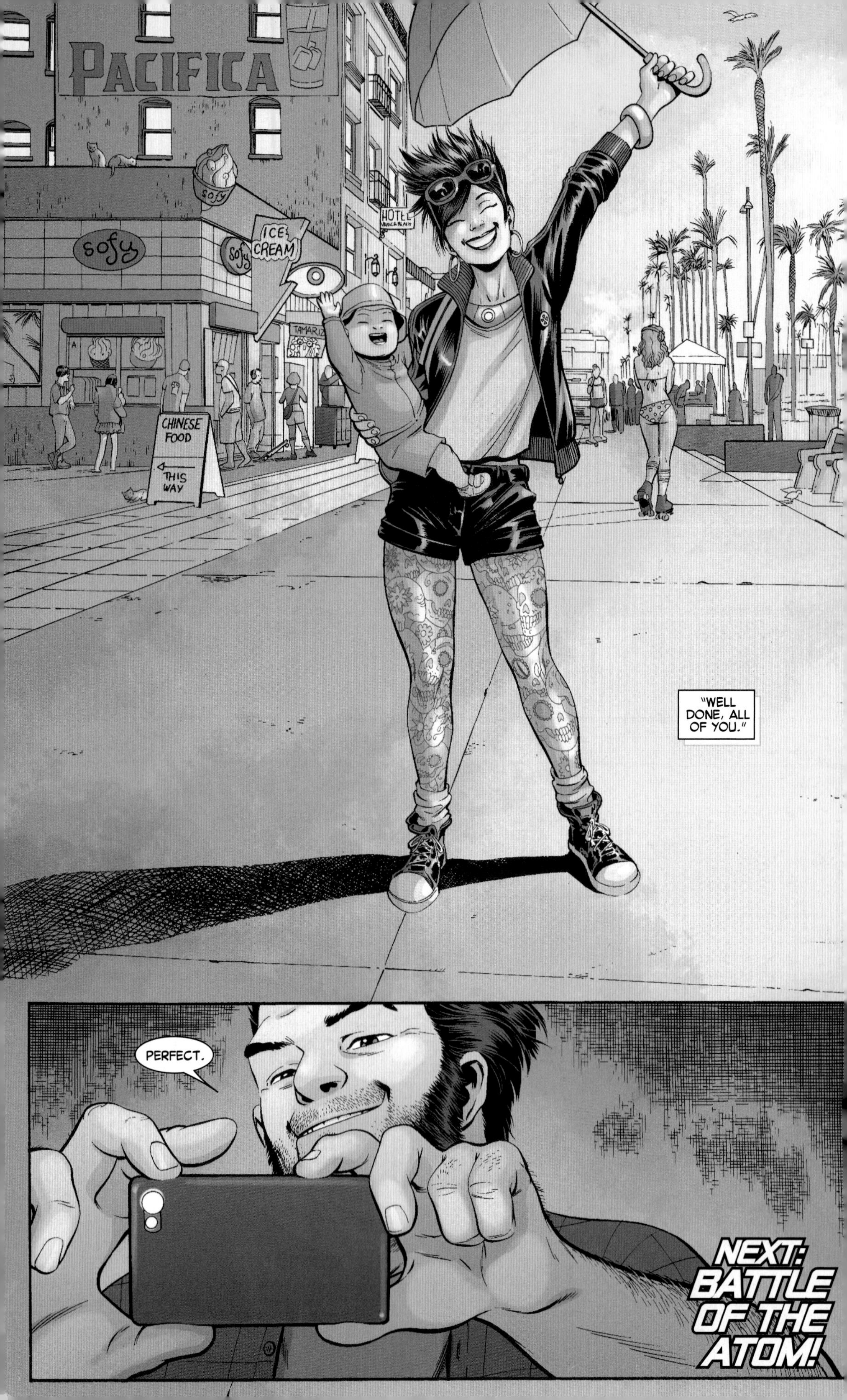
PACIFICA
sofy
sofy
sofy
ICE CREAM
HOTEL
TAMARIZ
CHINESE FOOD
THIS WAY
"WELL DONE, ALL OF YOU."
PERFECT.
NEXT: BATTLE OF THE ATOM!

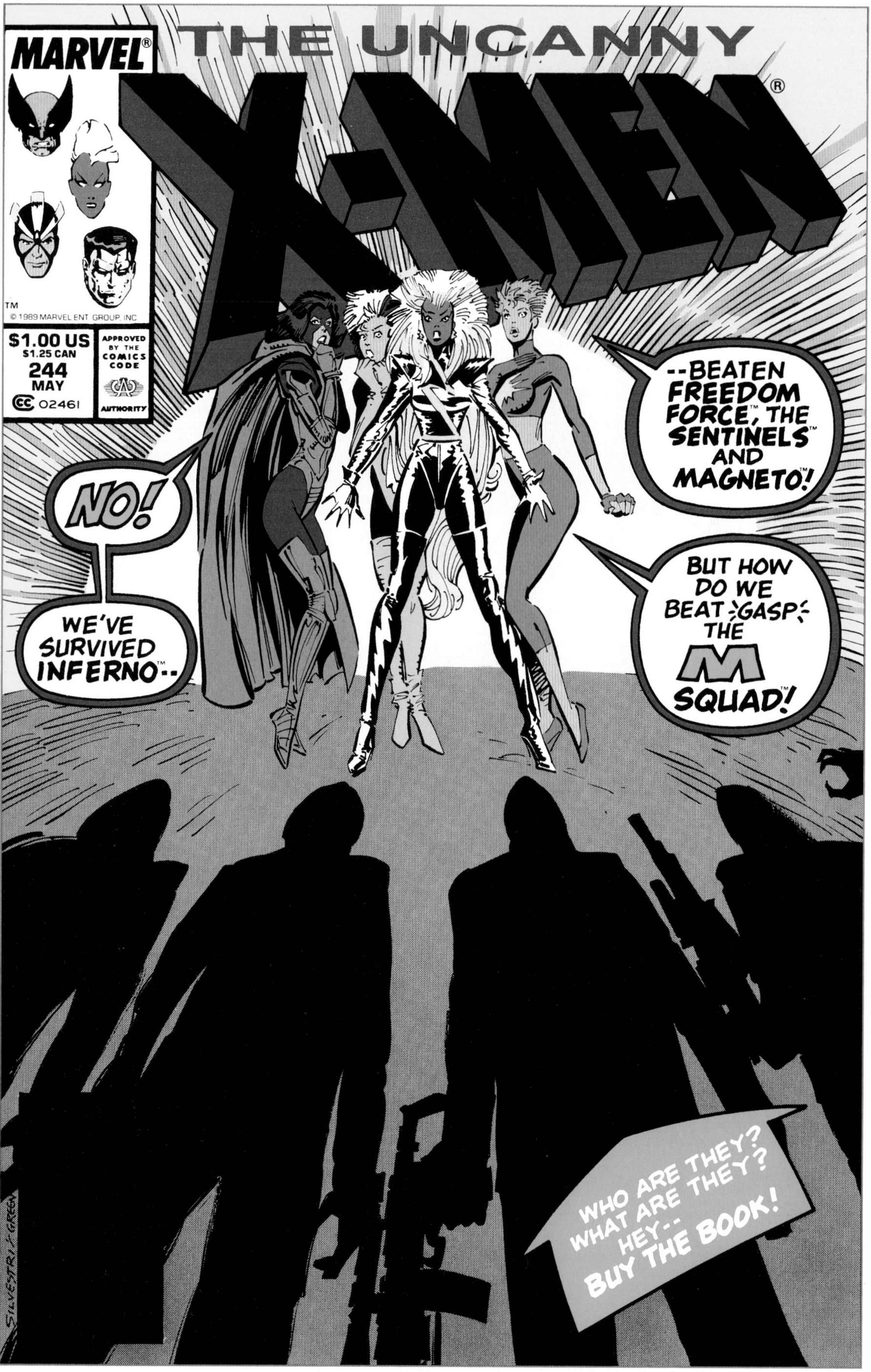
MARVEL
THE UNCANNY
X-MEN
TM
© 1989 MARVEL ENT. GROUP, INC.
$1.00 US
$1.25 CAN
244
MAY
CC 02461
APPROVED BY THE COMICS CODE AUTHORITY
NO!
WE'VE SURVIVED INFERNO--
--BEATEN FREEDOM FORCE, THE SENTINELS AND MAGNETO!
BUT HOW DO WE BEAT -GASP- THE M SQUAD!
WHO ARE THEY? WHAT ARE THEY? HEY-- BUY THE BOOK!
SILVESTRI/GREEN

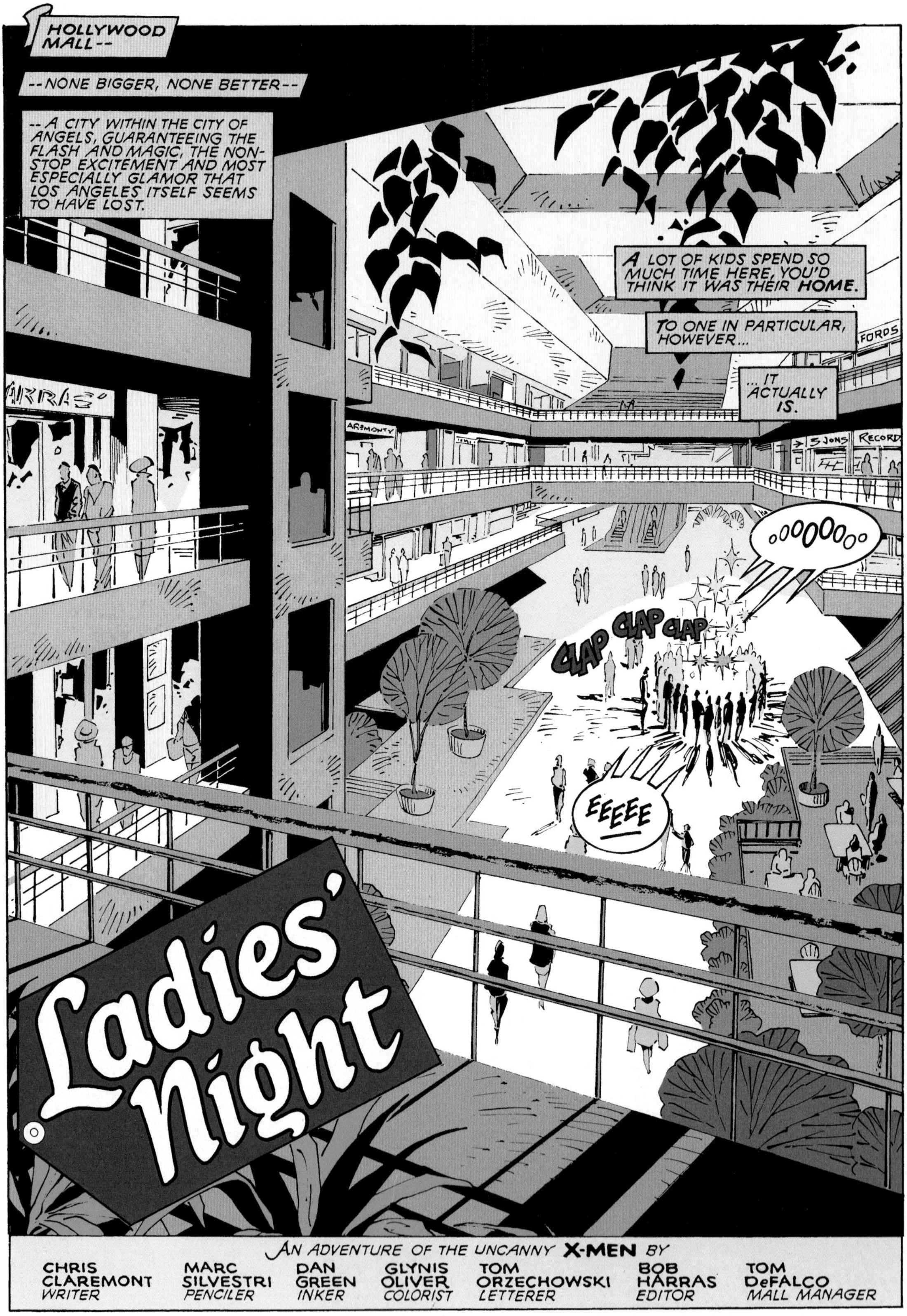
HOLLYWOOD MALL--
--NONE BIGGER, NONE BETTER--
--A CITY WITHIN THE CITY OF ANGELS, GUARANTEEING THE FLASH AND MAGIC, THE NON-STOP EXCITEMENT AND MOST ESPECIALLY GLAMOR THAT LOS ANGELES ITSELF SEEMS TO HAVE LOST.
A LOT OF KIDS SPEND SO MUCH TIME HERE, YOU'D THINK IT WAS THEIR HOME.
TO ONE IN PARTICULAR, HOWEVER...
...IT ACTUALLY IS.
oooOOOoo
CLAP CLAP CLAP
EEEEE
Ladies' Night

AN ADVENTURE OF THE UNCANNY **X-MEN** BY

CHRIS CLAREMONT	MARC SILVESTRI	DAN GREEN	GLYNIS OLIVER	TOM ORZECHOWSKI	BOB HARRAS	TOM DeFALCO
WRITER	*PENCILER*	*INKER*	*COLORIST*	*LETTERER*	*EDITOR*	*MALL MANAGER*

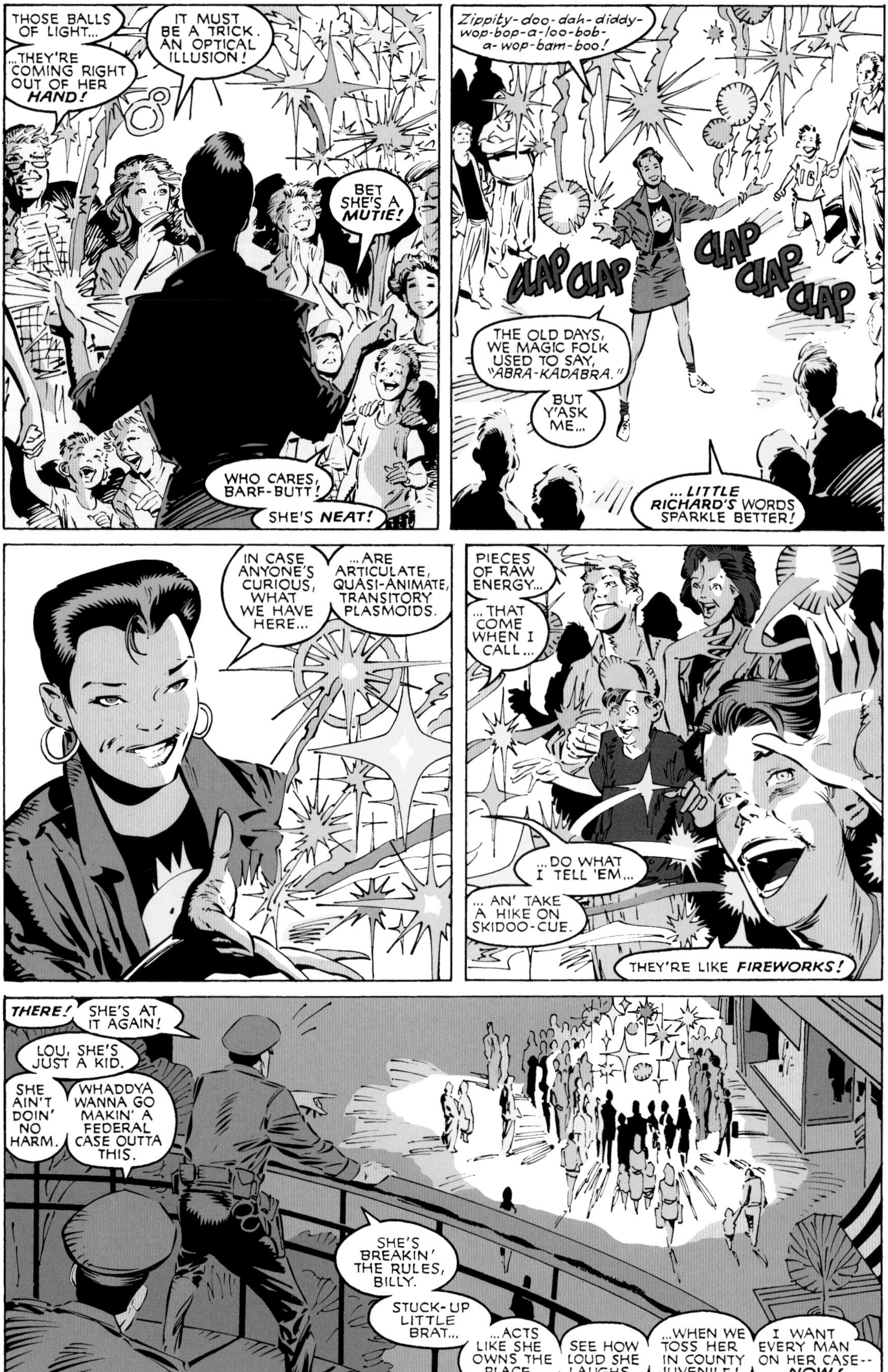
THOSE BALLS OF LIGHT...
...THEY'RE COMING RIGHT OUT OF HER **HAND!**
IT MUST BE A TRICK. AN OPTICAL ILLUSION!
BET SHE'S A **MUTIE!**
WHO CARES, BARF-BUTT!
SHE'S **NEAT!**
Zippity-doo-dah-diddy-wop-bop-a-loo-bob-a-wop-bam-boo!
CLAP CLAP
CLAP CLAP CLAP
THE OLD DAYS, WE MAGIC FOLK USED TO SAY, "*ABRA-KADABRA.*"
BUT Y'ASK ME...
...**LITTLE RICHARD'S** WORDS SPARKLE BETTER!
IN CASE ANYONE'S CURIOUS, WHAT WE HAVE HERE...
...ARE ARTICULATE, QUASI-ANIMATE, TRANSITORY PLASMOIDS.
PIECES OF RAW ENERGY...
...THAT COME WHEN I CALL...
...DO WHAT I TELL 'EM...
...AN' TAKE A HIKE ON SKIDOO-CUE.
THEY'RE LIKE **FIREWORKS!**
THERE!
SHE'S AT IT AGAIN!
LOU, SHE'S JUST A KID.
SHE AIN'T DOIN' NO HARM.
WHADDYA WANNA GO MAKIN' A FEDERAL CASE OUTTA THIS.
SHE'S BREAKIN' THE RULES, BILLY.
STUCK-UP LITTLE BRAT...
...ACTS LIKE SHE OWNS THE PLACE.
SEE HOW LOUD SHE LAUGHS...
...WHEN WE TOSS HER IN COUNTY JUVENILE!
I WANT EVERY MAN ON HER CASE-- **NOW!**

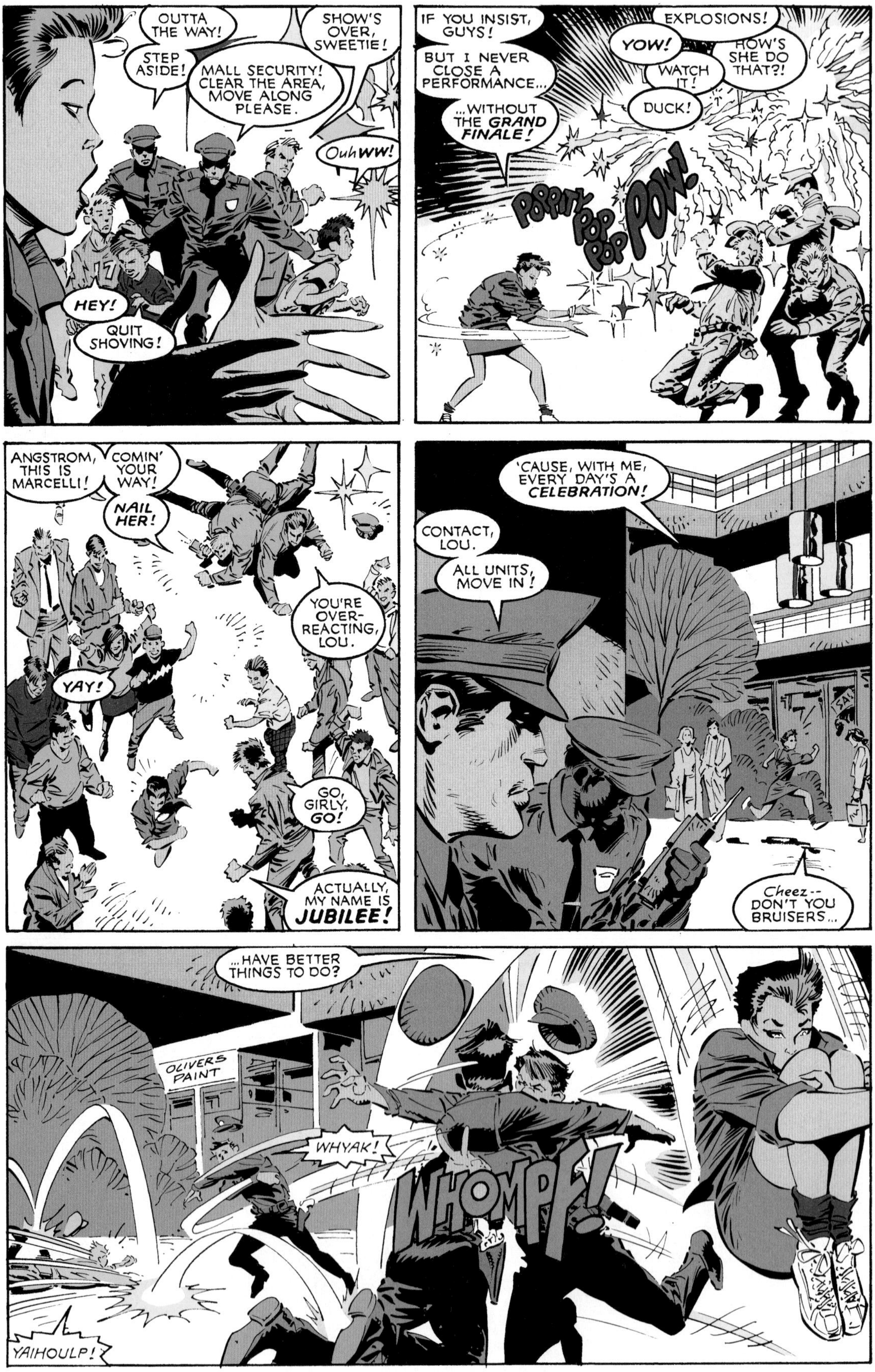
OUTTA THE WAY!
SHOW'S OVER, SWEETIE!
STEP ASIDE!
MALL SECURITY! CLEAR THE AREA, MOVE ALONG PLEASE.
OuhWW!
HEY!
QUIT SHOVING!
IF YOU INSIST, GUYS!
BUT I NEVER CLOSE A PERFORMANCE...
...WITHOUT THE GRAND FINALE!
EXPLOSIONS!
YOW!
HOW'S SHE DO THAT?!
WATCH IT!
DUCK!
POPPITY POP POP POW!
ANGSTROM, THIS IS MARCELLI!
COMIN' YOUR WAY!
NAIL HER!
YOU'RE OVER-REACTING, LOU.
YAY!
GO, GIRLY, GO!
ACTUALLY, MY NAME IS JUBILEE!
'CAUSE, WITH ME, EVERY DAY'S A CELEBRATION!
CONTACT, LOU.
ALL UNITS, MOVE IN!
Cheez-- DON'T YOU BRUISERS...
...HAVE BETTER THINGS TO DO?
OLIVERS PAINT
WHYAK!
WHOMPF!
YAIHOULP!

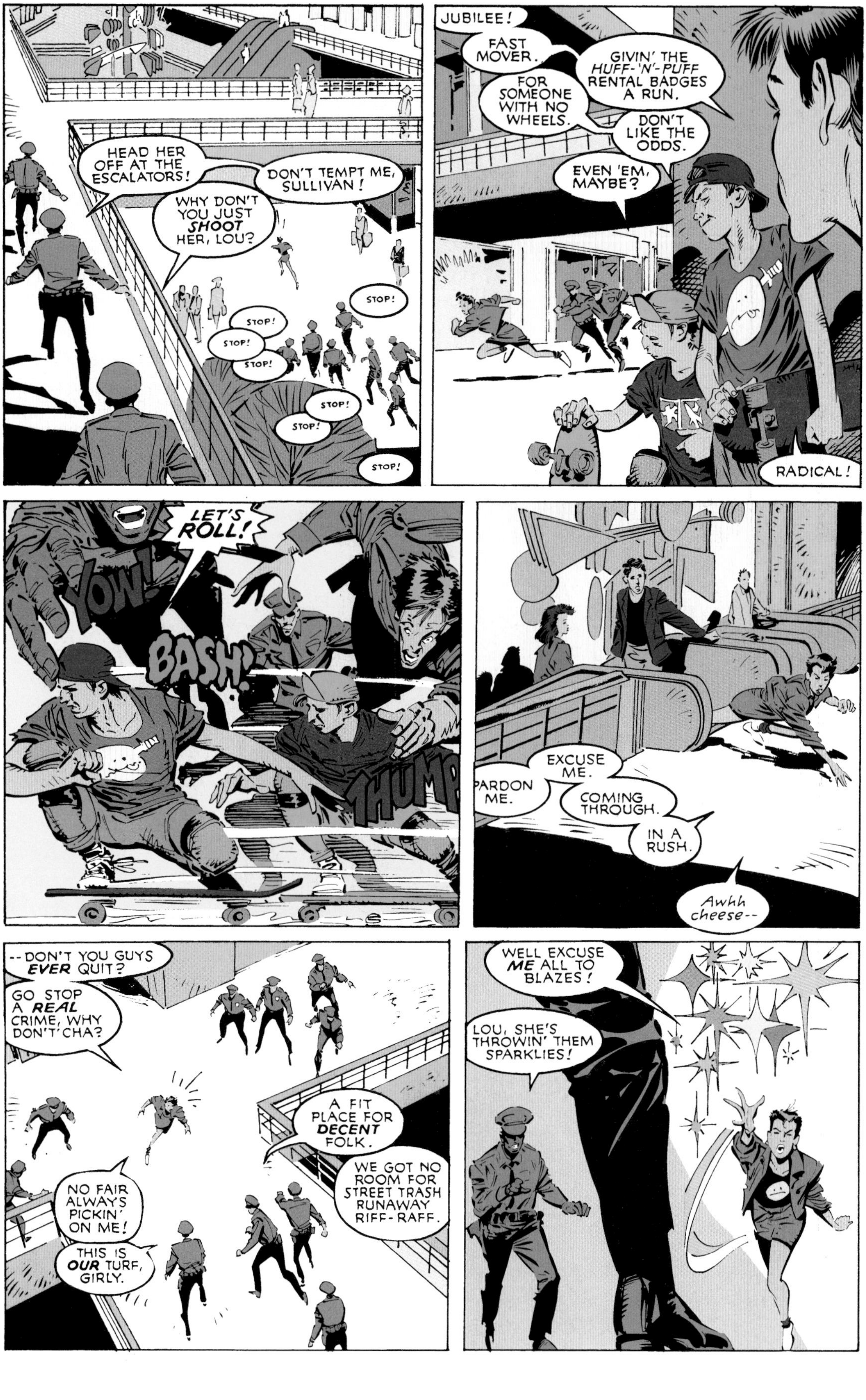
HEAD HER OFF AT THE ESCALATORS!
DON'T TEMPT ME, SULLIVAN!
WHY DON'T YOU JUST SHOOT HER, LOU?
STOP!
STOP!
STOP!
STOP!
STOP!
STOP!
STOP!
JUBILEE!
FAST MOVER.
FOR SOMEONE WITH NO WHEELS.
GIVIN' THE HUFF-'N'-PUFF RENTAL BADGES A RUN.
DON'T LIKE THE ODDS.
EVEN 'EM, MAYBE?
RADICAL!
LET'S ROLL!
YOW!
BASH!
THUMP
EXCUSE ME.
PARDON ME.
COMING THROUGH.
IN A RUSH.
Awhh cheese--
--DON'T YOU GUYS EVER QUIT?
GO STOP A REAL CRIME, WHY DON'T'CHA?
A FIT PLACE FOR DECENT FOLK.
WE GOT NO ROOM FOR STREET TRASH RUNAWAY RIFF-RAFF.
NO FAIR ALWAYS PICKIN' ON ME!
THIS IS OUR TURF, GIRLY.
WELL EXCUSE ME ALL TO BLAZES!
LOU, SHE'S THROWIN' THEM SPARKLIES!

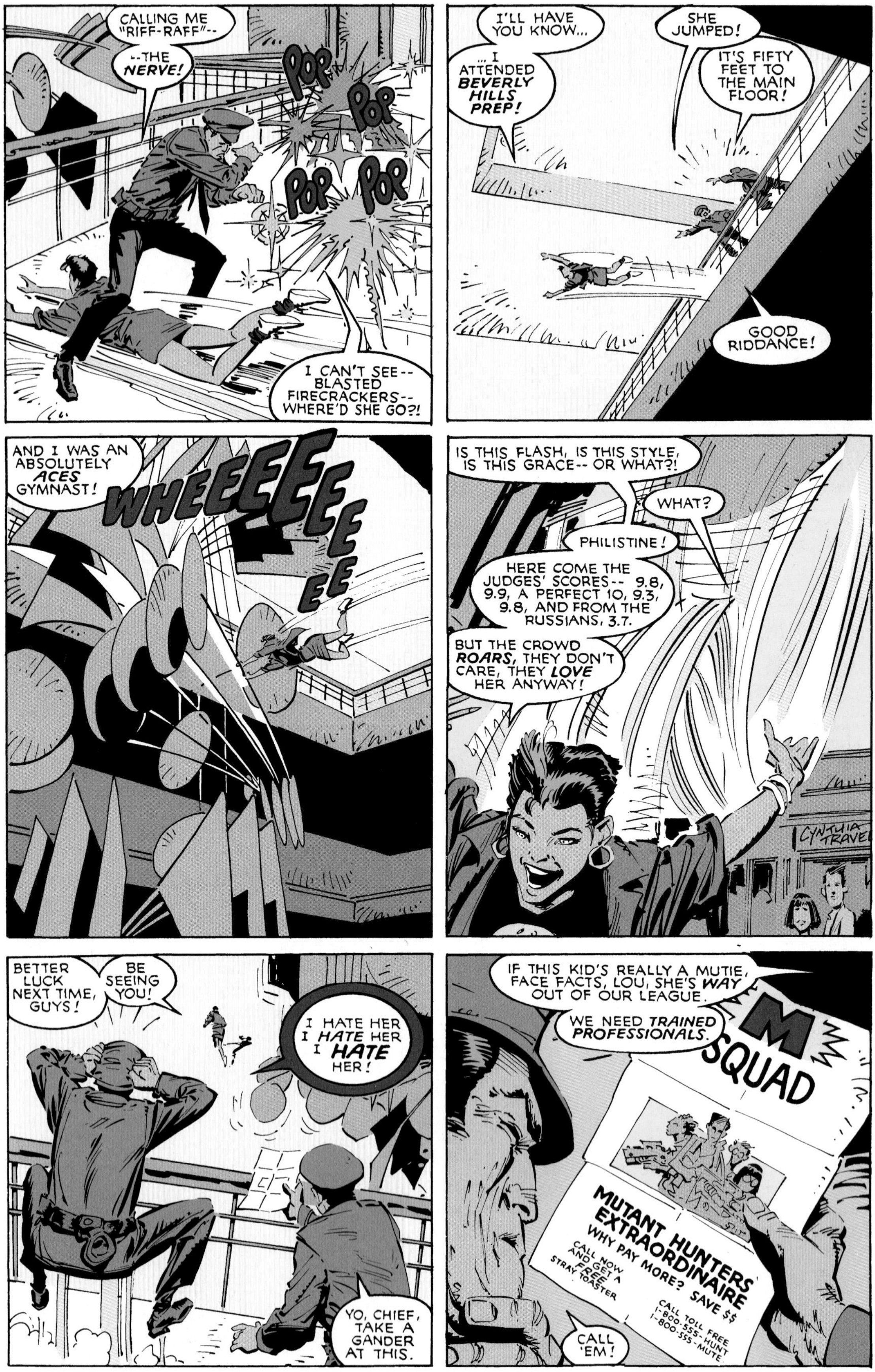
CALLING ME "RIFF-RAFF"--
--THE NERVE!
POP POP POP POP
I CAN'T SEE-- BLASTED FIRECRACKERS-- WHERE'D SHE GO?!
I'LL HAVE YOU KNOW...
... I ATTENDED BEVERLY HILLS PREP!
SHE JUMPED!
IT'S FIFTY FEET TO THE MAIN FLOOR!
GOOD RIDDANCE!
AND I WAS AN ABSOLUTELY ACES GYMNAST!
WHEEEEEEEEE
IS THIS FLASH, IS THIS STYLE, IS THIS GRACE-- OR WHAT?!
WHAT?
PHILISTINE!
HERE COME THE JUDGES' SCORES-- 9.8, 9.9, A PERFECT 10, 9.3, 9.8, AND FROM THE RUSSIANS, 3.7.
BUT THE CROWD ROARS, THEY DON'T CARE, THEY LOVE HER ANYWAY!
BETTER LUCK NEXT TIME, GUYS!
BE SEEING YOU!
I HATE HER I HATE HER I HATE HER!
YO, CHIEF, TAKE A GANDER AT THIS.
IF THIS KID'S REALLY A MUTIE, FACE FACTS, LOU, SHE'S WAY OUT OF OUR LEAGUE.
WE NEED TRAINED PROFESSIONALS.
M SQUAD
MUTANT HUNTERS EXTRAORDINAIRE
WHY PAY MORE? SAVE $$
CALL NOW AND GET A FREE STRAY TOASTER
CALL TOLL FREE 1-800-555-HUNT 1-800-555-MUTE
CALL 'EM!

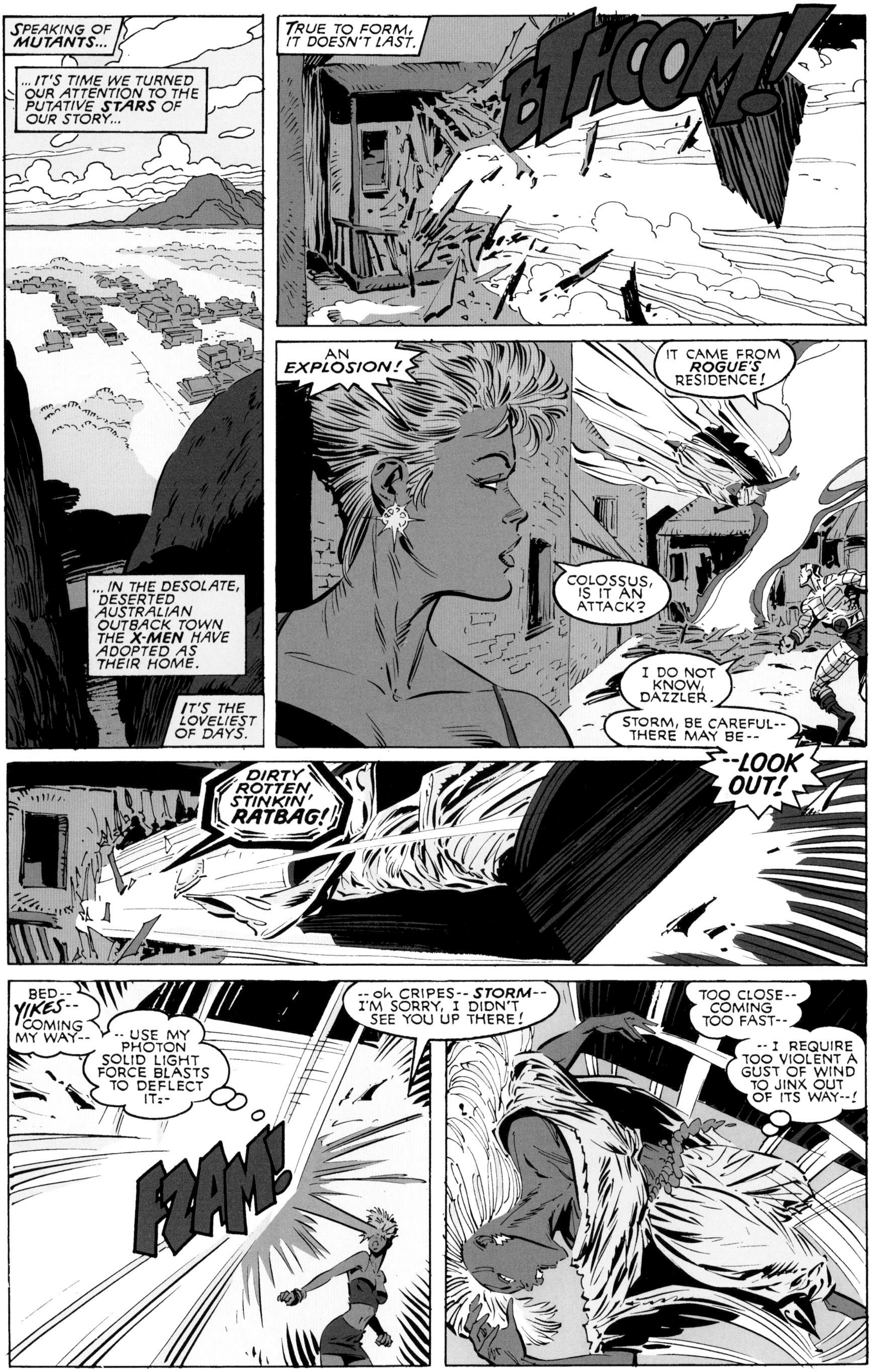
SPEAKING OF MUTANTS...
...IT'S TIME WE TURNED OUR ATTENTION TO THE PUTATIVE STARS OF OUR STORY...
...IN THE DESOLATE, DESERTED AUSTRALIAN OUTBACK TOWN THE X-MEN HAVE ADOPTED AS THEIR HOME.
IT'S THE LOVELIEST OF DAYS.
TRUE TO FORM, IT DOESN'T LAST.
BTHOOM!
AN EXPLOSION!
IT CAME FROM ROGUE'S RESIDENCE!
COLOSSUS, IS IT AN ATTACK?
I DO NOT KNOW, DAZZLER.
STORM, BE CAREFUL-- THERE MAY BE--
--LOOK OUT!
DIRTY ROTTEN, STINKIN' RATBAG!
BED-- YIKES-- COMING MY WAY--
-- USE MY PHOTON SOLID LIGHT FORCE BLASTS TO DEFLECT IT:-
FZAM!
-- oh CRIPES-- STORM-- I'M SORRY, I DIDN'T SEE YOU UP THERE!
TOO CLOSE-- COMING TOO FAST--
-- I REQUIRE TOO VIOLENT A GUST OF WIND TO JINX OUT OF ITS WAY--!

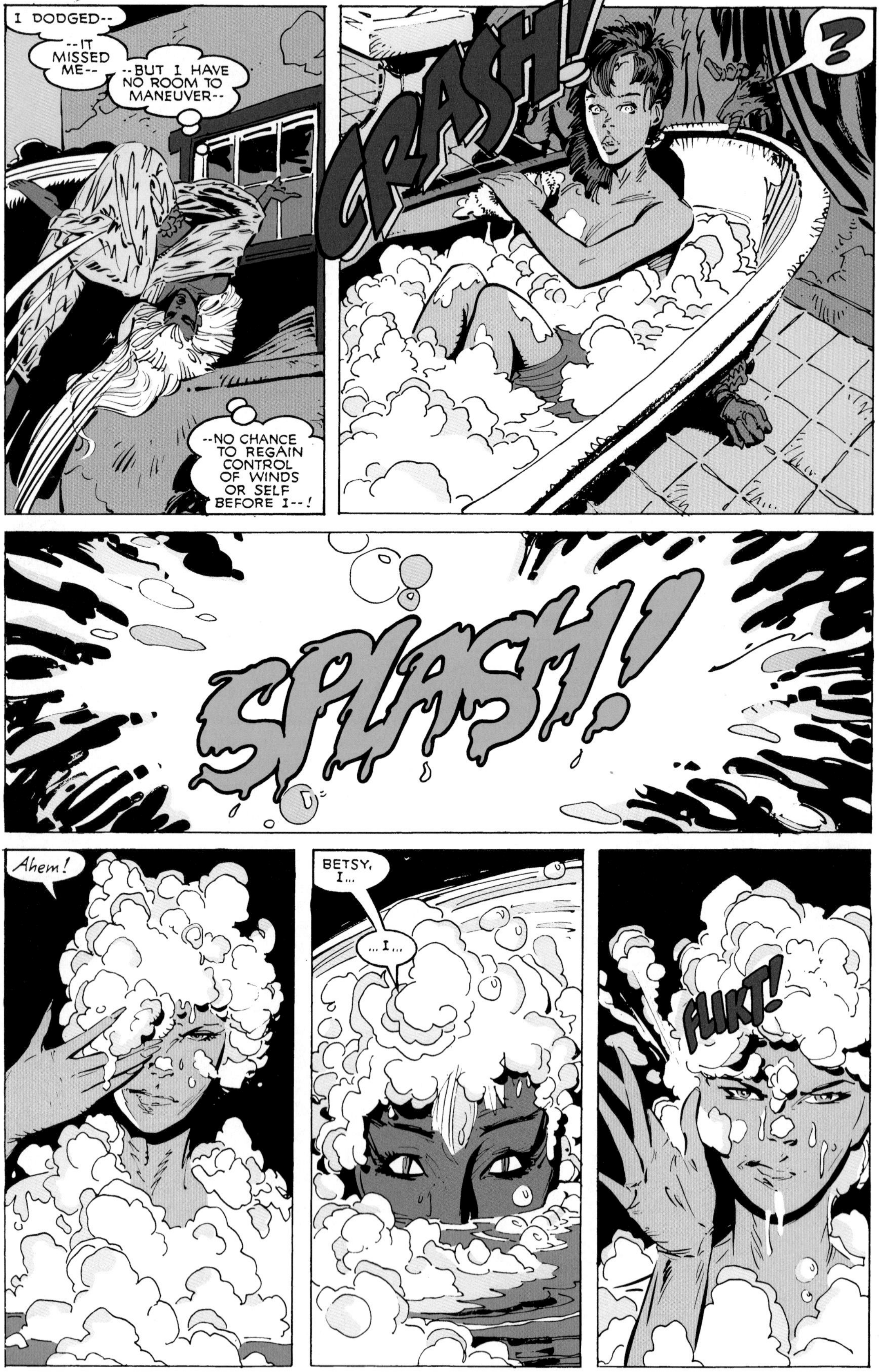

I DODGED--
--IT MISSED ME--
--BUT I HAVE NO ROOM TO MANEUVER--
--NO CHANCE TO REGAIN CONTROL OF WINDS OR SELF BEFORE I--!
CRASH!
?
SPLASH!
Ahem!
BETSY, I...
...I...
FLIKT!

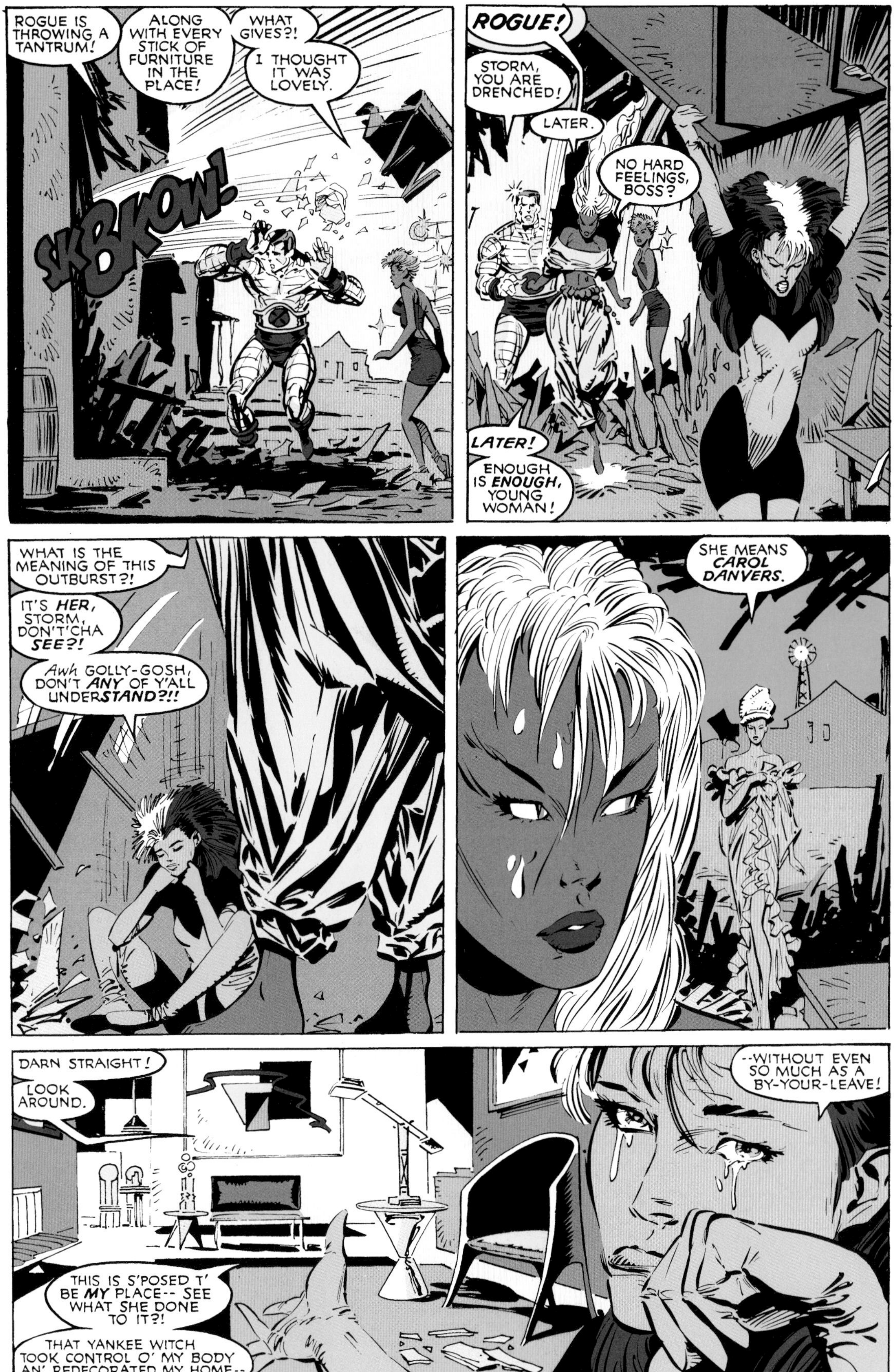
ROGUE IS THROWING A TANTRUM!
ALONG WITH EVERY STICK OF FURNITURE IN THE PLACE!
WHAT GIVES?!
I THOUGHT IT WAS LOVELY.
SKBKOW!
ROGUE!
STORM, YOU ARE DRENCHED!
LATER.
NO HARD FEELINGS, BOSS?
LATER!
ENOUGH IS ENOUGH, YOUNG WOMAN!
WHAT IS THE MEANING OF THIS OUTBURST?!
IT'S HER, STORM, DON'T'CHA SEE?!
Awh GOLLY-GOSH, DON'T ANY OF Y'ALL UNDERSTAND?!!
SHE MEANS CAROL DANVERS.
DARN STRAIGHT!
LOOK AROUND.
THIS IS S'POSED T' BE MY PLACE-- SEE WHAT SHE DONE TO IT?!
THAT YANKEE WITCH TOOK CONTROL O' MY BODY AN' REDECORATED MY HOME--
--WITHOUT EVEN SO MUCH AS A BY-YOUR-LEAVE!

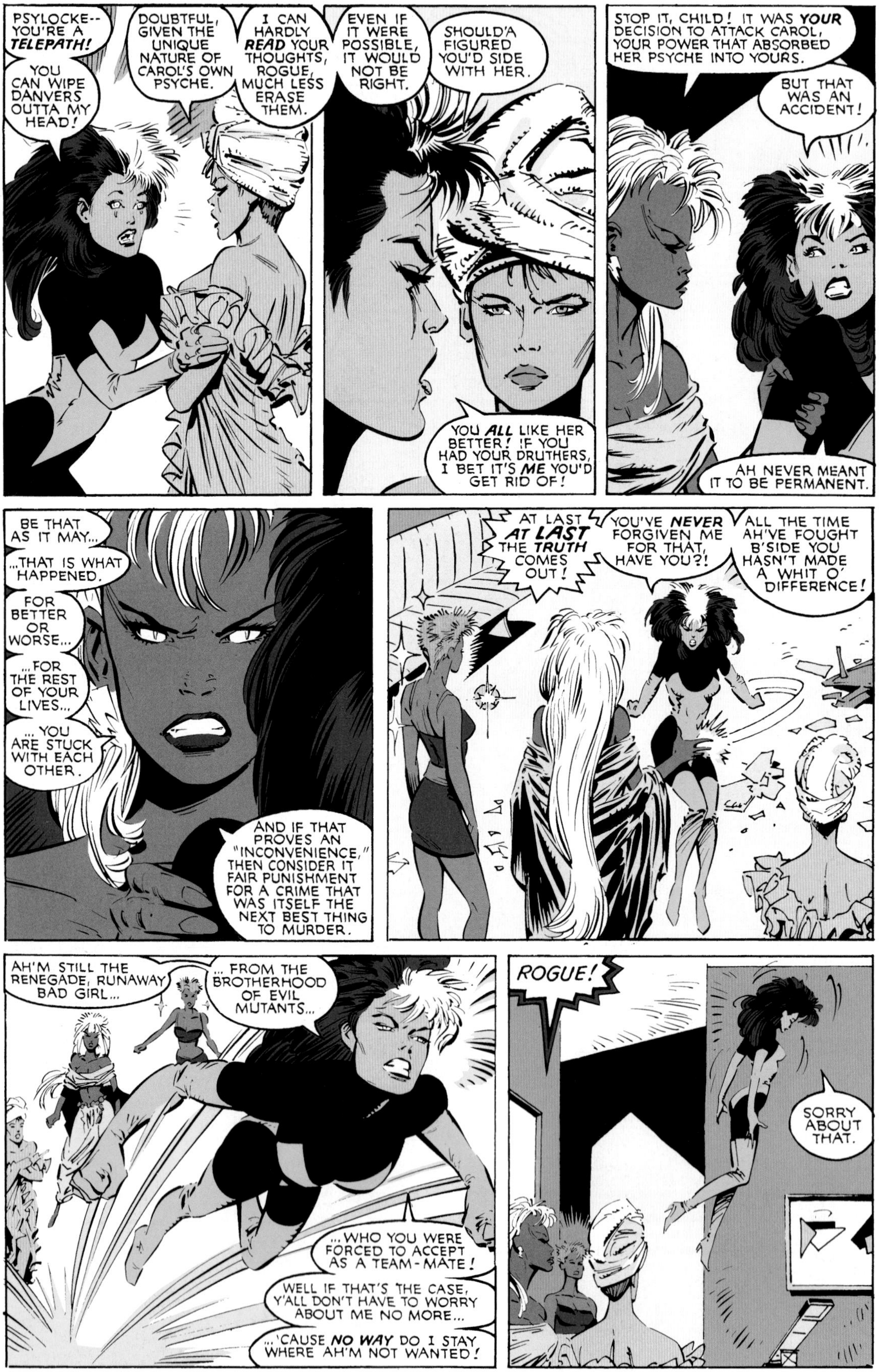
PSYLOCKE-- YOU'RE A TELEPATH!
YOU CAN WIPE DANVERS OUTTA MY HEAD!
DOUBTFUL, GIVEN THE UNIQUE NATURE OF CAROL'S OWN PSYCHE.
I CAN HARDLY READ YOUR THOUGHTS, ROGUE, MUCH LESS ERASE THEM.
EVEN IF IT WERE POSSIBLE, IT WOULD NOT BE RIGHT.
SHOULD'A FIGURED YOU'D SIDE WITH HER.
YOU ALL LIKE HER BETTER! IF YOU HAD YOUR DRUTHERS, I BET IT'S ME YOU'D GET RID OF!
STOP IT, CHILD! IT WAS YOUR DECISION TO ATTACK CAROL, YOUR POWER THAT ABSORBED HER PSYCHE INTO YOURS.
BUT THAT WAS AN ACCIDENT!
AH NEVER MEANT IT TO BE PERMANENT.
BE THAT AS IT MAY...
...THAT IS WHAT HAPPENED.
FOR BETTER OR WORSE...
...FOR THE REST OF YOUR LIVES...
... YOU ARE STUCK WITH EACH OTHER.
AND IF THAT PROVES AN "INCONVENIENCE," THEN CONSIDER IT FAIR PUNISHMENT FOR A CRIME THAT WAS ITSELF THE NEXT BEST THING TO MURDER.
AT LAST AT LAST THE TRUTH COMES OUT!
YOU'VE NEVER FORGIVEN ME FOR THAT, HAVE YOU?!
ALL THE TIME AH'VE FOUGHT B'SIDE YOU HASN'T MADE A WHIT O' DIFFERENCE!
AH'M STILL THE RENEGADE, RUNAWAY BAD GIRL...
... FROM THE BROTHERHOOD OF EVIL MUTANTS...
...WHO YOU WERE FORCED TO ACCEPT AS A TEAM-MATE!
WELL IF THAT'S THE CASE, Y'ALL DON'T HAVE TO WORRY ABOUT ME NO MORE...
...'CAUSE NO WAY DO I STAY WHERE AH'M NOT WANTED!
ROGUE!
SORRY ABOUT THAT.

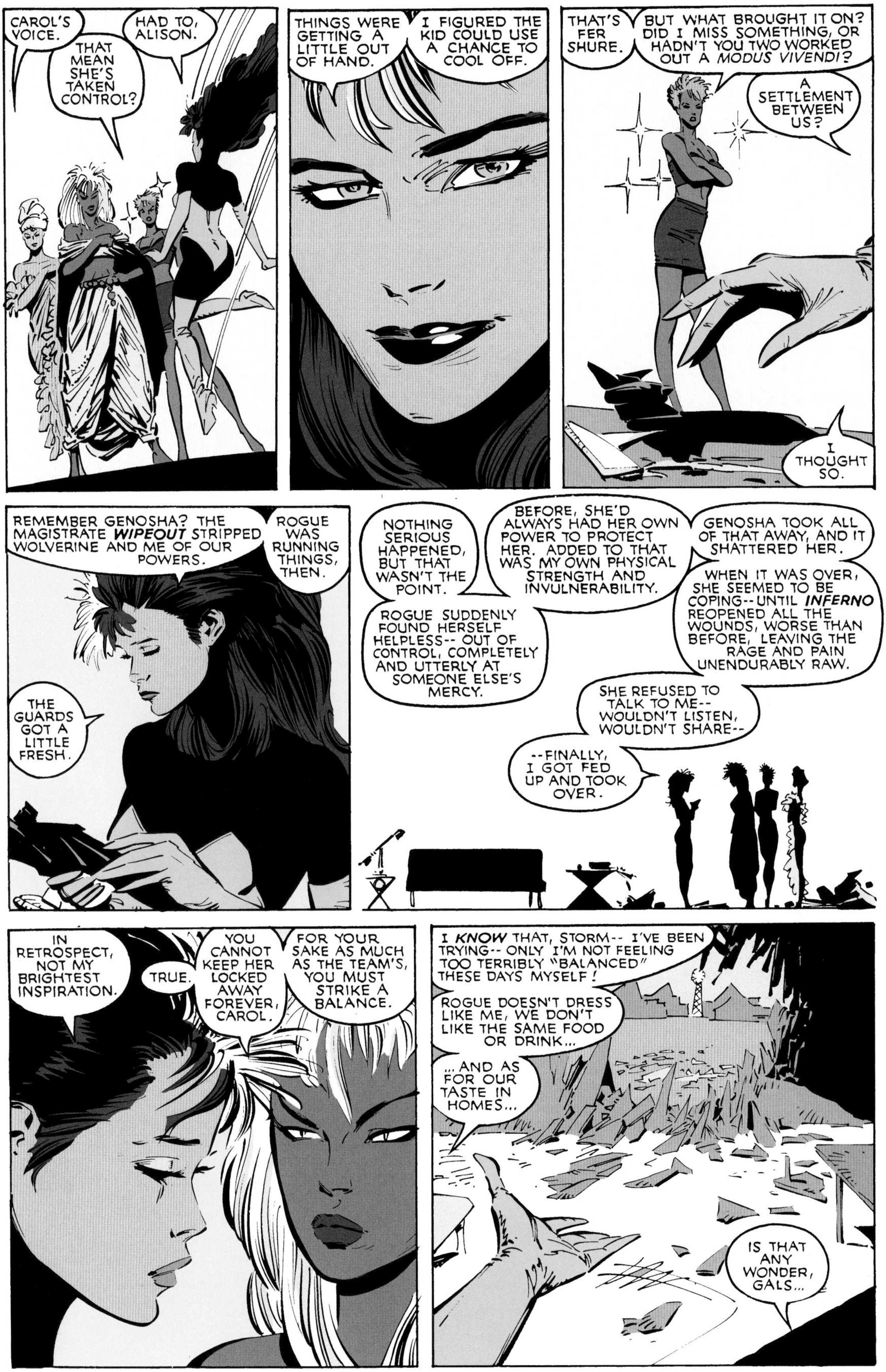

CAROL'S VOICE.
THAT MEAN SHE'S TAKEN CONTROL?
HAD TO, ALISON.
THINGS WERE GETTING A LITTLE OUT OF HAND.
I FIGURED THE KID COULD USE A CHANCE TO COOL OFF.
THAT'S FER SHURE.
BUT WHAT BROUGHT IT ON? DID I MISS SOMETHING, OR HADN'T YOU TWO WORKED OUT A *MODUS VIVENDI?*
A SETTLEMENT BETWEEN US?
I THOUGHT SO.
REMEMBER GENOSHA? THE MAGISTRATE **WIPEOUT** STRIPPED WOLVERINE AND ME OF OUR POWERS.
ROGUE WAS RUNNING THINGS, THEN.
THE GUARDS GOT A LITTLE FRESH.
NOTHING SERIOUS HAPPENED, BUT THAT WASN'T THE POINT.
ROGUE SUDDENLY FOUND HERSELF HELPLESS-- OUT OF CONTROL, COMPLETELY AND UTTERLY AT SOMEONE ELSE'S MERCY.
BEFORE, SHE'D ALWAYS HAD HER OWN POWER TO PROTECT HER. ADDED TO THAT WAS MY OWN PHYSICAL STRENGTH AND INVULNERABILITY.
GENOSHA TOOK ALL OF THAT AWAY, AND IT SHATTERED HER.
WHEN IT WAS OVER, SHE SEEMED TO BE COPING--UNTIL ***INFERNO*** REOPENED ALL THE WOUNDS, WORSE THAN BEFORE, LEAVING THE RAGE AND PAIN UNENDURABLY RAW.
SHE REFUSED TO TALK TO ME-- WOULDN'T LISTEN, WOULDN'T SHARE--
--FINALLY, I GOT FED UP AND TOOK OVER.
IN RETROSPECT, NOT MY BRIGHTEST INSPIRATION.
TRUE.
YOU CANNOT KEEP HER LOCKED AWAY FOREVER, CAROL.
FOR YOUR SAKE AS MUCH AS THE TEAM'S, YOU MUST STRIKE A BALANCE.
I **KNOW** THAT, STORM-- I'VE BEEN TRYING-- ONLY I'M NOT FEELING TOO TERRIBLY "BALANCED" THESE DAYS MYSELF!
ROGUE DOESN'T DRESS LIKE ME, WE DON'T LIKE THE SAME FOOD OR DRINK...
...AND AS FOR OUR TASTE IN HOMES...
IS THAT ANY WONDER, GALS...

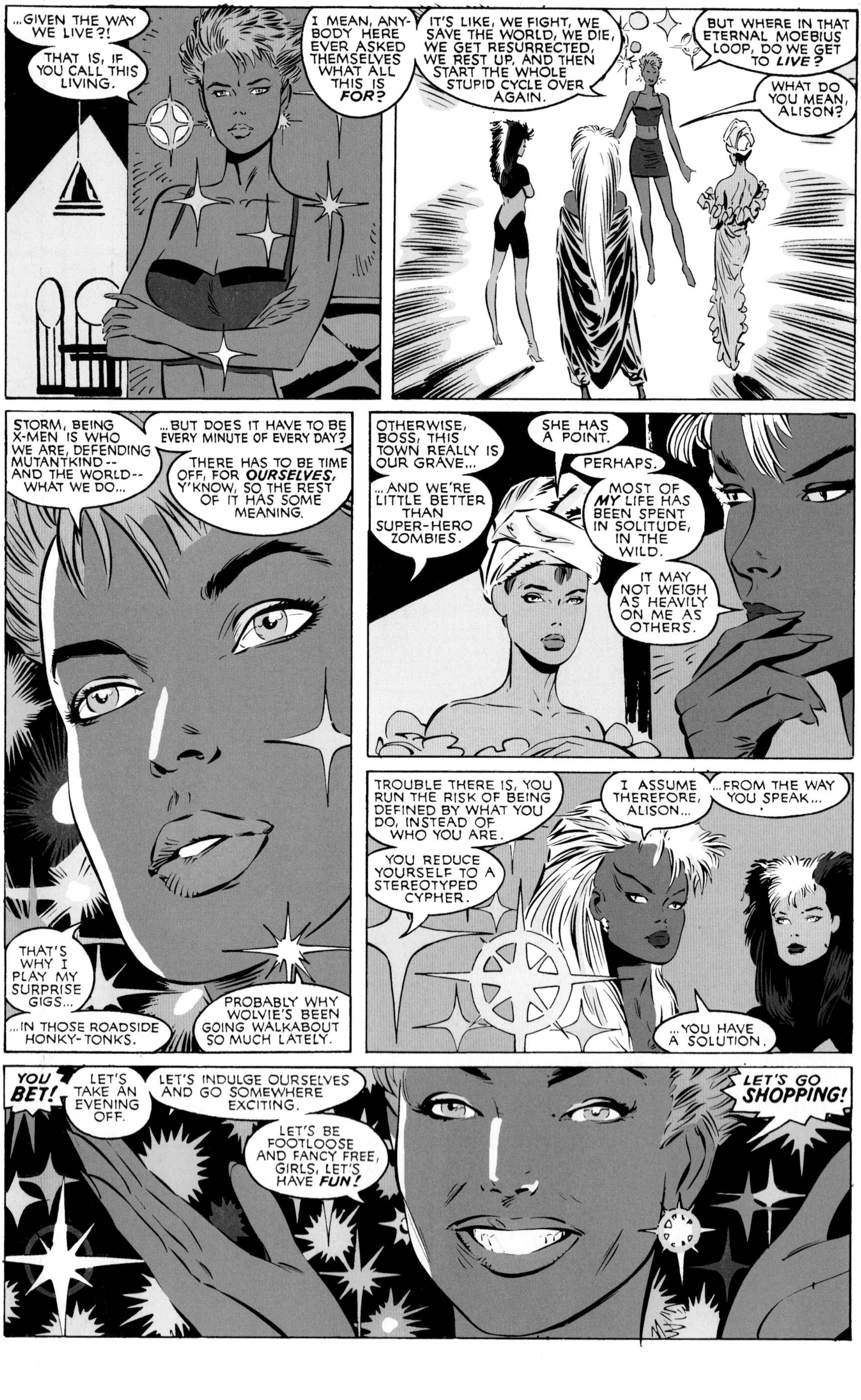
...GIVEN THE WAY WE LIVE?!
THAT IS, IF YOU CALL THIS LIVING.
I MEAN, ANYBODY HERE EVER ASKED THEMSELVES WHAT ALL THIS IS *FOR*?
IT'S LIKE, WE FIGHT, WE SAVE THE WORLD, WE DIE, WE GET RESURRECTED, WE REST UP, AND THEN START THE WHOLE STUPID CYCLE OVER AGAIN.
BUT WHERE IN THAT ETERNAL MOEBIUS LOOP, DO WE GET TO *LIVE*?
WHAT DO YOU MEAN, ALISON?
STORM, BEING X-MEN IS WHO WE ARE, DEFENDING MUTANTKIND-- AND THE WORLD-- WHAT WE DO...
...BUT DOES IT HAVE TO BE EVERY MINUTE OF EVERY DAY?
THERE HAS TO BE TIME OFF, FOR ***OURSELVES,*** Y'KNOW, SO THE REST OF IT HAS SOME MEANING.
THAT'S WHY I PLAY MY SURPRISE GIGS...
...IN THOSE ROADSIDE HONKY-TONKS.
PROBABLY WHY WOLVIE'S BEEN GOING WALKABOUT SO MUCH LATELY.
OTHERWISE, BOSS, THIS TOWN REALLY IS OUR GRAVE...
...AND WE'RE LITTLE BETTER THAN SUPER-HERO ZOMBIES.
SHE HAS A POINT.
PERHAPS.
MOST OF *MY* LIFE HAS BEEN SPENT IN SOLITUDE, IN THE WILD.
IT MAY NOT WEIGH AS HEAVILY ON ME AS OTHERS.
TROUBLE THERE IS, YOU RUN THE RISK OF BEING DEFINED BY WHAT YOU DO, INSTEAD OF WHO YOU ARE.
YOU REDUCE YOURSELF TO A STEREOTYPED CYPHER.
I ASSUME THEREFORE, ALISON...
...FROM THE WAY YOU SPEAK...
...YOU HAVE A SOLUTION.
YOU BET!
LET'S TAKE AN EVENING OFF.
LET'S INDULGE OURSELVES AND GO SOMEWHERE EXCITING.
LET'S BE FOOTLOOSE AND FANCY FREE, GIRLS, LET'S HAVE ***FUN!***
LET'S GO SHOPPING!

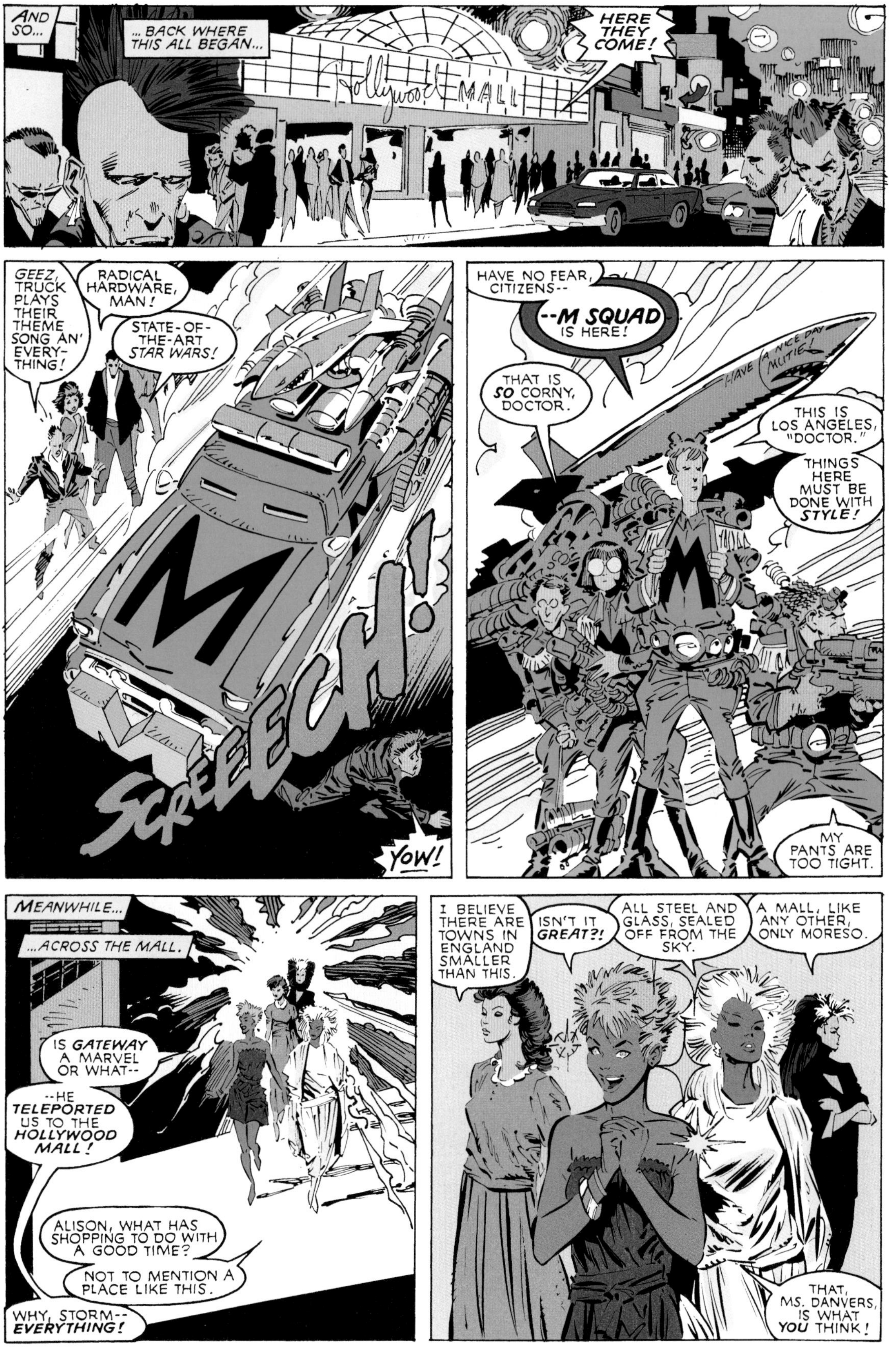
AND SO...
...BACK WHERE THIS ALL BEGAN...
HERE THEY COME!
GEEZ, TRUCK PLAYS THEIR THEME SONG AN' EVERYTHING!
RADICAL HARDWARE, MAN!
STATE-OF-THE-ART STAR WARS!
SCREEECH!
YOW!
HAVE NO FEAR, CITIZENS--
--M SQUAD IS HERE!
THAT IS SO CORNY, DOCTOR.
HAVE A NICE DAY MUTIE!
THIS IS LOS ANGELES, "DOCTOR."
THINGS HERE MUST BE DONE WITH STYLE!
MY PANTS ARE TOO TIGHT.
MEANWHILE...
...ACROSS THE MALL.
IS GATEWAY A MARVEL OR WHAT--
--HE TELEPORTED US TO THE HOLLYWOOD MALL!
ALISON, WHAT HAS SHOPPING TO DO WITH A GOOD TIME?
NOT TO MENTION A PLACE LIKE THIS.
WHY, STORM-- EVERYTHING!
I BELIEVE THERE ARE TOWNS IN ENGLAND SMALLER THAN THIS.
ISN'T IT GREAT?!
ALL STEEL AND GLASS, SEALED OFF FROM THE SKY.
A MALL, LIKE ANY OTHER, ONLY MORESO.
THAT, MS. DANVERS, IS WHAT YOU THINK!

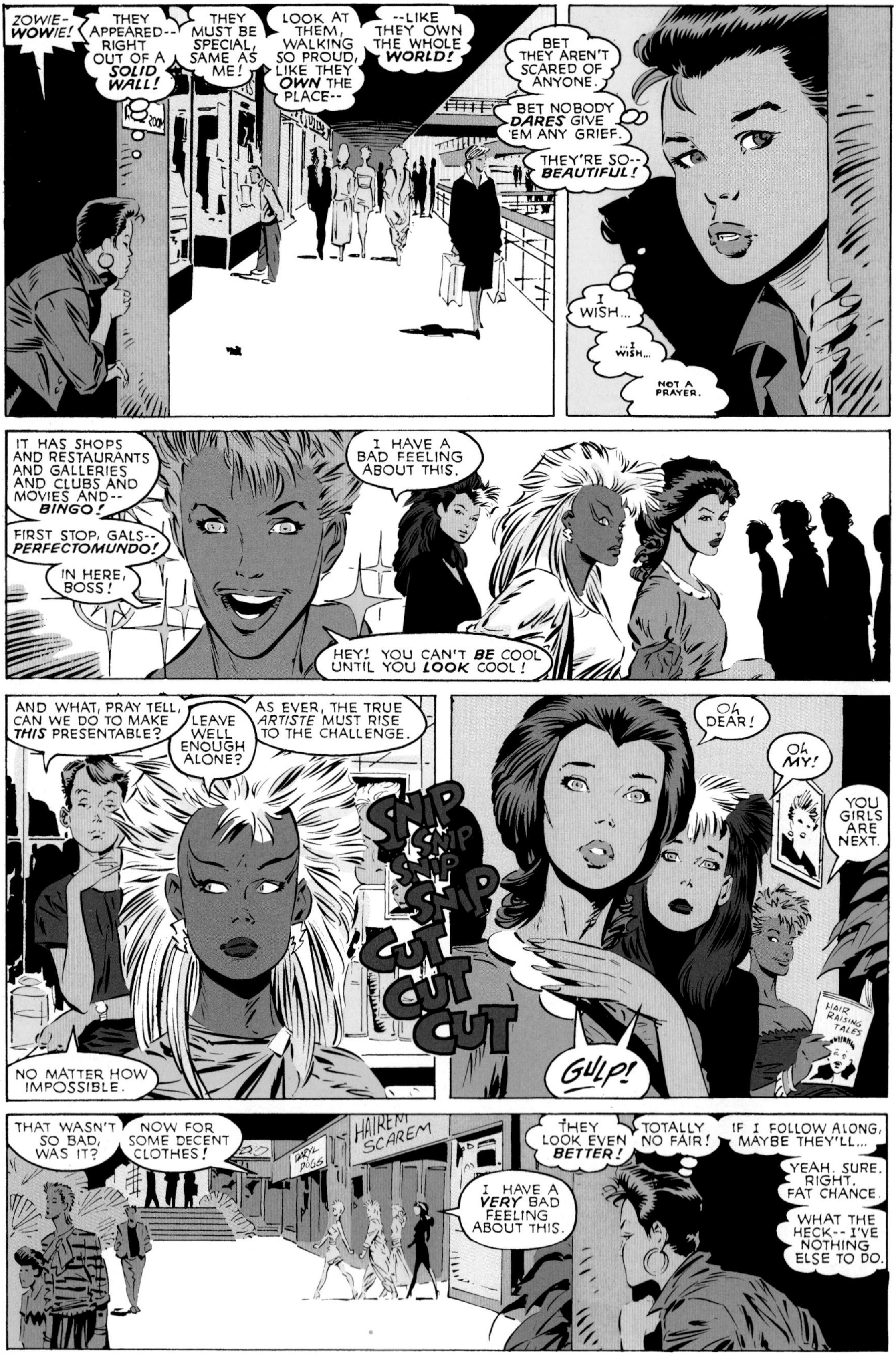
ZOWIE-WOWIE!
THEY APPEARED-- RIGHT OUT OF A SOLID WALL!
THEY MUST BE SPECIAL, SAME AS ME!
LOOK AT THEM, WALKING SO PROUD, LIKE THEY OWN THE PLACE--
--LIKE THEY OWN THE WHOLE WORLD!
BET THEY AREN'T SCARED OF ANYONE.
BET NOBODY DARES GIVE 'EM ANY GRIEF.
THEY'RE SO-- BEAUTIFUL!
I WISH...
...I WISH...
NOT A PRAYER.
IT HAS SHOPS AND RESTAURANTS AND GALLERIES AND CLUBS AND MOVIES AND-- BINGO!
FIRST STOP, GALS-- PERFECTOMUNDO!
IN HERE, BOSS!
I HAVE A BAD FEELING ABOUT THIS.
HEY! YOU CAN'T BE COOL UNTIL YOU LOOK COOL!
AND WHAT, PRAY TELL, CAN WE DO TO MAKE THIS PRESENTABLE?
LEAVE WELL ENOUGH ALONE?
AS EVER, THE TRUE ARTISTE MUST RISE TO THE CHALLENGE.
NO MATTER HOW IMPOSSIBLE.
SNIP SNIP SNIP SNIP
CUT CUT CUT
Oh DEAR!
Oh MY!
YOU GIRLS ARE NEXT.
GULP!
HAIR RAISING TALES
THAT WASN'T SO BAD, WAS IT?
NOW FOR SOME DECENT CLOTHES!
HAIREM SCAREM
I HAVE A VERY BAD FEELING ABOUT THIS.
THEY LOOK EVEN BETTER!
TOTALLY NO FAIR!
IF I FOLLOW ALONG, MAYBE THEY'LL...
YEAH. SURE. RIGHT. FAT CHANCE.
WHAT THE HECK-- I'VE NOTHING ELSE TO DO.

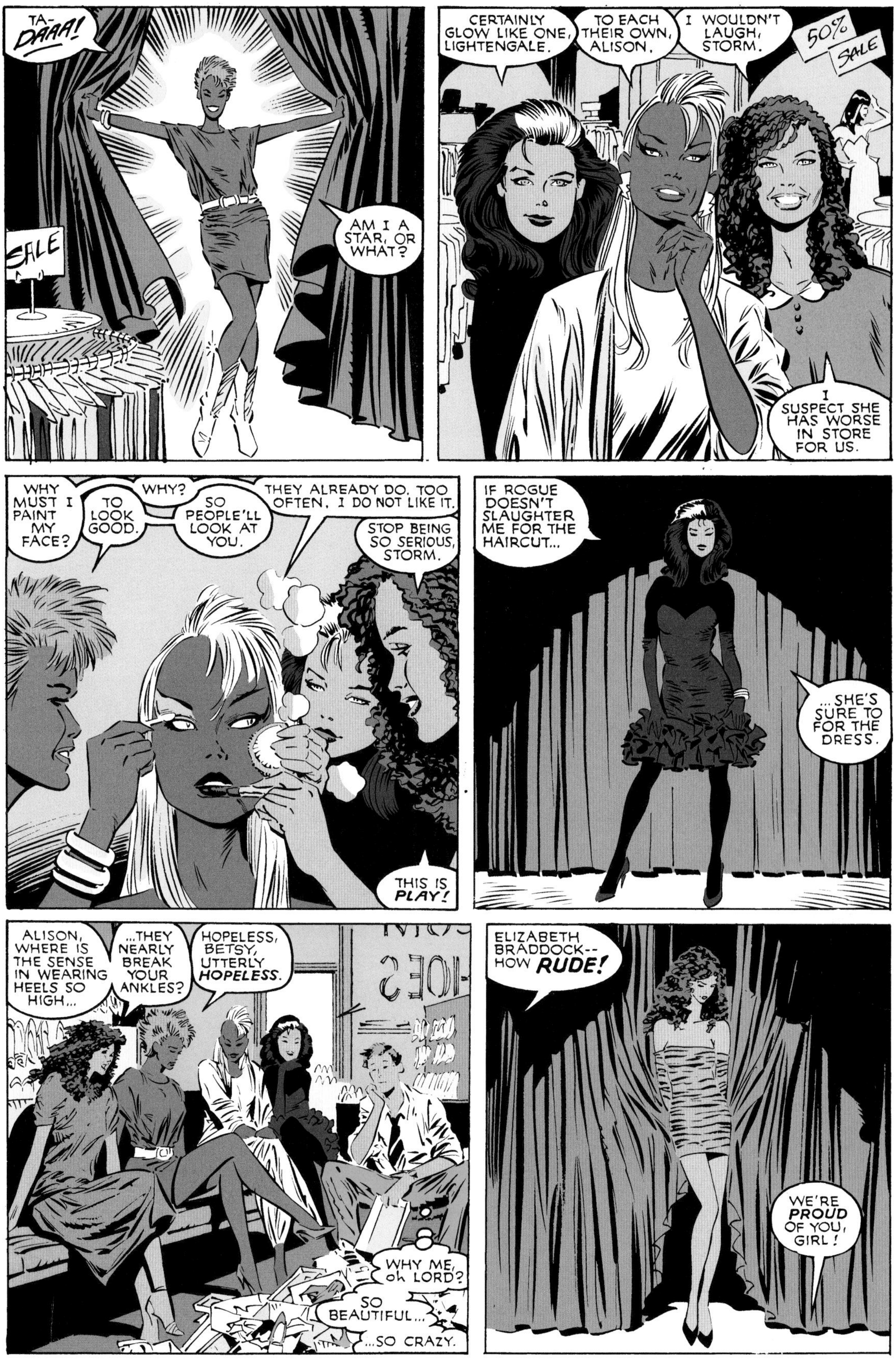
TA-DAAA!
AM I A STAR, OR WHAT?
CERTAINLY GLOW LIKE ONE, LIGHTENGALE.
TO EACH THEIR OWN, ALISON.
I WOULDN'T LAUGH, STORM.
50% SALE
I SUSPECT SHE HAS WORSE IN STORE FOR US.
SALE
WHY MUST I PAINT MY FACE?
TO LOOK GOOD.
WHY?
SO PEOPLE'LL LOOK AT YOU.
THEY ALREADY DO. TOO OFTEN. I DO NOT LIKE IT.
STOP BEING SO SERIOUS, STORM.
THIS IS PLAY!
IF ROGUE DOESN'T SLAUGHTER ME FOR THE HAIRCUT...
...SHE'S SURE TO FOR THE DRESS.
ALISON, WHERE IS THE SENSE IN WEARING HEELS SO HIGH...
...THEY NEARLY BREAK YOUR ANKLES?
HOPELESS, BETSY, UTTERLY HOPELESS.
WHY ME, oh LORD?
SO BEAUTIFUL...
...SO CRAZY.
ELIZABETH BRADDOCK--HOW RUDE!
WE'RE PROUD OF YOU, GIRL!

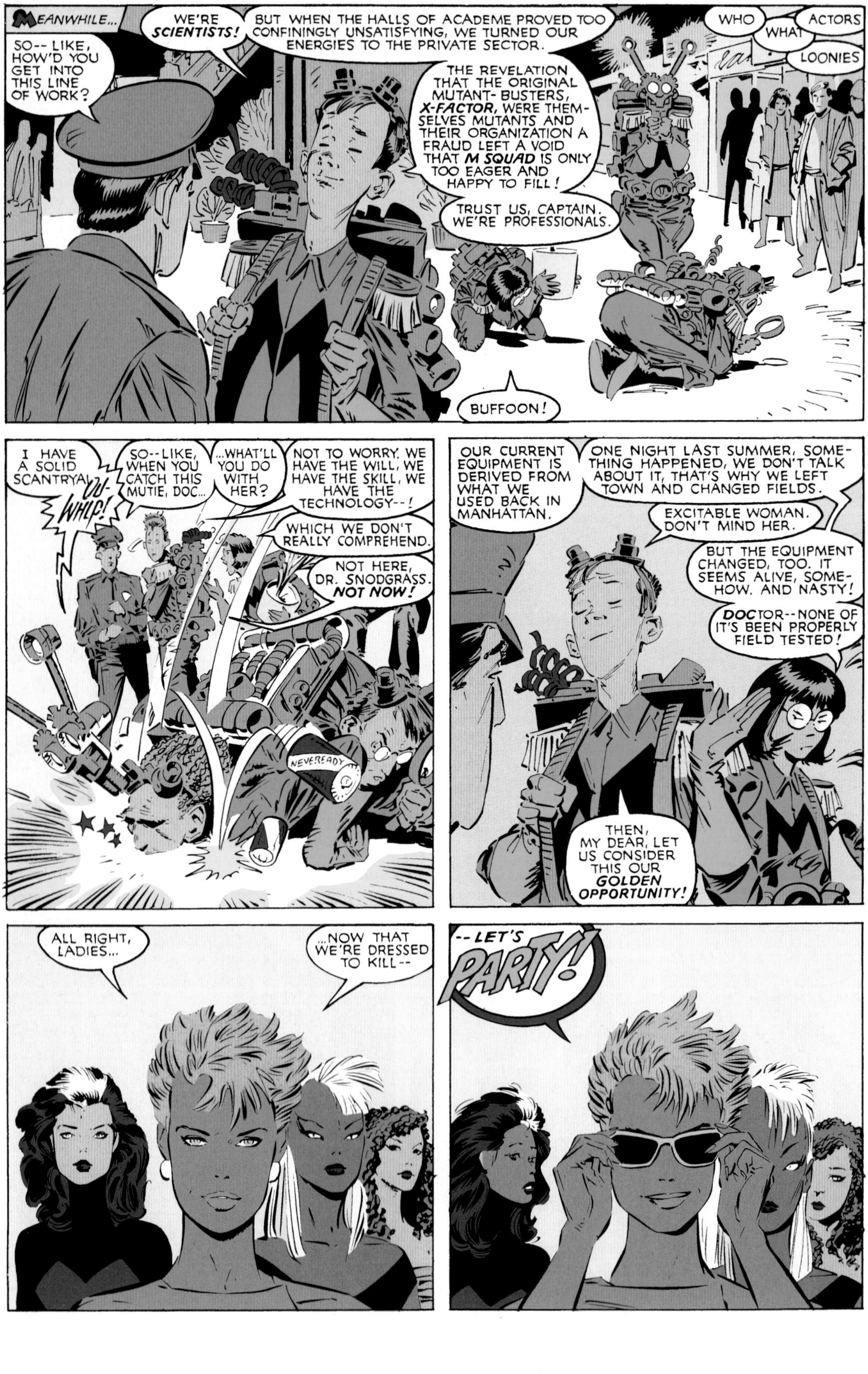
MEANWHILE...
SO-- LIKE, HOW'D YOU GET INTO THIS LINE OF WORK?
WE'RE SCIENTISTS!
BUT WHEN THE HALLS OF ACADEME PROVED TOO CONFININGLY UNSATISFYING, WE TURNED OUR ENERGIES TO THE PRIVATE SECTOR.
THE REVELATION THAT THE ORIGINAL MUTANT-BUSTERS, X-FACTOR, WERE THEMSELVES MUTANTS AND THEIR ORGANIZATION A FRAUD LEFT A VOID THAT M SQUAD IS ONLY TOO EAGER AND HAPPY TO FILL!
TRUST US, CAPTAIN. WE'RE PROFESSIONALS.
WHO
WHAT
ACTORS
LOONIES
BUFFOON!
I HAVE A SOLID SCANTRYAL
UU-WHLP!
SO--LIKE, WHEN YOU CATCH THIS MUTIE, DOC...
...WHAT'LL YOU DO WITH HER?
NOT TO WORRY. WE HAVE THE WILL, WE HAVE THE SKILL, WE HAVE THE TECHNOLOGY--!
WHICH WE DON'T REALLY COMPREHEND.
NOT HERE, DR. SNODGRASS. NOT NOW!
NEVEREADY
OUR CURRENT EQUIPMENT IS DERIVED FROM WHAT WE USED BACK IN MANHATTAN.
ONE NIGHT LAST SUMMER, SOMETHING HAPPENED, WE DON'T TALK ABOUT IT, THAT'S WHY WE LEFT TOWN AND CHANGED FIELDS.
EXCITABLE WOMAN. DON'T MIND HER.
BUT THE EQUIPMENT CHANGED, TOO. IT SEEMS ALIVE, SOMEHOW. AND NASTY!
DOCTOR--NONE OF IT'S BEEN PROPERLY FIELD TESTED!
THEN, MY DEAR, LET US CONSIDER THIS OUR GOLDEN OPPORTUNITY!
ALL RIGHT, LADIES...
...NOW THAT WE'RE DRESSED TO KILL--
--LET'S PARTY!

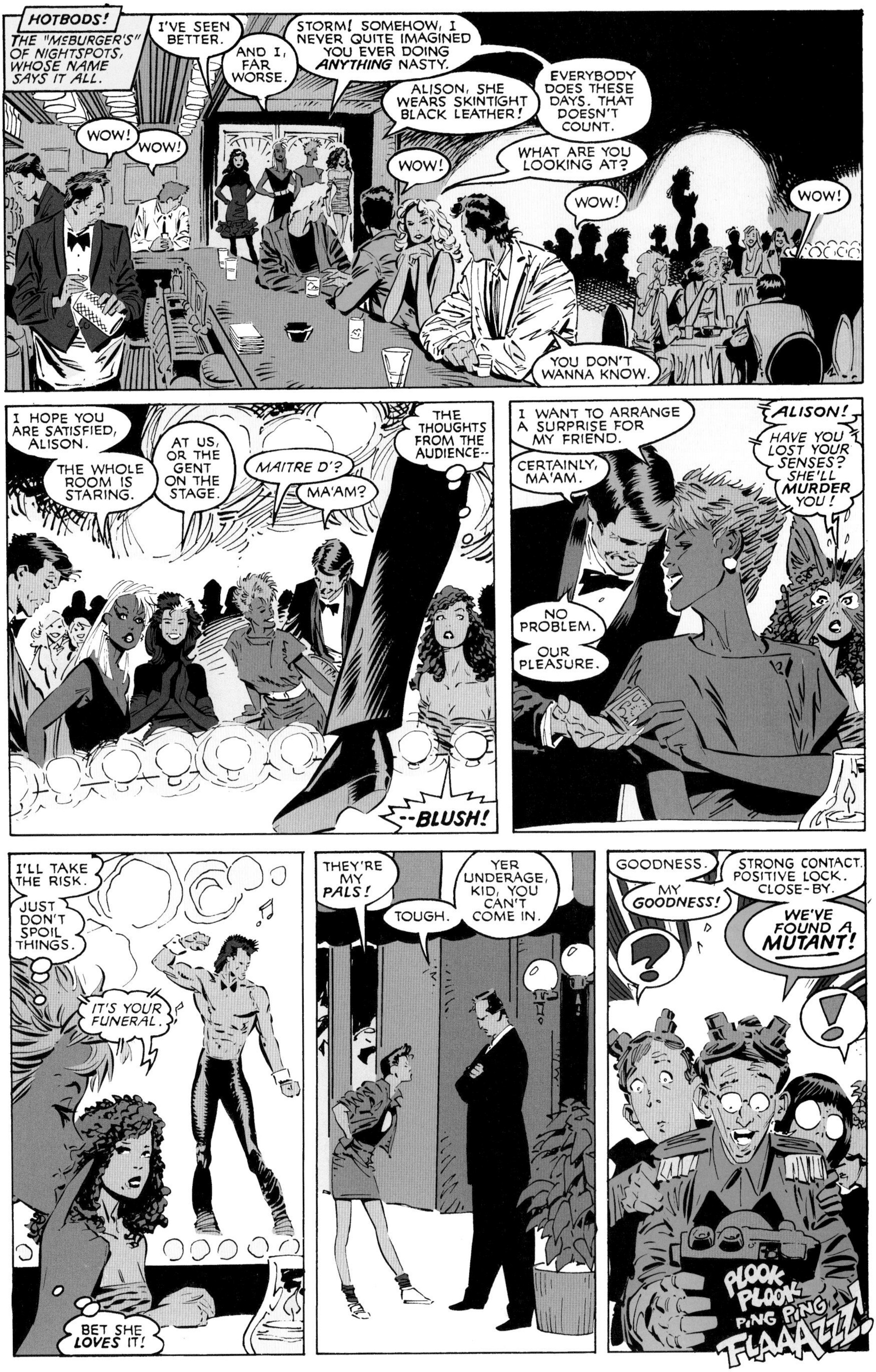
HOTBODS!
THE "McBURGER'S" OF NIGHTSPOTS, WHOSE NAME SAYS IT ALL.
I'VE SEEN BETTER.
AND I, FAR WORSE.
STORM! SOMEHOW, I NEVER QUITE IMAGINED YOU EVER DOING ANYTHING NASTY.
ALISON, SHE WEARS SKINTIGHT BLACK LEATHER!
EVERYBODY DOES THESE DAYS. THAT DOESN'T COUNT.
WOW!
WOW!
WOW!
WHAT ARE YOU LOOKING AT?
WOW!
WOW!
YOU DON'T WANNA KNOW.
I HOPE YOU ARE SATISFIED, ALISON.
THE WHOLE ROOM IS STARING.
AT US, OR THE GENT ON THE STAGE.
MAITRE D'?
MA'AM?
THE THOUGHTS FROM THE AUDIENCE--
--BLUSH!
I WANT TO ARRANGE A SURPRISE FOR MY FRIEND.
CERTAINLY, MA'AM.
ALISON!
HAVE YOU LOST YOUR SENSES? SHE'LL MURDER YOU!
NO PROBLEM.
OUR PLEASURE.
I'LL TAKE THE RISK.
JUST DON'T SPOIL THINGS.
IT'S YOUR FUNERAL.
BET SHE LOVES IT!
THEY'RE MY PALS!
YER UNDERAGE, KID, YOU CAN'T COME IN.
TOUGH.
GOODNESS.
MY GOODNESS!
STRONG CONTACT. POSITIVE LOCK. CLOSE-BY.
WE'VE FOUND A MUTANT!
?
!
PLOOK PLOOK PING PING FLAAAZZZ!

I'M TOLD **YOU'RE** A LADY...

...WHO LOVES TO **DANCE**!

WHAT?! I CANNOT!!

HA HA HO HO hee hee!

Oh ALISON-- --THE THINNEST OF THIN ICE.

SURE YOU CAN. FEEL THE MUSIC.

SEIZE THE MOMENT. LET YOURSELF **GO!**

TRUST ME, YOU'LL **LOVE** IT!

I... I... I...

GIVE IT A WHIRL, GIRL!

YOU'VE NOTHING TO LOSE BUT YOUR DIGNITY!

DON'T BE A **WEENIE**, BOSS!

REMEMBER, STORM-- --PLAY!

Tweeet ♪ Whweeet! ♪

THAT'S THE SPIRIT!

IS THIS **FUN**, OR WHAT?

MEANWHILE, RIGHT OUTSIDE...

Uh-oh!

THAT'S YOUR MUTANT, DOCTOR?

GOOD GRIEF, SHE'S JUST A **CHILD**!

IRRELEVANT, DOCTOR. MY SCANNERS CONFIRM DR. SHINER'S INITIAL CONTACT.

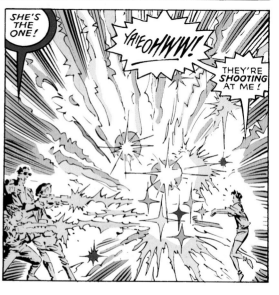

SHE'S THE ONE!

YAEOHWW!

THEY'RE **SHOOTING** AT ME!

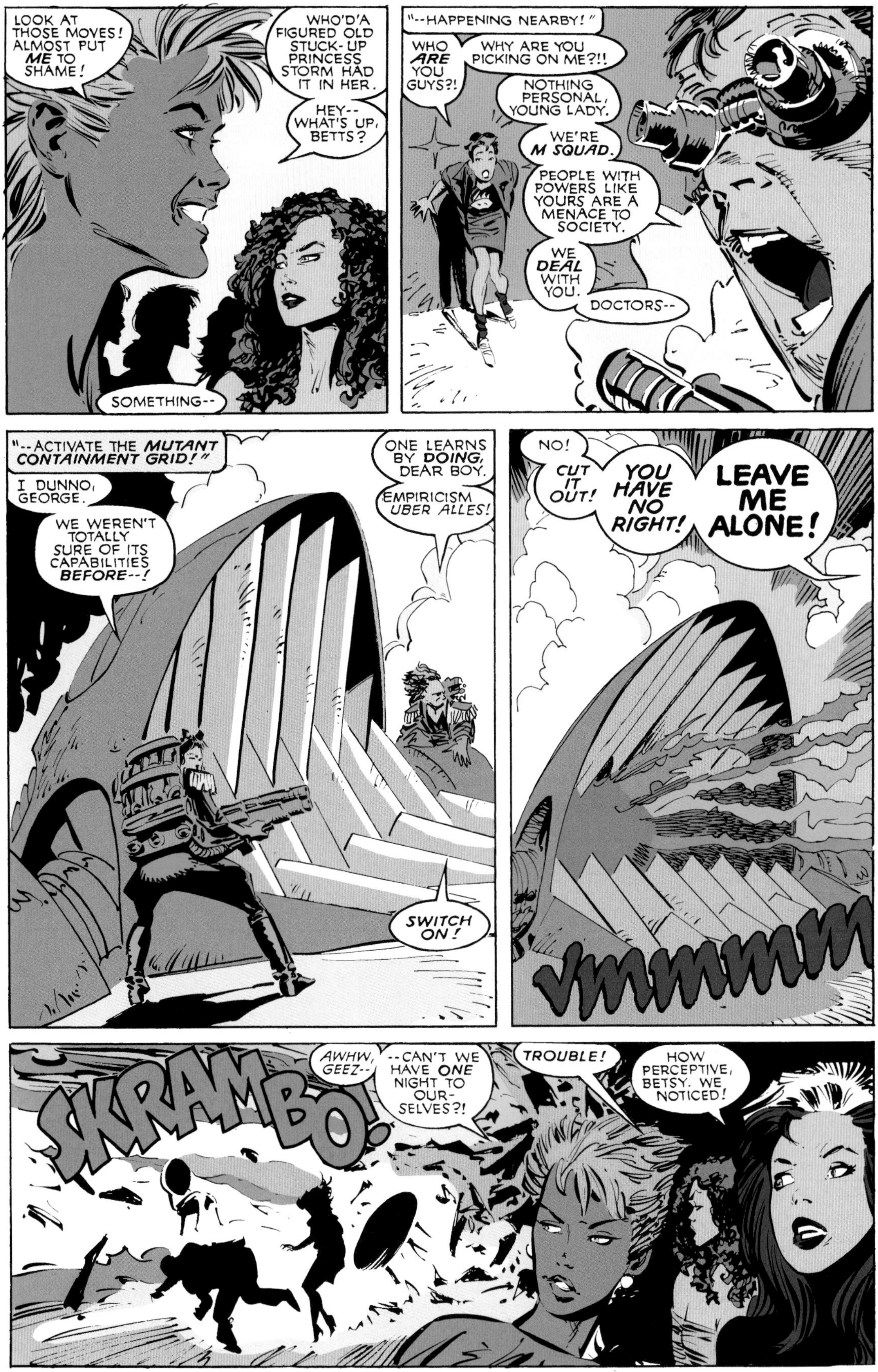
LOOK AT THOSE MOVES! ALMOST PUT ME TO SHAME!
WHO'D'A FIGURED OLD STUCK-UP PRINCESS STORM HAD IT IN HER.
HEY-- WHAT'S UP, BETTS?
SOMETHING--
"--HAPPENING NEARBY!"
WHO ARE YOU GUYS?!
WHY ARE YOU PICKING ON ME?!!
NOTHING PERSONAL, YOUNG LADY.
WE'RE M SQUAD.
PEOPLE WITH POWERS LIKE YOURS ARE A MENACE TO SOCIETY.
WE DEAL WITH YOU.
DOCTORS--
"--ACTIVATE THE MUTANT CONTAINMENT GRID!"
I DUNNO, GEORGE.
WE WEREN'T TOTALLY SURE OF ITS CAPABILITIES BEFORE--!
ONE LEARNS BY DOING, DEAR BOY.
EMPIRICISM UBER ALLES!
SWITCH ON!
NO!
CUT IT OUT!
YOU HAVE NO RIGHT!
LEAVE ME ALONE!
VMMMM
SKRAMBO!
AWHW, GEEZ--
--CAN'T WE HAVE ONE NIGHT TO OUR-SELVES?!
TROUBLE!
HOW PERCEPTIVE, BETSY. WE NOTICED!

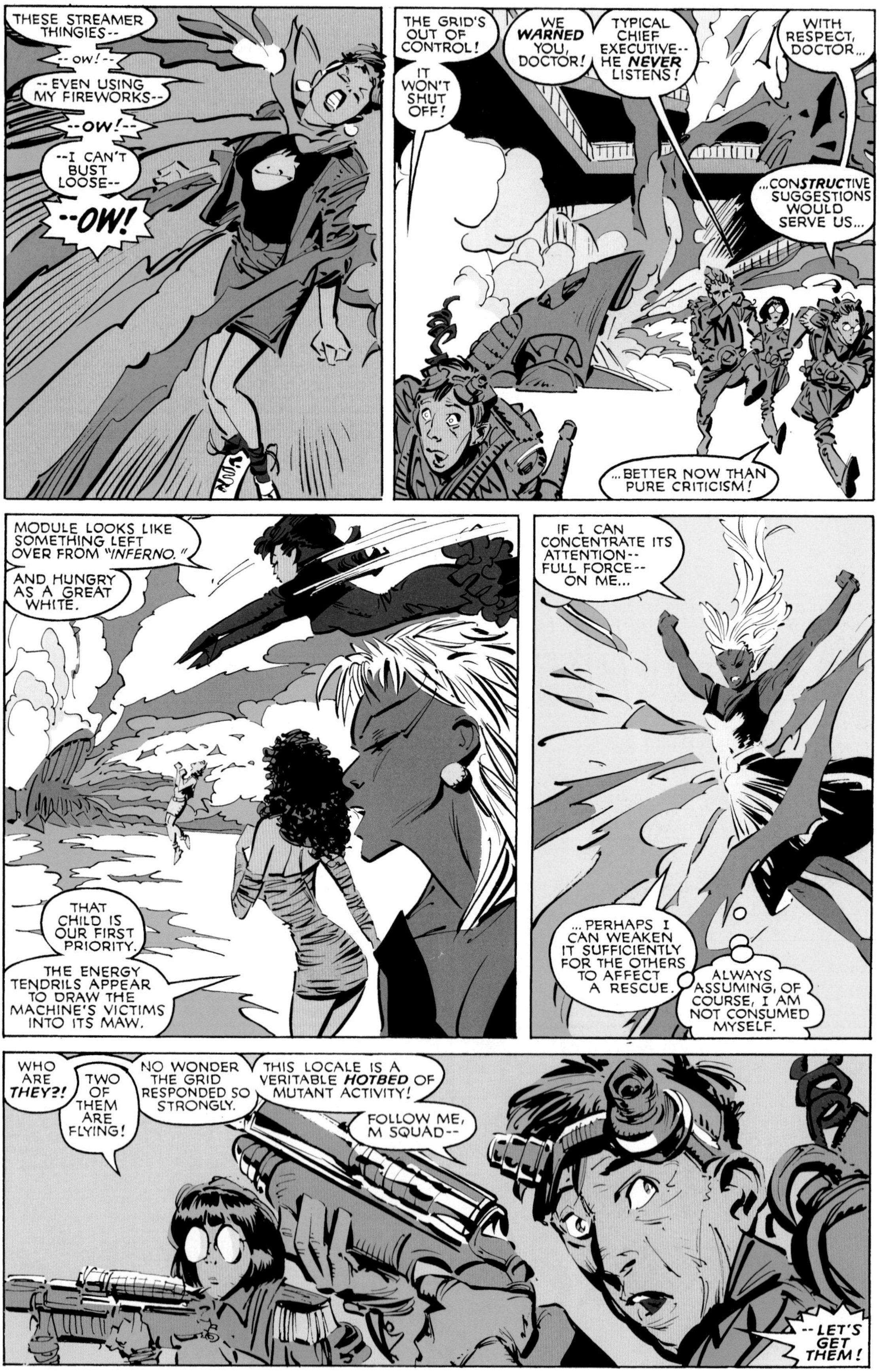
THESE STREAMER THINGIES--
--OW!--
--EVEN USING MY FIREWORKS--
--OW!--
--I CAN'T BUST LOOSE--
--OW!
THE GRID'S OUT OF CONTROL!
IT WON'T SHUT OFF!
WE WARNED YOU, DOCTOR!
TYPICAL CHIEF EXECUTIVE-- HE NEVER LISTENS!
WITH RESPECT, DOCTOR...
...CONSTRUCTIVE SUGGESTIONS WOULD SERVE US...
...BETTER NOW THAN PURE CRITICISM!
MODULE LOOKS LIKE SOMETHING LEFT OVER FROM "INFERNO."
AND HUNGRY AS A GREAT WHITE.
THAT CHILD IS OUR FIRST PRIORITY.
THE ENERGY TENDRILS APPEAR TO DRAW THE MACHINE'S VICTIMS INTO ITS MAW.
IF I CAN CONCENTRATE ITS ATTENTION-- FULL FORCE-- ON ME...
...PERHAPS I CAN WEAKEN IT SUFFICIENTLY FOR THE OTHERS TO AFFECT A RESCUE.
ALWAYS ASSUMING, OF COURSE, I AM NOT CONSUMED MYSELF.
WHO ARE THEY?!
TWO OF THEM ARE FLYING!
NO WONDER THE GRID RESPONDED SO STRONGLY.
THIS LOCALE IS A VERITABLE HOTBED OF MUTANT ACTIVITY!
FOLLOW ME, M SQUAD--
--LET'S GET THEM!

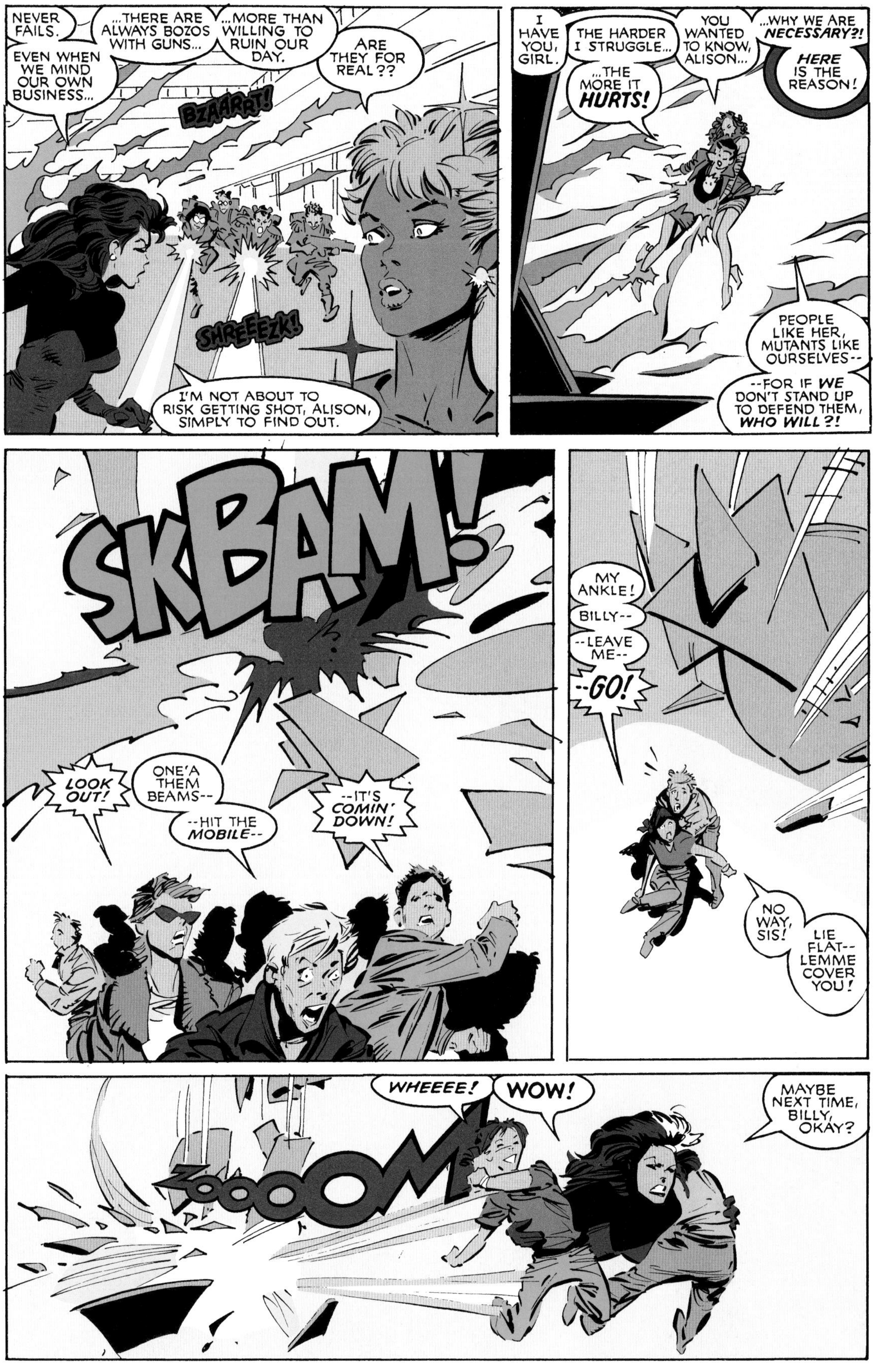
NEVER FAILS.
EVEN WHEN WE MIND OUR OWN BUSINESS...
...THERE ARE ALWAYS BOZOS WITH GUNS...
...MORE THAN WILLING TO RUIN OUR DAY.
ARE THEY FOR REAL??
BZAARRT!
SHREEEZK!
I'M NOT ABOUT TO RISK GETTING SHOT, ALISON, SIMPLY TO FIND OUT.
I HAVE YOU, GIRL.
THE HARDER I STRUGGLE...
...THE MORE IT HURTS!
YOU WANTED TO KNOW, ALISON...
...WHY WE ARE NECESSARY?!
HERE IS THE REASON!
PEOPLE LIKE HER, MUTANTS LIKE OURSELVES--
--FOR IF WE DON'T STAND UP TO DEFEND THEM, WHO WILL?!
SKBAM!
LOOK OUT!
ONE'A THEM BEAMS--
--HIT THE MOBILE--
--IT'S COMIN' DOWN!
MY ANKLE!
BILLY--
--LEAVE ME--
--GO!
NO WAY, SIS!
LIE FLAT--LEMME COVER YOU!
WHEEEE!
WOW!
ZOOOOOM
MAYBE NEXT TIME, BILLY, OKAY?

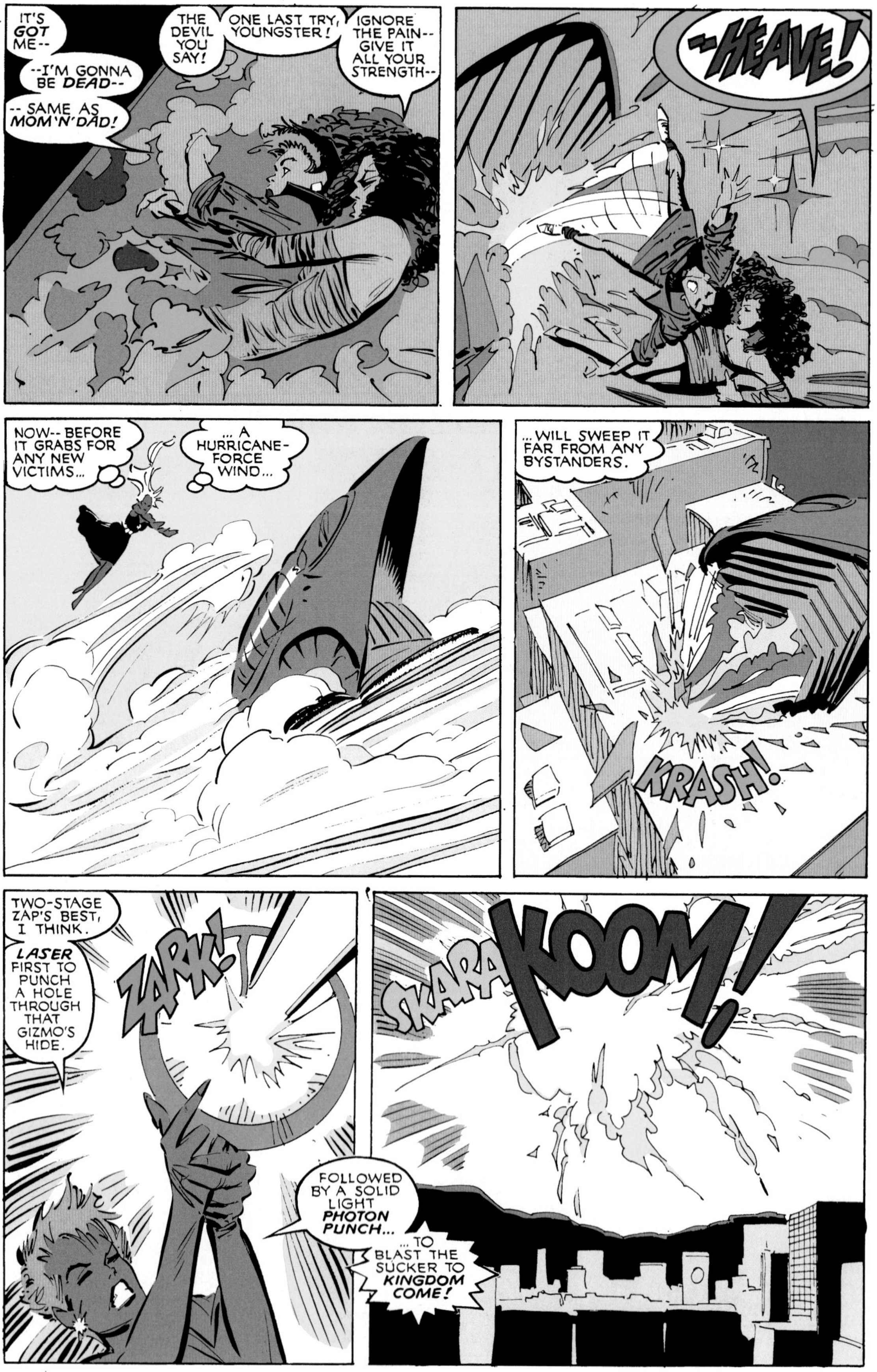
IT'S **GOT** ME--
--I'M GONNA BE **DEAD**--
-- SAME AS **MOM 'N' DAD**!
THE DEVIL YOU SAY!
ONE LAST TRY, YOUNGSTER!
IGNORE THE PAIN-- GIVE IT ALL YOUR STRENGTH--
--HEAVE!
NOW-- BEFORE IT GRABS FOR ANY NEW VICTIMS...
... A HURRICANE-FORCE WIND...
... WILL SWEEP IT FAR FROM ANY BYSTANDERS.
KRASH!
TWO-STAGE ZAP'S BEST, I THINK.
LASER FIRST TO PUNCH A HOLE THROUGH THAT GIZMO'S HIDE.
ZARK!
SKARAKOOOM!
FOLLOWED BY A SOLID LIGHT **PHOTON PUNCH**...
... TO BLAST THE SUCKER TO **KINGDOM COME**!

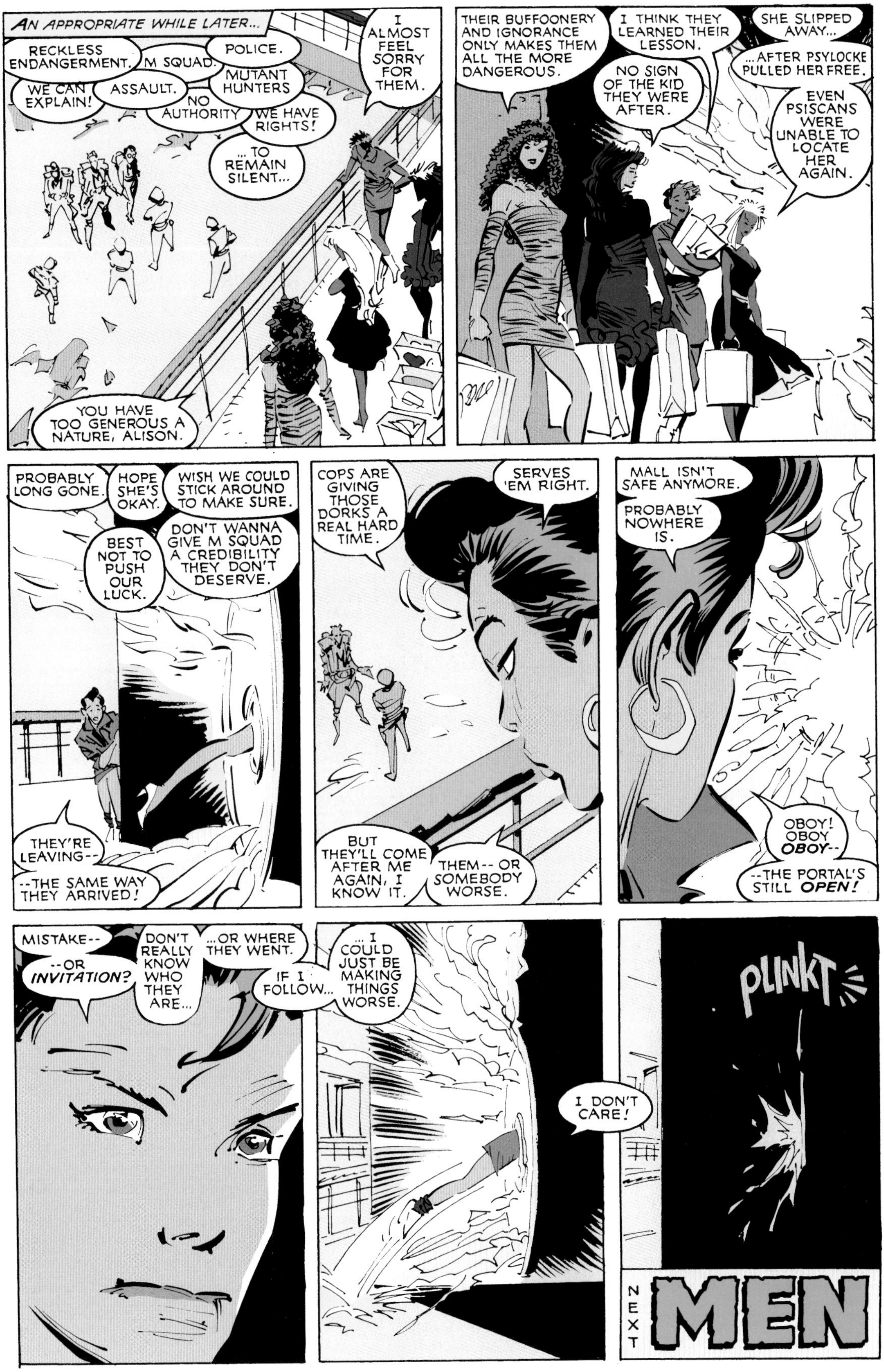
AN APPROPRIATE WHILE LATER...
RECKLESS ENDANGERMENT.
M SQUAD.
POLICE.
MUTANT HUNTERS
WE CAN EXPLAIN!
ASSAULT.
NO AUTHORITY
WE HAVE RIGHTS!
... TO REMAIN SILENT...
I ALMOST FEEL SORRY FOR THEM.
YOU HAVE TOO GENEROUS A NATURE, ALISON.
THEIR BUFFOONERY AND IGNORANCE ONLY MAKES THEM ALL THE MORE DANGEROUS.
I THINK THEY LEARNED THEIR LESSON.
NO SIGN OF THE KID THEY WERE AFTER.
SHE SLIPPED AWAY...
...AFTER PSYLOCKE PULLED HER FREE.
EVEN PSISCANS WERE UNABLE TO LOCATE HER AGAIN.
PROBABLY LONG GONE.
HOPE SHE'S OKAY.
WISH WE COULD STICK AROUND TO MAKE SURE.
BEST NOT TO PUSH OUR LUCK.
DON'T WANNA GIVE M SQUAD A CREDIBILITY THEY DON'T DESERVE.
THEY'RE LEAVING--
--THE SAME WAY THEY ARRIVED!
COPS ARE GIVING THOSE DORKS A REAL HARD TIME.
SERVES 'EM RIGHT.
BUT THEY'LL COME AFTER ME AGAIN, I KNOW IT.
THEM-- OR SOMEBODY WORSE.
MALL ISN'T SAFE ANYMORE.
PROBABLY NOWHERE IS.
OBOY! OBOY OBOY--
--THE PORTAL'S STILL OPEN!
MISTAKE--
--OR INVITATION?
DON'T REALLY KNOW WHO THEY ARE...
...OR WHERE THEY WENT.
IF I FOLLOW...
... I COULD JUST BE MAKING THINGS WORSE.
I DON'T CARE!
PLINKT
NEXT
MEN

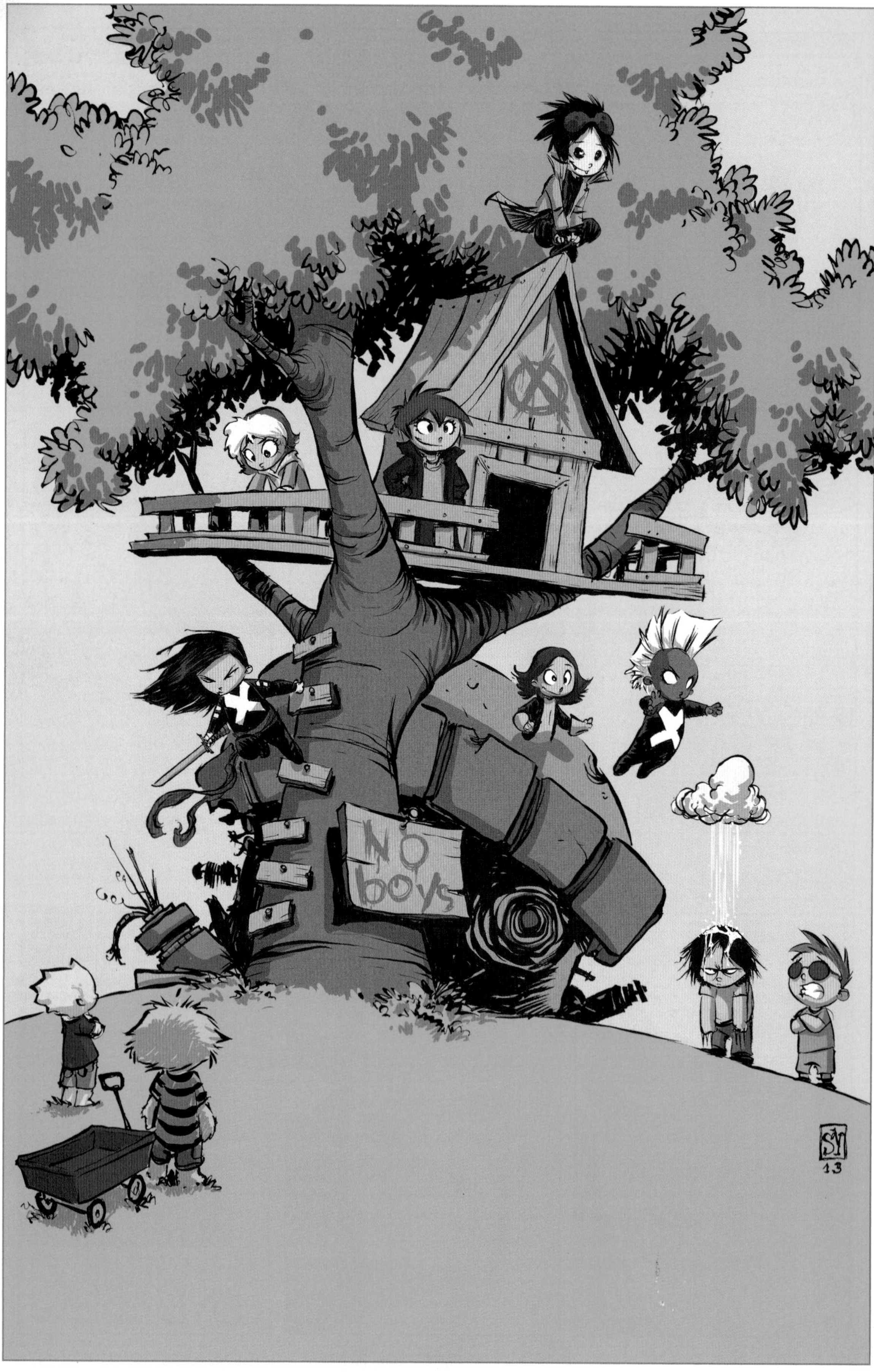
NO boys
SY 13

X-MEN #1 VARIANT
BY SKOTTIE YOUNG

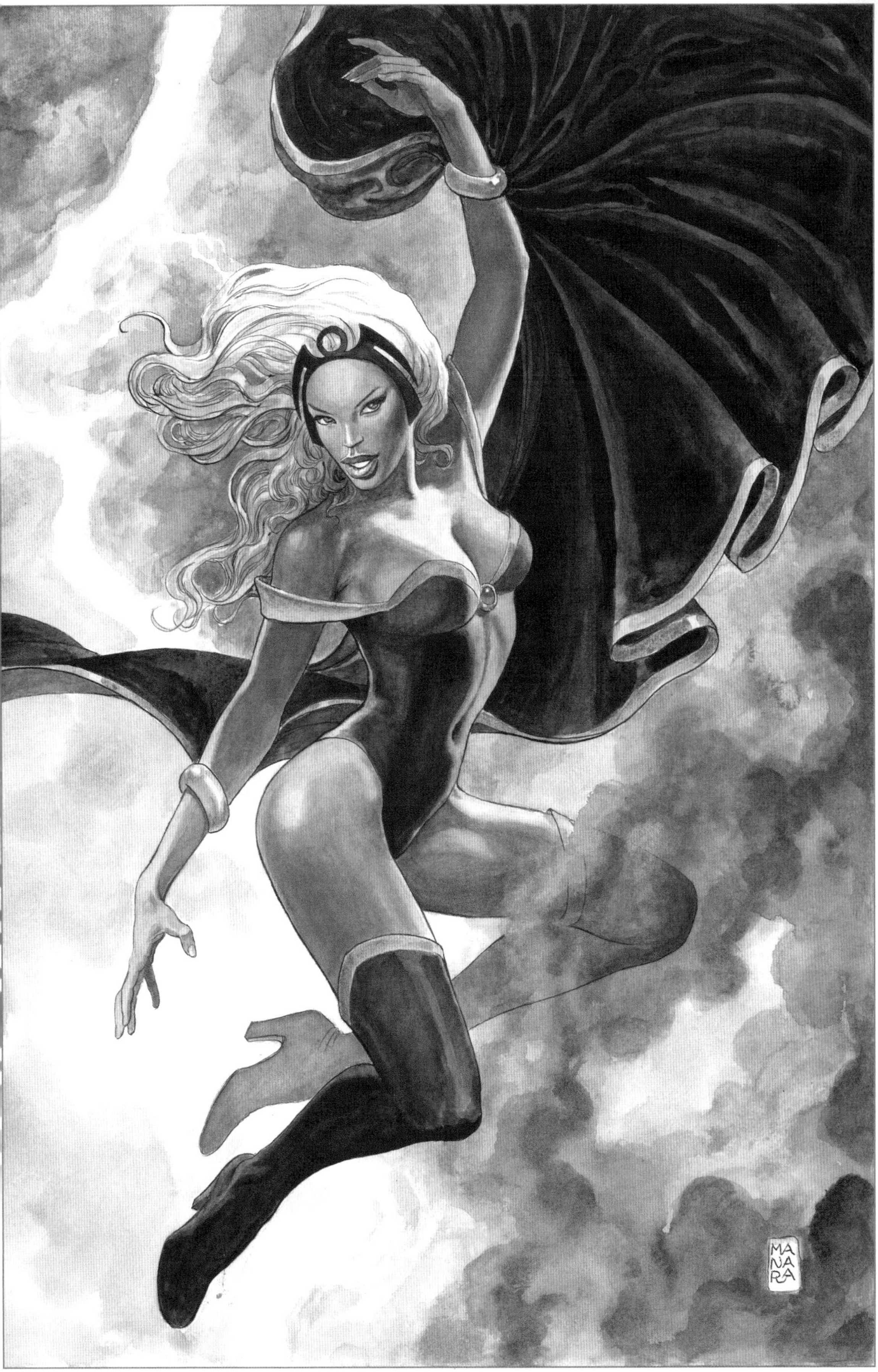
MA
NA
RA

X-MEN #1 VARIANT
BY MILO MANARA

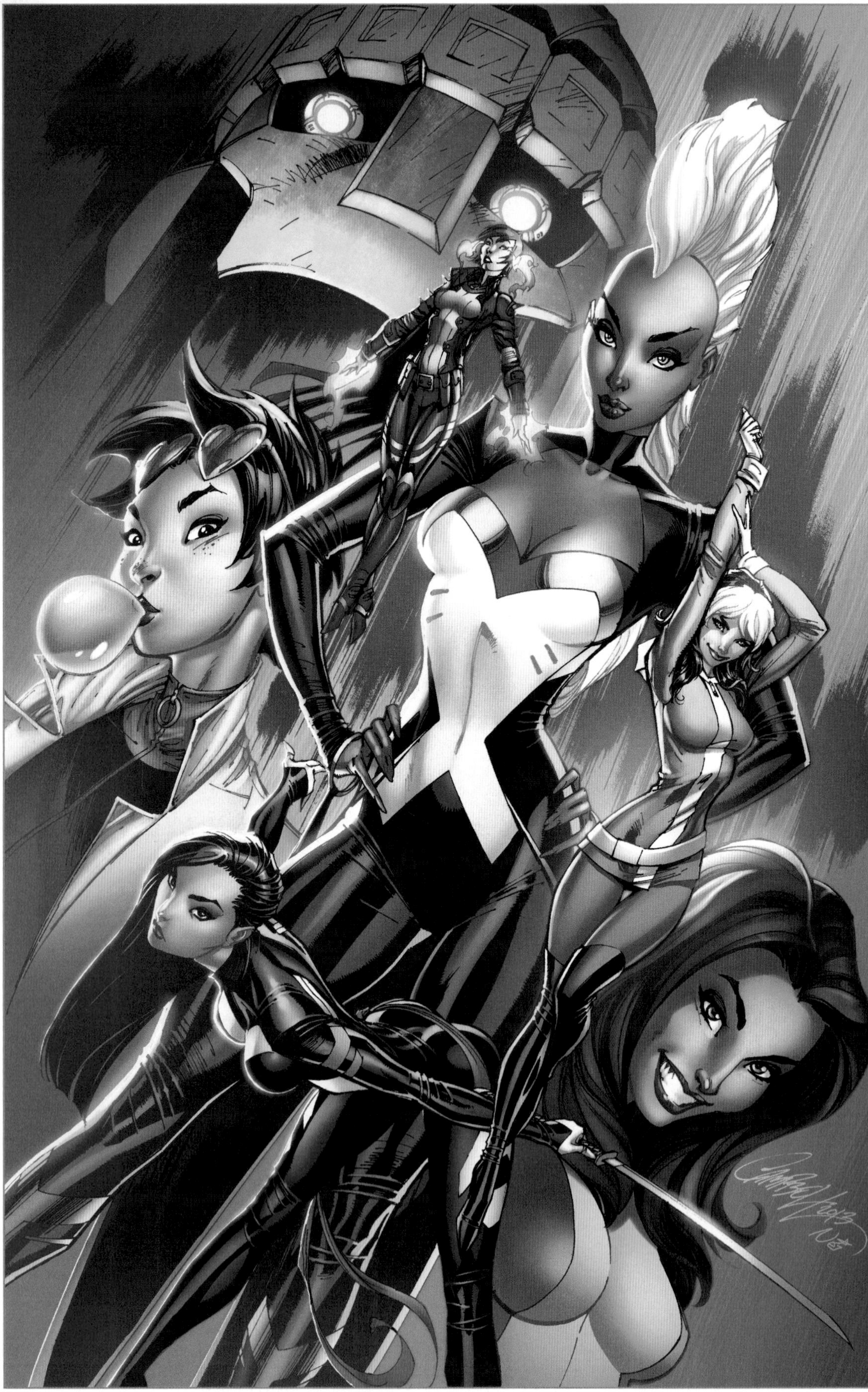

X-MEN #1 VARIANT
BY J. SCOTT CAMPBELL & NEI RUFFINO

X-MEN #1 VARIANT
BY MARK BROOKS

X-MEN #1 VARIANT
BY TERRY DODSON & RACHEL DODSON

X-MEN #1 50TH ANNIVERSARY VARIANT
BY JOE MADUREIRA & JASON KEITH

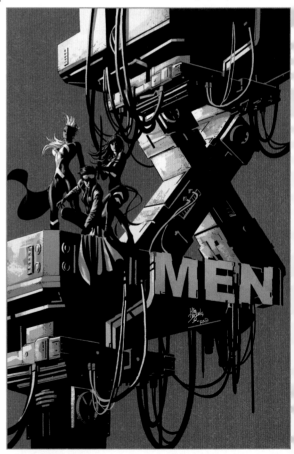

X-MEN #1 MILE HIGH COMICS VARIANT
BY MIKE DEADATO & RAIN BEREDO

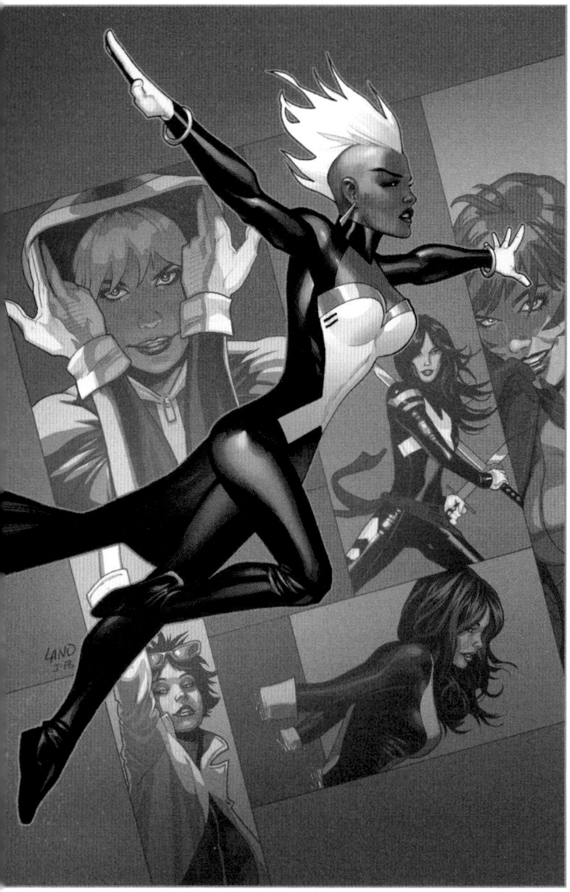
LAND

X-MEN #1 DRAGON'S LAIR VARIANT
BY GREG LAND & JUSTIN PONSOR

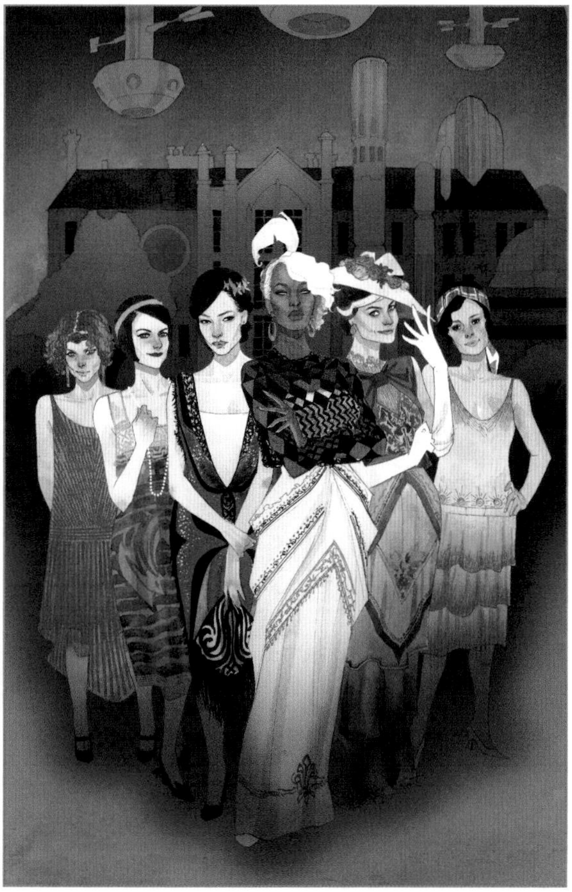

X-MEN #1 HASTINGS VARIANT
BY KEVIN WADA

X-MEN #1 LIMITED EDITION COMIX VARIANT
BY ED McGUINNESS & MORRY HOLLOWELL

X-MEN #1 MILE HIGH COMICS VARIANT
BY HUMBERTO RAMOS & EDGAR DELGADO

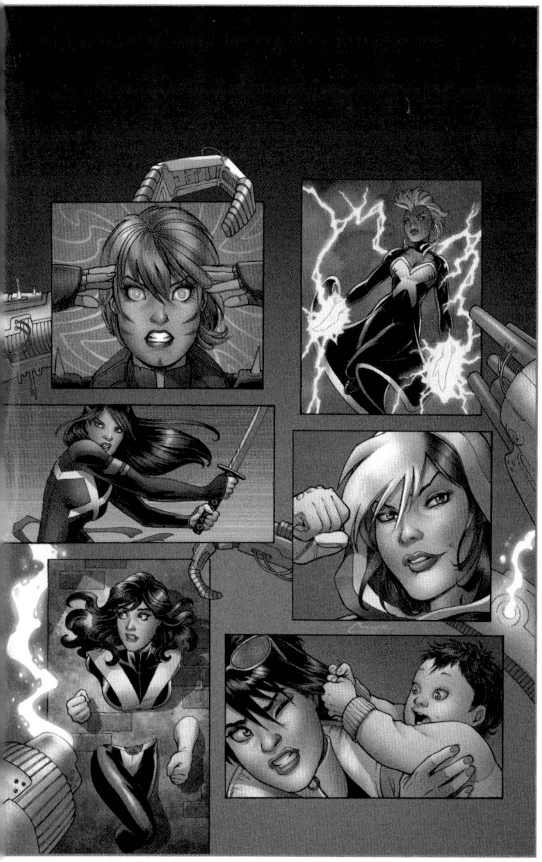

X-MEN #2 VARIANT
BY AMANDA CONNER & PAUL MOUNTS

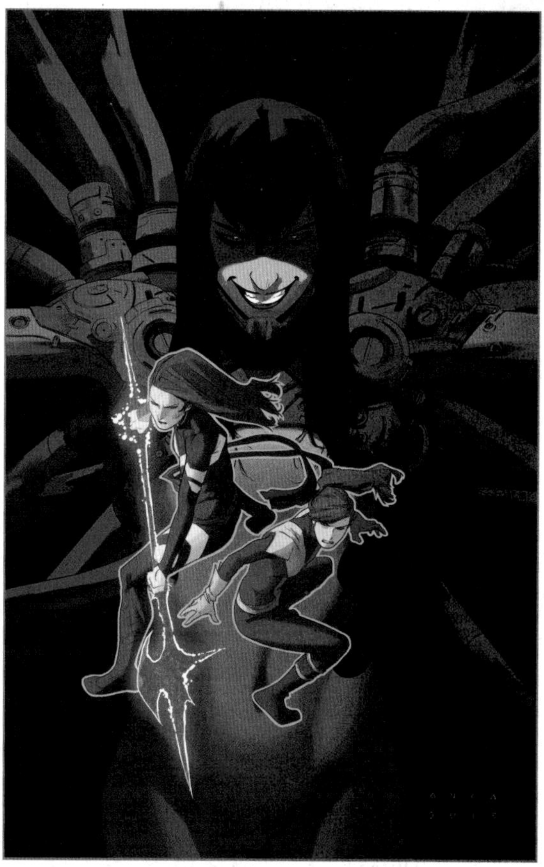

X-MEN #3 VARIANT
BY KRIS ANKA

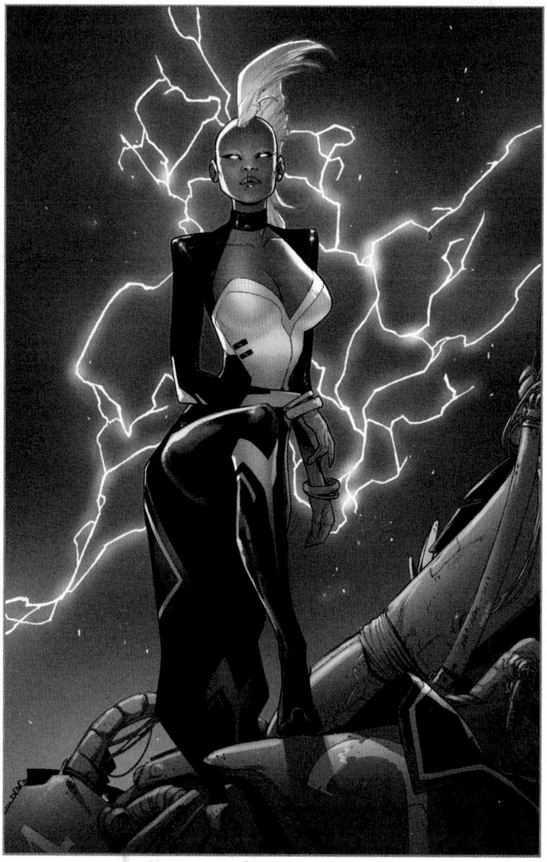

X-MEN #4 VARIANT
BY SARA PICHELLI & EDGAR DELGADO